Sixties Europe

Sixties Europe examines the border-crossing uprisings of the 1960s in Europe on both sides of the Cold War divide. Placing European developments within a global context formed by Third World liberation struggles and Cold War geopolitics, Timothy Scott Brown highlights the importance of transnational exchanges across bloc boundaries. New Left ideas and cultural practices easily crossed bloc boundaries, but Brown demonstrates that the 1960s in Europe did not simply unfold according to a normative western model. Everywhere, innovations in the arts and popular culture synergized radical politics as advocates of workers' democracy emerged to pursue longstanding demands predating the Cold War divide. Tracing the development of a distinctive blend of cultural and political activism across diverse national settings, *Sixties Europe* examines an important, historically recent attempt to address unresolved questions about human social organization that remain relevant in the present, and it offers an original history of Europe across a transformative decade.

Timothy Scott Brown is Professor and Chair of History at Northeastern University and Senior Fellow at the Institute for European Studies at the University of California, Berkeley. He is a historian of twentieth-century transnational social movements. A two-time Fulbright recipient, he is winner of the 2016 Berlin Prize of the American Academy in Berlin and a 2016–2017 Fellow of the American Council of Learned Societies. His books include *West Germany in the Global Sixties: The Anti-Authoritarian Revolt, 1962–1978* (2013), *Weimar Radicals: Nazis and Communists between Authenticity and Performance* (2009), and *The Global Sixties in Sound and Vision: Media, Counterculture, Revolt* (2014) with Andrew Lison.

NEW APPROACHES TO EUROPEAN HISTORY

Series editors
T. C. W. BLANNING, *Sidney Sussex College, Cambridge*
BRENDAN SIMMS, *Peterhouse, Cambridge*

New Approaches to European History is an important textbook series that provides concise but authoritative surveys of major themes and problems in European history since the Renaissance. Written at a level and length accessible to advanced school students and undergraduates, each book in the series addresses topics or themes that students of European history encounter daily: the series embraces both some of the more "traditional" subjects of study and those cultural and social issues to which increasing numbers of school and college courses are devoted. A particular effort is made to consider the wider international implications of the subject under scrutiny. To aid the student reader, scholarly apparatus and annotation is light, but each work has full supplementary bibliographies and notes for further reading: where appropriate, chronologies, maps, diagrams, and other illustrative material are also provided.

For a complete list of titles published in the series, please see: www.cambridge.org/newapproaches

Sixties Europe

Timothy Scott Brown

Northeastern University

CAMBRIDGE
UNIVERSITY PRESS

CAMBRIDGE
UNIVERSITY PRESS

University Printing House, Cambridge CB2 8BS, United Kingdom

One Liberty Plaza, 20th Floor, New York, NY 10006, USA

477 Williamstown Road, Port Melbourne, VIC 3207, Australia

314–321, 3rd Floor, Plot 3, Splendor Forum, Jasola District Centre,
New Delhi – 110025, India

79 Anson Road, #06–04/06, Singapore 079906

Cambridge University Press is part of the University of Cambridge.

It furthers the University's mission by disseminating knowledge in the pursuit of
education, learning, and research at the highest international levels of excellence.

www.cambridge.org
Information on this title: www.cambridge.org/9781107122383
DOI: 10.1017/9781316388327

First published 2020

Printed in the United Kingdom by TJ International Ltd, Padstow Cornwall

A catalogue record for this publication is available from the British Library.

Library of Congress Cataloging-in-Publication Data
Names: Brown, Timothy Scott, author
Title: Sixties Europe / Timothy Scott Brown, Northeastern University, Boston.
Other title: 60s Europe
Description: Cambridge, United Kingdom; New York, NY: Cambridge
University Press, 2020. | Series: New approaches to European history |
Includes bibliographical references and index.
Identifiers: LCCN 2020005698 | ISBN 9781107122383 (hardback) |
ISBN 9781107552906 (paperback) | ISBN 9781316388327 (epub)
Subjects: LCSH: Europe – Civilization – 1945– | Nineteen sixties. | Politics and
culture – Europe – History – 20th century. | Revolutions – Europe –
History – 20th century. | Social movements – Europe – History – 20th century. |
Counterculture – Europe – History – 20th century. | Radicalism –
Europe – History – 20th century.
Classification: LCC D1055 .B78 2020 | DDC 940.55/6–dc23
LC record available at https://lccn.loc.gov/2020005698

ISBN 978-1-107-12238-3 Hardback
ISBN 978-1-107-55290-6 Paperback

Contents

Figures

Acknowledgments

I would like to thank the colleagues and students with whom I've spent the last decade discussing and writing about the global 1968. Understanding the 1960s has been as much a collective project as making them.

Introduction

"[A]fter more than forty years of counterrevolutionary history," proclaimed the journal *Internationale Situationniste* in late 1969, "the revolution is being reborn everywhere, striking terror into the hearts of the masters of the East as well as those of the West, attacking them both in their differences and in their deep affinity."[1] The immediate concern of the piece was the crushing of the Prague Spring in Czechoslovakia the previous year. The Situationists diagnosed the event as a product of the "advanced decay of Stalinism," although they had no idea at the time how many decades it would take for the rot to become fatal.[2] The Situationist International exerted a sometimes-hidden, sometimes-overt influence on the moment of continent-spanning rebellion of which the Prague Spring was a part – the revolt of "1968."[3] Across Western and Central Europe, small groups of anarchist-bohemian cultural saboteurs used the Situationist toolkit of cultural provocation to catalyze more broadly based rebellions. Under the state socialist dictatorships of Eastern Europe, the toolkit was less useful; as the West German student leader Rudi Dutschke, himself an émigré from East Germany, once observed: "I was never a Situationist, in the GDR I didn't have the opportunity."[4] Yet, if Situationist tactics of provocation were difficult to transfer into the more closed societies of the East, Situationist analysis nevertheless encompassed both sides of the East-West divide. Identifying the deep logics underlying the surface antagonisms of the Cold War binary, the Situationists rejected both capitalism and state socialism as two sides of the same oppressive coin. Their position – that despite being formally opposed to one another, both capitalism and state socialism produced

---

[1] "Reform and counter-reform in bureaucratic power," *Internationale Situationniste*, 12 (September 1969), 35–43, 43.

[2] "Reform and counter-reform in bureaucratic power."

[3] Gerd-Rainer Horn, *The Spirit of '68: Rebellion in Western Europe and North America, 1956–1976* (Oxford: Oxford University Press, 2006).

[4] Quoted in Timothy Scott Brown, *West Germany and the Global Sixties: The Anti-Authoritarian Revolt, 1962–1978* (New York: Cambridge University Press, 2013; 2015), 46.

1

parallel states of alienation and un-freedom – was a central and widely shared insight of the rebellions of 1968.

The antiauthoritarian rebellion to which the Situationists referred assumed its symbolic importance in part through the spectacular impression left by two events of the year 1968: the "French May" and the "Prague Spring."[5] The former was a spontaneous uprising in which a short-lived but powerful alliance between students and workers came close to bringing the French state to its knees. The latter was a movement of reform within the ruling Communist Party that expanded into a radical-democratic explosion that was only suppressed by Soviet force of arms. Together, they mounted a two-fold challenge to the reigning orthodoxies of the Cold War, leaving an indelible mark on the radical imagination of the 1960s. These rebellions were significant in the first instance for offering ideas and slogans – "all power to the imagination," "socialism with a human face" – that pointed to the possibility of a radically different arrangement of daily life stretching across the Cold War divide. More broadly, they were significant as part of a globe-spanning rebellion stretching from Berkeley to Beijing, from Tokyo to Tunis, from Turin to Tashkent. The Prague Spring and the French May occurred in the year 1968, but it was the global context that made them part of "1968."[6]

The sheer scope of the rebellion revealed in the latest research, as well as a recognition of the differing timelines from country to country and region to region, has led scholars increasingly to speak less of "1968" than of a "global 1960s." New and emerging scholarship on the global 1960s has been marked by interest in the relationship of Europe and North America to the Global South, or in the terminology of the era, the Third World. In some cases, the focus on this relationship has threatened to devolve into an argument about where the "real" 1968 was located – that is, has threatened to become an argument around the proposition that it was events like the French May that were epiphenomenal to anticolonial rebellions in the Third World and not the other way around.[7]

Europe's key importance in the global 1960s is nevertheless undeniable, not least because it functioned, in Martin Klimke and Joachim

[5] Martin Klimke, Jacco Pekelder, and Joachim Scharloth (eds.), *Between Prague Spring and French May: Opposition and Revolt in Europe, 1960–1980* (New York: Berghahn, 2011).

[6] On the globe-spanning remit of "1968" see Chen Jian, Martin Klimke, Masha Kirasirova, Mary Nolan, Marilyn Young, and Joanna Waley-Cohen, *The Routledge Handbook of the Global Sixties: Between Protest and Nation-Building* (London: Routledge, 2018).

[7] A tendency notable in the 2016 conferences at NYU Shanghai and NYU Abu Dhabi that gave rise to *The Routledge Handbook of the Global Sixties*.

Scharloth's words, as "a microcosm for global political events."[8] Europe was the region in which the Cold War scenario was generated, and it forcefully experienced its effects, not least in the physical and psychic partition of the continent; Europe was the region responsible for colonialism, and thus a sensitive register of the effects of its dismantling, and Europe was a crucial generator of the *ideas* of 1968, alongside America – in the form of the counterculture and the Free Speech and Civil Rights Movements – and the Third World, via the writings of Castro, Che, Mao, and other leading theorists of anticolonial national liberation. Above all, Europe was, along with America, a key repository of postmaterialist values that arose as a significant force primarily only in settings where basic questions of national sovereignty were already settled (i.e. the First and Second Worlds) and without reference to which any reading of 1968 is partial at best.

Even at the level of the "local" (variously defined), 1968 was not a unitary phenomenon. The globality of 1968 was less a matter of geographic scope than of the intersection of globalizing influences across local terrains. "Global," as a leading scholar has pointed out, "does not mean everywhere."[9] Wherever they might lie across the terrain of the "three worlds," all 1968s were simultaneously local *and* global. The collapsing of space, not just through transnational mobility but through the creation of alternative geographies of radical belonging, is, consequently, a central theme of this book.[10]

Another is the telescoping of time. In Paris and Prague, scenes of barricades and insurrectionary graffiti called up rich associations with revolutionary traditions stretching back to 1789. But the Situationists' response to the Prague Spring touched on a specific historical conflict, stretching back to the Russian Revolution, in which competing versions of socialism were at odds: one radical-democratic, bottom up, valorizing spontaneity and self-determination; the other centralized, bureaucratic, and monopolistic. To posit, as the Situationists did before the fact, the existence of an uprising like 1968, or to explain it once it had broken out, was to disrupt the Bolshevik teleology of history in which 1917 loomed

---

[8] Martin Klimke and Joachim Scharloth, "Introduction," in Martin Klimke and Joachim Scharloth (eds.), *1968 in Europe: A History of Protest and Activism, 1956–1977* (London: Palgrave Macmillan, 2008), 1–9, 2.

[9] Jeremy Varon, at the conference "Revisiting 1968 and the Global Sixties," NYU Abu Dhabi, September 20, 2016.

[10] See Wilfried Mausbach, "America's Vietnam in Germany – Germany in America's Vietnam: On the relocation of spaces and the appropriation of history," in Belinda Davis, Wilfried Mausbach, Martin Klimke, and Carla MacDougall (eds.), *Changing the World, Changing Oneself: Political Protest and Collective Identities in West Germany and the US in the 1960s and 1970s* (New York: Berghahn, 2010), 41–64.

large while other dates were erased. To analyze its content, simultaneously, was to reclaim Marxism from state-sanctioned dialectical materialism while insisting on the links between revolution and daily life. As the statement of a "Yugoslav comrade" circulated in Western radical circles around 1968 put it: "To change the conditions of life, to know how to die, to practice free love, to live one's daily life, to hope for despair, is to understand 1905, Kronstadt, Catalonia, Budapest 1956."[11]

This invocation of great insurrectionary moments in history – liminal moments of refusal (Russia 1905), mass democracy (Russia 1921), workers' self-management (Spain 1936), and heroic resistance against authoritarianism (Hungary 1956) – did more than pay respect to the revolutionary lost causes of the past; it insisted on the utopian possibility in the present. Highlighting the linkage between these moments and the possibility of a transformative rupture in *ways of living*, moreover, it insisted on the importance of what had been lost in much of what remained of the so-called Old Left and what was central to the New Left: the possibility of a creative utopia free of hierarchy, bureaucracy, and lies. The centrality of this utopian urge helps account for the importance of *culture* in 1968, which was due not just to new and expanding possibilities of mass media or the worldwide spread of new forms of youth culture and popular culture in the postwar decades but to a convergence of radical politics and radical art. Actively pursued by the Situationists, among many others, this convergence sought to channel a widespread and powerful urge to create new and authentic ways of living and being in the world.

In this way, the Situationists captured the zeitgeist of a rebellion that ranged itself simultaneously against all forms of domination and unjust authority on both sides of the "Iron Curtain." Here, they occupied analytic terrain that remains important today, for 1968 was a response to longstanding issues and dilemmas regarding the organization of human societies, a response that refused to conform to the artificial boundaries of the Cold War. The dissident Polish intellectual Leszek Kołakowski touched on this point in his reflections on the meaning and tasks of the political left. To be "left," he suggested, was to establish a radical independence of thought that rejected two "rights" – the one represented by "Stalinist inertia," the other by "the inertia of capitalism."[12] The left

---

[11] A Yugoslav Comrade who knows the ropes, "We are nothing if not everything," in Peter Stansill and David Zane Mairowitz (eds.), *BAMN (By Any Means Necessary): Outlaw Manifestos and Ephemera, 1965–1970* (New York: Autonomedia, 1999), 124.

[12] Leszek Kołakowski, "The concept of the left," in Carl Oglesby (ed.), *The New Left Reader* (New York: Grove, 1969), 157. Originally published in Leszek Kołakowski, *Toward a Marxist Humanism: Essays on the Left Today* (New York: Grove), 1968.

must, he wrote, simultaneously "reject socialist phraseology as a façade for police states and democratic phraseology as a disguise for bourgeois rule."[13]

It was precisely because 1968 reopened longstanding questions about the organization of human society that its shape and content were so bewildering to contemporaries and to scholars. Far from being a monolithic phenomenon, 1968 channeled a multiplicity of impulses and energies pursued by actors with frequently contradictory goals and competing ideas about how to achieve them. If the core impulse of 1968 was antiauthoritarianism – the unifying principle that underpinned radical energies on both sides of the Cold War divide – the content of that impulse had to be filled through active processes of knowledge creation. It is unsurprising that the writings of the German-American philosopher Herbert Marcuse were so popular on both sides of the East-West divide during the 1960s. Marcuse's notion of a "great refusal" captured the radical imagination in a moment of widespread resistance to totalizing, bloc-spanning systems of control and domination.[14] The question of the means by which Marcuse's refusal was to be carried out, however – that is, the question of the concrete politics through which a *sensibility* would be enacted – was open. Everyone was talking about "cultural revolution" around 1968, but what cultural revolution actually meant was the subject of heated dispute.

The story of sixties radicalism is by and large not one of fixed groups linked to distinct ideological positions; rather, radical activism involved the working through of concepts and organizational forms, some new, some drawn from revolutionary moments past. This recapitulative gesture, by which a profusion of doctrines and approaches were tried on for size, lent sixties radicalism a strongly syncretic character. It also made sixties radicalism very much about the definition of political terms. Radicals around 1968 had a well-developed understanding of what the political "right" was – it was generally pro-capitalist (true of liberalism as well); fought colonial wars like the American one in Southeast Asia; supported various types of traditional hierarchy established in terms of gender, race, and class; was "top down" instead of "bottom up"; and stood in opposition to impulses toward democratic participation. In short, the right rejected all or part of the tripartite goal of human emancipation – liberty, fraternity, and equality – elaborated in the French Revolution of 1789.

[13] Kołakowski, "The concept of the left."
[14] Herbert Marcuse, *One-Dimensional Man: Studies in the Ideology of Advanced Industrial Society* (Boston: Beacon, 1964), 256–257.

What did it mean, by contrast, to be on the "left"? The answer to this question was the sought-after prize of 1968, the attempt to find it *the* ideological task that underpinned all others. In Western Europe, under capitalist systems that defined themselves to a greater or lesser degree in opposition to the socialist tradition(s), the tasks of the left were at least partly defined by circumstances, even if the correct means of accomplishing them was open to debate. It was the great analytic failure of a minority on the Western left to take state socialism's emancipatory claims at face value, while it was the analytic success of others to recognize in revolts against state socialism (Hungary 1956, Czechoslovakia 1968) the drive toward socialist emancipation that had stalled in Russia practically even before its influence was felt in the rest of Europe. In Eastern Europe, the question of what "left" meant was complicated by a formally left-wing context that made the task of establishing the parameters of a truly emancipatory politics all the more urgent and difficult, but everywhere, the attempt to uncover the form and content of an effective emancipatory politics was the central ideological and organizational task of 1968.

Analyses of the Soviet Union played a key role in determining understandings of the left political landscape. At stake was the question of what a "revolution" was and whether the Bolsheviks had successfully enacted one. For followers of the exiled Bolshevik militant Leon Trotsky – "Trotskyists" – the Bolshevik regime instituted in 1917 actually was a form of the socialism predicted by Marx, but it had become a "degenerated workers state" under Stalin. Adherents of Chairman Mao Zedong – "Maoists" – interpreted the USSR in accordance with Chinese Communist orthodoxy as a revisionist state that had given up its revolutionary credentials through peaceful coexistence with the West. Traditions such as left communism and council communism – the latter associated especially with figures such as Cornelius Castoriadis and Anton Pannekoek – argued that the Soviet Union was not a true workers state but a form of "state capitalism" in which a bureaucracy had replaced a capitalist class as the owners of the means of production.[15] Anarchists ("libertarian socialists"[16]) meanwhile rejected a Bolshevik regime that

---

[15] See Anton Pannekoek, "State Capitalism and Dictatorship," *Rätekorrespondenz*, 1936. English translation: *International Council Correspondence*, vol. 3, no. 1, January 1937. The "state capitalism" thesis originated with dissident Trotskyists who disagreed with Trotsky's contention that the USSR's nationalization of property established its credentials as a "workers' state" no matter its subsequent bureaucratic "degeneration." The thesis was also central to the development of Marxist humanism through the work of figures like Raya Dunayevskaya, C. L. R. James, and Tony Cliff.

[16] The term "libertarian socialist" deserves special comment. In the European tradition, a libertarian is not, as in the modern American sense, an individualist advocate of free market capitalism; rather, a "libertarian" is an anarchist: a socialist who rejects the state in

had crushed rank-and-file socialist militancy whenever it threatened party rule, notably in the suppression of the 1921 rebellion in the Baltic Sea naval base of Kronstadt.[17] The Situationists inherited the anarchist critique. In their uncompromising parlance, "bureaucracy" was a synonym for "state socialism" on the Soviet model, while "bureaucrat" – the Situationist insult *par excellence* – served to dismiss Stalinist apparatchiks and their camp followers in the Communist parties of the West simultaneously. As much as anything else, as we shall see in the following pages, 1968 was about the definition of terms.

This book does not assume an even terrain across Europe. Taking as a given that the energies of 1968 manifested differently in different locations in response to unique circumstances, it follows the emerging scholarly consensus in claiming that there were characteristic features of 1968 that were able to become more or less universal while others were stillborn in locations where authoritarian political structures could not be overcome.[18] The study thus does not offer a survey of all European nation states, something that has already been accomplished in varying configurations in a number of fine essay collections.[19] While some nation states receive dedicated treatment in this study, others instead appear throughout the text where aspects of their histories highlight issues of transnational reception or shed light on particular historiographical or theoretical points that illuminate sixties Europe as a whole. Focusing instead on

favor of democratically organized, anticapitalist mass action from below. In accordance with European terminological convention, *libertarian socialism* in this study is a synonym for anarchism. Anarchism was important in the 1960s in an individualist or countercultural iteration consonant with "doing your own thing," but it was equally important for serious political theorists on the left in its collectivist iteration, as a synonym for workplace democracy, an impulse for which, for sixties radicals, "Spain 1936" and "Hungary 1956" operated as key metonyms.

[17] On Kronstadt see Israel Getzler, *Kronstadt 1917–1921: The Fate of a Soviet Democracy* (Cambridge: Cambridge University Press, 1983); Paul Avrich, *Kronstadt 1921* (Princeton: Princeton University Press, 1970). For accounts from the anarchist perspective, see Ida Mett, *The Kronstadt Uprising* (London: Solidarity, 1967); Emma Goldman, *Trotsky Protests Too Much* (Glasgow: The Anarchist Communist Federation, 1938); Alexander Berkman, "The Kronstadt Rebellion," in *Der Sindikalist* (Berlin: 1922). For an account sympathetic to the Bolsheviks, see Victor Serge, *Memoirs of a Revolutionary, 1901–41* (Oxford: Oxford University Press, 1963). See also Maurice Brinton, *The Bolsheviks and Workers' Control: The State and Counter-Revolution* (London: Solidarity, 1970).

[18] Here the study follows the precedent of an important recent collection of essays on the Global Sixties that, by placing "nation-building" alongside "protest" in its title, acknowledges that the priorities and repertoires associated with 1968, while present in various degrees around the globe, were not available in their full range in situations where first-order problems of national self-determination – or of basic democratic rights – were yet to be resolved; Jian, et al. (eds.), *The Routledge Handbook of the Global Sixties*.

[19] Readers interested in such a comparative approach would do well to refer to Klimke and Scharloth, *1968 in Europe*.

classical problems of revolutionary theory and organization as they were manifested in sixties Europe, the study gives pride of place to cases where those were manifested most forcefully and consequentially.

The first chapter of this book examines how "1968" or "the sixties" has been constructed in the scholarship, situating the events the terms describe within their spatial and temporal coordinates. Chapter 2 examines the prehistory of the revolt, showing how it grew out of and continued to draw upon both older histories of war and revolution and a developing context of decolonization and superpower conflict. Chapter 3 traces 1968's origins to the realm of culture, examining the sphere of social action and cultural production populated by artists and anarchists, dropouts and youth rebels with a cause. Chapter 4 examines the development of fully fledged political movements in Europe on both sides of the Cold War divide, showing how youth and student rebellion intersected with powerful impulses for workers' democracy with deep historical roots and strong ongoing relevance around 1968. Finally, Chapter 5 explores a post-1968 moment characterized by a continued search for effective means of social action involving new actors, strategies, and goals.

1   Mapping Sixties Europe

In June 1968, with the embers of the May uprising in Paris not yet fully cooled, a BBC broadcast entitled "Students in Revolt" tried to come to grips with the unrest roiling Europe. Featuring activists such as Daniel Cohn-Bendit (France), Dragana Stavijel (Yugoslavia), Alan Geismar (France), Tariq Ali (England), Leo Nauweds (Belgium), Jan Kavan (Czechoslovakia), Yasuo Ishii (Japan), Ekkehart Krippendorff (West Germany), Lewis Cole (United States), and Alberto Martin de Hijas (Spain), the program showcased the efforts of student Marxists to join forces across national borders. Photographs of the event reveal a signature image of the 1960s: youth and beauty combined with political militancy and radical self-confidence. Yet internationalist photo opportunities could conceal as much as they revealed. Behind the scenes, Tariq Ali quarreled with Dragana Stavijel over her vocal support for dictator Josip Broz Tito, who at the time was busy persecuting critically minded university professors in Yugoslavia.[1] Jan Kavan was only a few months away from being forced to emigrate to the UK after the Soviet invasion of Czechoslovakia. And Alberto Martin de Hijas was to be imprisoned by the right-wing Franco regime upon his return to Spain. Left-wing critiques possible in the relatively open political space of the Western democracies – space that, as we will see, was indeed only *relatively* open – had to be undertaken with great care in the right-wing dictatorships of southern Europe or the state socialist police states of Eastern Europe.

The BBC's attempt to grapple with what was most obvious and striking about 1968 as it was happening – the new prominence of students, their explicit internationalism, and the similarities of the claims they were making across national and Cold War borders – illustrates the extent to which the question of what 1968 *meant* was

---

[1] Reporting on the event, the leading anarchist newspaper *Freedom* lamented "the Yugoslav girl [for whom] Tito could do no wrong; a disappointing analysis from somebody representing the Yugoslav movement"; *Freedom*, 29(19) (June 22, 1968).

1.1 Participants in the BBC broadcast "Students in Revolt" sing the "Internationale," June 12, 1968. From left to right: Dragana Stavijel, Ekkehart Krippendorff, Daniel Cohn-Bendit, Luca Meldolese, Tariq Ali, Lewis Cole, Alan Geismar (Associated Press).

imbedded in the moment itself. A key part of that question concerned the relationship between the whole and the parts. It seemed obvious to contemporaries, as it does to historians today, that disparate national upheavals were connected – but how and why? Student internationalism was one answer, but not a complete one. Typical were the reflections of the editors of London's flagship countercultural journal the *International Times*, who at the beginning of the 1970s were still puzzling over what they called the "curious international tendency towards parallel thinking which operated throughout the late '60s."[2] Everywhere at that time, insurgent youth seemed to be on the move, adopting the same fashions, music, and texts, sharing views on sexuality (in favor) and authority (against). Little wonder that historians, following the sense of contemporaries, have written about the 1960s using terms like "spirit," "imagination," and "eros" – the era's qualities of simultaneity, synergy, and velocity seem almost to strain against purely empirical analysis.[3]

---

[2] Reprinted in Peter Stansill and David Zane Mairowitz (eds.), *BAMN (By Any Means Necessary): Outlaw Manifestos and Ephemera, 1965–1970* (New York: Autonomedia, 1999), 41.

[3] Gerd-Rainer Horn, *The Spirit of '68: Rebellion in Western Europe and North America, 1956–1976* (Oxford: Oxford University Press, 2006); George Katsiaficas, *The Imagination of the New Left: A Global Analysis of 1968* (Boston, MA: South End, 1987).

1.2 The internationalist imagination in 1968. Cover of the journal *Black Dwarf*, edited by Tariq Ali (Barry Amiel and Norman Melburn Trust Archive).

Space, Time, and Interpretation

The scholarship of the last decade and a half has nevertheless increasingly established ways of imposing analytic order on the disparate energies making up the global 1968. The initial phase of the historiography on 1968 dealt primarily with Western Europe and the United States.[4] A second phase – still ongoing – saw the integration of the Third World, both as an influence within Europe and on its own terms. This intervention has encompassed the examination both of *actual* Third World histories in 1968 (as opposed to the Third World's status as a projection screen for Western radical fantasies[5]) and the concrete role played by Third World activists *within* Europe.[6] More recently, scholars have posited the existence of a "Socialist Sixties" in the Communist dictatorships of Eastern Europe.[7] Even more recently, they have sought to incorporate right-wing dictatorships in Spain, Portugal, Greece, and Turkey – the latter two exemplars of a distinct "Mediterranean Sixties."[8] With this expansion in the scholarly remit in mind, we can usefully think in terms of three "zones" of Europe: one made up of Communist Eastern Europe, the other two of the two sectors of capitalist Europe – the parliamentary democracies of Western Europe and the capitalist-authoritarian regimes of Southern Europe (Spain, Portugal, and – from 1967 – Greece). Here the analytic task becomes one of understanding how Europe's 1968 manifested not just in individual countries but in different political-economic regimes where very different prospects for activism attained.

As mentioned in the introduction, the geographic expansion in the scholarship has only been possible in connection with a temporal one. Much of the initial historiography focused on the symbolic date 1968, simply because so much of the epoch's signature events took place in that year. The decade of the 1960s has since been designated as "long," in order to capture the

---

[4] See Ronald Fraser (ed.), *1968: A Student Generation in Revolt* (New York: Pantheon, 1988); Katsiaficas, *The Imagination of the New Left*.

[5] See the essays in Samantha Christiansen and Zachary A. Scarlett (eds.), *The Third World in the Global 1960s* (New York: Berghahn, 2013).

[6] Quinn Slobodian, *Foreign Front: Third World Politics in Sixties West Germany* (Durham, NC: Duke University Press, 2012); Christoph Kalter, *The Discovery of the Third World: Decolonization and the Rise of the New Left in France, c. 1950–1976* (Cambridge: Cambridge University Press, 2016).

[7] Anne E. Gorsuch and Diane P. Koenker (eds.), *The Socialist Sixties: Crossing Borders in the Second World* (Bloomington: Indiana University Press, 2013).

[8] Kenan Behzat Sharpe, "A Mediterranean Sixties. Cultural politics in Turkey, Greece, and Beyond," in Chen Jian, Martin Klimke, Masha Kirasirova, Mary Nolan, Marilyn Young, and Joanna Waley-Cohen (eds.), *The Routledge Handbook of the Global Sixties: Between Protest and Nation-Building* (London: Routledge, 2018); Leonidas Karakatsanis and Nikolaos Papadogiannis, *The Politics of Culture in Turkey, Greece and Cyprus: Performing the Left Since the Sixties* (London: Routledge, 2017).

importance of the trajectory on either side of the events of 1968, and "global" as a means of suggesting that "1968" in any one national location has to be seen as a part of a larger whole. The "global 1968" is simultaneously thus both a spatial and a temporal designation, for analytic time-tables and geographies have had to expand together when the outlines of the historic conjuncture vary considerably by country and region.

None of the temporal designations is purely chronological in any case; each marks a different way of referring to a political and cultural rebellion that took different shapes in different locations according to unique time-tables. Here there exists in the scholarship a tension between *event* and *process*. The use of the date 1968 as a stand-in for a world-historical protest moment has stood very much in line with a focus on the former: protests, street battles, assassinations, and massacres. One obvious shortcoming of this approach is that the focus on confrontational events, falling within the ambit of "politics" as traditionally understood, obscures radical-democratic and antiauthoritarian innovations in the sphere of culture (e.g. in the counterculture and the arts) that were equally if not more salient in their effect on society.

A more fundamental problem is that the notion of a "watershed year of 1968" obscures the long-term processes that made the protest explosion possible. The work of the last decade and a half has increasingly emphasized trends toward cultural liberalization in which the radicalism of "1968" appears as much a product of changing patterns of youth consumption as of neo-Marxist theory and student activism.[9] This focus on cultural change has sometimes threatened to almost fully depoliticize – and thereby dehistoricize – the 1960s.[10] Elsewhere, a "long sixties" periodization has been keyed more closely to political as opposed to cultural developments.[11] Without downplaying the centrality of politics, other scholars have highlighted the role played by long-term social change in general and by changing patterns of consumption in particular.[12] So far

[9] See Axel Schildt, Detlef Siegfried, and Karl Christian Lammers (eds.), *Dynamische Zeiten: Die 60er Jahre in den beiden deutschen Gesellschaften* (Hamburg: Wallstein, 2000). See also Detlef Siegfried, *Time Is on My Side: Konsum und Politik in der Westdeutschen Jugendkultur der 60er Jahre* (Göttingen: Wallstein, 2006).

[10] Arthur Marwick's influential notion of a "long 1960s" (roughly from 1958 to 1974) is keyed to the rise and fall of the period of economic stability and optimism that he argues made the 1960s possible. This "cultural revolution" marked by changing patterns of consumption and shifting social mores plays a much greater role, for Marwick, than the ideology and activism of student and labor activists; Arthur Marwick, *The Sixties: Cultural Revolution in Britain, France, Italy, and the United States, c.1958–c.1974* (Oxford: Oxford University Press, 1998).

[11] Horn, *The Spirit of '68*.

[12] See the essays in Axel Schildt and Detlef Siegfried, *Between Marx and Coca-Cola: Youth Cultures in Changing European Societies, 1960–1980* (New York: Berghahn, 2006).

in the cultural direction had the weight shifted in the historiography around the fortieth anniversary of 1968 that one American historian could lament the loss of focus on the "big eventedness" of 1968, that is, regret the almost complete erasure of political revolution in favor of cultural evolution.[13] Now, just past the fiftieth anniversary of 1968, the "long" nature of the 1960s has come to be taken for granted, even as scholars seek to integrate event and process in more sophisticated ways.

An important feature of the latest scholarship on the global 1968 is a turn toward oral history, which, alongside its documentary relevance, is supplying perspectives previously underrepresented in the scholarship. First, it is recording the voices of nonnotable actors, everyday activists who have previously been erased in favor of a handful of well-educated and articulate spokesmen. The choice of "spokes*men*" in the previous sentence is deliberate, since the notable voice on 1968 has been overwhelmingly male. The oral-historical turn is capturing the voices of women, in the process shifting the picture of what was at stake around 1968 in the direction of the politics of daily life. This shift has a class angle as well, as the new scholarship provides spaces for participants outside the realm of elite education and media presence.[14] Finally, the oral-historical turn is helping erase the artificial boundary between East and West by capturing the voices of activists behind the Iron Curtain in a way that would previously not have been possible.[15]

One thing these new approaches have in common is to demonstrate the interconnection between culture and politics around 1968. To be sure, not every young person was a revolutionary in sixties Europe, but every young person – and many an older person! – was affected by the revolution in mores, the disruption of traditional outlooks, the explosion of images, ideas, texts, new possibilities of travel, and a geo-political situation in which conflict between the Cold War blocs and between the First World and the Third World inhabited the global consciousness. Critically, however, all these "revolutions" took place against the backdrop of, and were inseparable from, a worldwide resurgence of left-wing politics. This is why the best of the scholarship emphasizing the

---

[13] Geoff Eley, "Telling stories about sixty-eight: Troublemaking, political passions, and the enabling of democracy," talk given at the annual meeting of the German Studies Association in St. Paul, Minnesota, October 4, 2008.

[14] Celia Hughes, *Young Lives on the Left: Sixties Activism and the Liberation of the Self* (Manchester: Manchester University Press, 2015). See also Mitchell Abidor (ed.), *May Made Me: An Oral History of the 1968 Uprising in France* (London: Pluto, 2018); Christina von Hodenberg, *Das andere Achtundsechzig: Gesellschaftsgeschichte einer Revolte* (Munich: C. H. Beck, 2018).

[15] See Robert Gildea, James Mark, and Anette Warring (eds.), *Europe's 1968: Voices of Revolt* (Oxford: Oxford University Press, 2013).

1.3 "Alternative Society Now." *International Times*, May/June 1968. Flagship publication of the London Underground featuring up-to-the-minute reportage from the student riots in Paris (*International Times* Archive).

importance of broad cultural transformations taking place in the realms of lifestyle and consumption does not attempt to separate revolutionary politics from popular culture but stresses their essential indivisibility around the radical moment of 1968.[16] Miniskirts and Beatle boots, television sets and rock music, may have represented a cultural revolution, but they were epiphenomenal to the great anticapitalist and antibureaucratic surge of the decade, which sought to do far more than burnish the surfaces of daily life. It was the ideology and activism of radical activists, in and outside Europe, that supplied the analytic spine to the otherwise invertebrate body of youth revolt.

What Was Politics in 1968?

However we interpret 1968, it is important to recognize that it was above all a political project or, more properly, a convergence of sometimes complementary, sometimes contradictory projects seeking to translate a generalized spirit of rebellion into a concrete program. One of the hallmarks of 1968, accordingly, was the search for political action forms appropriate to the spiritual content of the rebellion, a search in which culture and politics were intimately bound together. The characteristic shape of sixties activism was conditioned by the search for right methods of radical action. This involved attempts to identify the *who* of the revolution – to establish the identity of the "revolutionary subject"; the *how* – to settle on the effective action forms; and the *what* – to determine proper revolutionary goals. These three quests were intimately related to a fourth having to do with source material. In a divided Europe with a largely Stalinized or bureaucratized mainstream left, where competing radical traditions had been marginalized or silenced, from whence were effective methods of radical action to come?

One answer was from Europe's own radical past. Activists scoured cultural memory for building-blocks, recovered symbolic dates, and repurposed old texts, slogans, and iconography. Another source was from revolutionary impulses abroad, whether the American counterculture or the movements of Third World liberation. Even as activists demanded redress for past national sins (e.g. Nazism in West Germany, the Algerian War in France, the Civil War in Greece, Stalinist show trials in Czechoslovakia), activists mined history for democratic or radical first principles, repurposing ideological and radical-tactical source material for use in the present. For all the sense of rapid acceleration into the future, many of 1968's "new" concerns were thus not entirely new, especially where they touched on longstanding problems of revolutionary

---

[16] For example, Siegfried, *Time Is on My Side*.

tactics and organization. As the French student radical Daniel Cohn-Bendit put it, "I am not, and do not want to be, anything but a plagiarist when it comes to the preaching of revolutionary theory and practice."[17]

If "plagiarism" functioned diachronically, in the search for usable traditions from the radical past, it also functioned synchronically in the border-crossing adoption of ideas and action forms of the global present. Because it was part of a global revolt, Europe partook heavily of exogenous cultural-political influences, above all those from America and, on the continent, from the UK. As the original source of key cultural innovations (rock 'n' roll, the writings of the Beat poets, the underground press, the hippie movement) and political manifestations (the Civil Rights and Free Speech Movements, mobilizations against the Vietnam War, the Women's Movement), and also because of its hegemonic role within Cold War Europe, the revolt in America exercised an outsized role in Europe. "Europe" was, in other words, not a closed system but a site at which global influences converged in response to unique local circumstances.

The relationship between the global and the local was operative in two registers, one concrete and one virtual. On the one hand, there were transnational exchanges involving the movement of people, cultural productions, and ideas; on the other, there were acts of the globalizing radical imagination by which activists inserted themselves into various global communities, whether the Third World liberation struggles, the American counterculture, or an international New Left. Much of the recent scholarship has focused on understanding how these twin phenomena – transnational exchanges and global imaginings – functioned around 1968. To begin with, each was made possible by new possibilities of movement for people and ideas, the former by the new availability of air travel and new routes of youth tourism and student exchange, the latter by the fresh and unprecedented role of television, radio, and print media.[18]

In Eastern Europe, transnational exchange was facilitated by varying degrees of cultural opening, accompanied by a notable increase in the permeability of borders from the middle of the decade. Czechoslovakia became a key node of international exchange, sending hundreds of thousands of students abroad as tourists or for international exchange and welcoming huge numbers of young visitors from abroad. In the summer of 1968, write James Mark and Anna von der Goltz, "the graffiti on Prague's city walls ... could be found in Czech, English, French,

---

[17] Daniel Cohn-Bendit and Gabriel Cohn-Bendit, *Obsolete Communism: The Left-Wing Alternative* (London: AK, 2000), 19.

[18] On the important role played by youth tourism, see Richard Ivan Jobs, *Backpack Ambassadors: How Youth Travel Integrated Europe* (Chicago: Chicago University Press, 2017).

German, Spanish and Italian."[19] In Hungary, the "Windows to the West" policy adopted by the regime in the mid-1960s created the possibility of consuming Western movies and music that displayed a critical relationship to Western society (e.g. *Easy Rider*), and the lyrics of the political folk music of artists like Pete Seeger and Bob Dylan were translated into Hungarian.[20] To be sure, the circulation of cultural texts was far from unrestricted in the East, even in more liberal state socialist regimes like Czechoslovakia and Hungary. In the latter, texts like Cohn-Bendit's *Obsolete Communism* and Marcuse's *One-Dimensional Man* were restricted to the party elite, even if Western countercultural texts like Abbie Hoffman's *Steal This Book* could find their way to Hungarian activists through smuggled channels.[21]

In many cases, however, cross-border exchanges were facilitated directly through official channels. In the East, indeed, the socialist way of life was explicitly imagined as transnational, and young people were understood to be its most important ambassadors.[22] Poland's relatively liberal travel policies allowed its student functionaries to travel in both East and West.[23] Czech students could visit Poland and find out about political clubs or forge links with other Eastern Bloc students by hitchhiking. Events like the April 1966 "We Accuse Imperialism" conference in Hungary or the January 1967 "Coexistence and the Third World" seminar in Prague, the latter attended by members of the West German Socialist German Students' League (SDS), provided sanctioned spaces for the mingling of Eastern and Western youth.[24] Such exchanges were not without unintended consequences, as was shown in July 1968 when, at the 9th World Youth Festival in Sofia, Bulgaria, West German SDS members put their Bulgarian student hosts in the uncomfortable situation of confronting authorities in ways to which they were not accustomed.[25] Nevertheless, the extent of the passage of cultural products and ideas through "gaps in the Iron Curtain" is striking.[26]

---

[19] Anna von der Goltz and James Mark, "Encounters," in Gildea, Mark, and Warring, *Europe's 1968*, 133–134.

[20] Von der Goltz and Mark, "Encounters," 134.

[21] Von der Goltz and Mark, "Encounters," 135–139.

[22] Zdenek Nebrensky, "Early voices of dissent: Czechoslovakian student opposition at the beginning of the 1960s," in Martin Klimke, Jacco Pekelder, and Joachim Scharloth (eds.), *Between Prague Spring and French May: Opposition and Revolt in Europe, 1960–1980* (New York: Berghahn, 2011), 32–48, 37.

[23] Nebrensky, "Early voices of dissent," 35.

[24] Von der Goltz and Mark, "Encounters," 147.

[25] Von der Goltz and Mark, "Encounters," 147–148; see also Nick Rutter, "Look left, drive right: Internationalism at the 1968 World Youth Festival," in Gorsuch and Koenker, *The Socialist Sixties*, 193–212.

[26] Von der Goltz and Mark, "Encounters," 133.

Because of their key role in these patterns of exchange, students became the radical actors of 1968 *par excellence*. In militant groups across Europe, the presence of foreign student radicals was the rule rather than the exception. In West Germany, African and Latin American Student Leagues cooperated with the SDS. West Berlin became home to sizable and active foreign activist communities made up of students from the Middle East, Latin America, and across Europe. In France, an Italian Worker-Student Action Committee worked in tandem with the Revolutionary Action Committee of the Sorbonne (CARS).[27] The diaspora caused by the dictatorship of the Colonels from 1967 saw Greek students become a significant presence in West Germany, France, Italy, and elsewhere. Spanish young people traveled the length and breadth of Europe, the Franco dictatorship notwithstanding.[28] Budapest hosted a "parade of international activists" ranging from Greek student exiles from the dictatorship of the Colonels to West German and American student activists come to pay homage at the court of György Lukács.[29]

What applied to young people in general and students in particular applied especially to the political avant-gardes who helped synergize the revolt across national boundaries. A radical "rock star" like Rudi Dutschke was everywhere, being interviewed in London's *International Times*, republished in American collections of the latest radical thought, and visiting students and intellectuals in Holland, Czechoslovakia, and Yugoslavia.[30] In exchanges ranging from summer camps and seminars to pilgrimages and personal visits, activists forged international networks that helped drive the revolts across national borders. As early as 1965, a libertarian socialist camping group brought together French anarchists and Dutch Provos, Italian trade unionists and British peace activists.[31] Anarchist youth gatherings took place in Paris in April 1966 and in Milan the following year.[32] The Amsterdam Provos visited West Germany, and West German activists including Rudi Dutschke and Dieter Kunzelmann

---

[27] Andrew Feenberg and Jim Freedman, *When Poetry Ruled the Streets: The French May Events of 1968* (Albany: State University of New York Press, 2001), 152.

[28] Kostis Kornetis, "Spain and Greece," in Martin Klimke and Joachim Scharloth (eds.), *1968 in Europe: A History of Protest and Activism, 1956–1977* (London: Palgrave Macmillan, 2008), 253–266, 255, 262.

[29] Von der Goltz and Mark, "Encounters," 135.

[30] See Niek Pas, "Subcultural movements: The Provos," in Martin Klimke and Joachim Scharloth, "Introduction," in Klimke and Scharloth, *1968 in Europe*, 13–22, 19.

[31] Jean-Pierre Duteuil, *Nanterre 1968: Notes on the Background to the 22 March Group* (ChristieBooks, electronic edition, 2014).

[32] The gathering attracted participants from France, Sweden, Holland, Belgium, Italy, Spain, West Germany, and Great Britain; "European meeting of young anarchists," *Freedom. Anarchist Weekly*, 27(12) (April 16, 1966).

visited the Provos in Amsterdam.[33] There was considerable traffic between the continent and the UK of both hard-political and counter-cultural varieties, of which the June 1968 BBC broadcast with which we began this chapter was only one salient example.

Transnational activists played a key role in the circulation of cultural products, whether Rudi Dutschke personally bringing back a copy of Marcuse's *One-Dimensional Man* from a trip to America or the Czech activist Peter Uhl bringing French texts back to Prague from Paris.[34] Transnational exchanges were far from one-way affairs. Radical periodicals from Europe found their way across the world. The American radical Penelope Rosemont remembers that the shelves of the Solidarity Bookshop in Chicago were filled with periodicals from anarchist presses like Freedom and Solidarity in London, from the SI and the Provos, and from radical groups in Spain, Italy, France, and Australia.[35] Access to the latest subversive products from abroad was not the exception in 1968 but the rule. And indeed, the forging of such access through personal contacts, importation, and various types of cultural initiative was a quintessential activity of 1968.

It is important to remember that although transnational exchange may have been an inevitable response to the reality of a moment in which border-crossing ideas, goods, and activists were the order of the day, it was also a reaction to the perceived deficits, political and cultural, of activists' own countries; activists were frequently forced to look abroad for inspiration in both the political and the cultural realms, seeking out the locally needed from the globally available. This act of border-crossing vision was intimately linked to the broader act of imagination that fueled the proliferation of radicalism around 1968. Through personal experience and connections, through imported texts and images, it was possible to learn about, be outraged by, or take inspiration from events in faraway locations. In this sense, the "parallel thinking" adduced by the *International Times* was more than just the result of a sort of cultural acceleration in which everything became more broadly available, to more people, than ever before; it was understood by activists themselves as a necessary pre-requisite for their political self-realization.

If the movements of 1968 were characterized, indeed, by "global vision," it was not just because activists watched each other across borders

[33] Niek Pas, "Mediatization of the Provos: From a local movement to a European phenomenon," in Klimke, Pekelder, and Scharloth, *Between Prague Spring and French May*, 157–176, 169.

[34] Von der Goltz and Mark, "Encounters," 133.

[35] Penelope Rosemont, *Dreams and Everyday Life: André Breton, Surrealism, Rebel Worker, SDS and the Seven Cities of Cibola* (Chicago: Charles H. Kerr, 2008).

or broadened their own activism to embrace an expanded conception of politics; their refusal of the ideological restrictions of the Cold War was underpinned by the assumption of the fundamental similarity of struggles across national borders. None of the struggles of 1968 took place in isolation, even those in the most closed societies. Polish students mobilized under the slogan "Poland awaits its Dubček."[36] Czechoslovakian protests broke out in response to the anti-Semitic campaign against the Polish left.[37] Activists often compared their own countries poorly to others. Relatively pacific London looked at West Germany and worried that it wasn't being "radical" enough. West Berlin looked at Paris and felt much the same way.[38] Students in France rebelled with an eye on West Germany, and Spanish workers inspired by France went on strike.[39] Italian students demonstrated against de Gaulle and clashed with police in front of the French embassy, occupying campuses and appealing for worker-student cooperation.[40] In all cases, activists tended to be aware of, and strongly support, the struggles of their opposite numbers both within and across bloc boundaries.

The student or countercultural radical around 1968 posited themselves as a new "revolutionary subject," that is, as an actor capable of bringing about revolutionary change, even in situations in which the traditional revolutionary subject – the proletariat – no longer seemed interested in revolution. The fundamental act of this radical subjectivity was a will to "connect the dots" – that is, to identify links between seemingly disparate phenomena. This meant more than just establishing connections between different political and social issues. This gesture expressed not only a desire to be transnational – that is, to refuse artificially inscribed national borders – but to be global, not merely in the sense of attending to global struggles but in the sense of attempting to apprehend the whole, to be *total*.

Even in their most constrained settings, activist energies around 1968 were rooted in two key meta-assumptions. The first of these was that all struggles were connected. The movements of 1968 were the opposite of what are today referred to as "single-issue movements." Around 1968,

---

[36] Mauricio Borrero, "Spring Thaw, Summer Frost: Eastern Europe in 1968," in Elaine Carey and Alfred J. Andrea (eds.), *Protests in the Streets: 1968 across the Globe* (Indianapolis: Hackett, 2016), 71.
[37] Borrero, "Spring Thaw, Summer Frost," 74.
[38] Hans Magnus Enzensberger in Bernhard Pollmann (ed.), *Lesebuch zur deutschen Geschichte, Vom deutschen Reich bis zur Gegenwart* (Dortmund: Chronik, 1984), vol. 3, 253–254.
[39] Katsiaficas, *The Imagination of the New Left*, 3.
[40] Rolf Werenskjold, "A Chronology of the Global 1968 Protest," *Report No. 13* (Volda: Volda University College, 2010), 179.

every movement was a *multi*-issue movement, a movement that assumed that no single cause could be addressed in isolation from any other. That perspective was forcefully articulated in the 1967–1968 "May Day Manifesto" of the British New Left, which spoke of a "single political system" that could only be opposed by taking into account the totality of its aspects. "We believe that the system we now oppose can only survive by a willed separation of issues, and the resulting fragmentation of consciousness," it read. "Our own first position is that all the issues, industrial and political, international and domestic, economic and cultural, humanitarian and radical, are deeply connected; that what we oppose is a political, economic and social system."[41] The second meta-position, a corollary to the first, was that all three "worlds" were connected – that what happened in Europe or America was inseparable from what was happening behind the Iron Curtain or in the Third World. It was considered impossible, for good reason, to analyze the structures governing the modern world on a merely national or regional basis.

These two assumptions fueled what we may refer to as a proliferation of the political around 1968 – that is, a penetration of the political into all spheres, or the emergence of a belief that all spheres could or should be political, followed by a range of different attempts to put that belief into practice. Two key impulses underpinned these attempts. The first and most foundational was antiauthoritarianism. As the revolt in Europe progressed, this imperative opened up more and more of the social landscape to the antiauthoritarian gaze, so that, where it was not blunted by direct state intervention, there was hardly an institution or area of human activity in which authority relations were not being challenged and upset. In Eastern Europe, as we have noted, the antiauthoritarian imperative came up against the hard power of the state and in many cases was tempered by political situations in which Communist parties themselves sought reform, creating at least the appearance of a common interest with young radicals. Nevertheless, antiauthoritarianism provided a critical motif for attempts to overturn existing power relations in very different sorts of societies.

A second key impulse, the will to self-organization, was a practical analog to the first. It corresponded to the impetus toward participatory democracy and autonomous social organization, driving the search for radical-democratic   alternatives   to   top-down   models   of   social

---

[41] May Day Manifesto Committee, "May Day Manifesto 1967–68. A re-issue of the text of the May Day Manifesto, with a new introduction by Michael Rustin," *Soundings* (2013), 2–3. The original May Day Manifesto was published in May 1967 under the editorship of Stuart Hall, Edward Thompson, and Raymond Williams; a second version edited solely by Williams was published by Penguin the following year. The citation here is from the second version, reprinted in *Soundings*.

organization.[42] This attempt came to expression in the school, the workplace, and in all the autonomous initiatives – underground publishers and bookstores; independent youth centers and childcare collectives; film, music, and theatrical collectives – where radical politics met independent cultural production. It also dovetailed, crucially, with the search for the revolutionary subject that drove the mobilization of an ever-wider segment of the young population. Self-organization was the organizational trope and mobilizing method *par excellence*, and one that could help paper over, at least temporarily, the political tensions and outright contradictions at the heart of antiauthoritarian projects.

The rebellion of 1968 took place during the social-scientific moment of the 1960s, in which fields like sociology and psychology were coming into their own as means of explaining rapid social change and in which sociologically minded thinkers like Herbert Marcuse and C. Wright-Mills enjoyed star status among student-left intelligentsias. The leading role played by students in the movements of 1968 ensured that political action would be grounded in theory, and the primacy of theory meant that all acts of rebellion, even those rooted in primal drives, would be justified in accordance with key texts and intellectual traditions. The fashionability of theory allowed it to spread beyond student circles, supplying a ready-made justification for whatever acts of revolt young people envisioned.

Simultaneously, activists privileged communication as political action, not just in verbal terms but in visual and performative acts as well. As much as it was about *protests* against the initiatives of state power, 1968 was also about *creative* acts – artistic, cultural-productive, self-organizational – undertaken from below. Central to this creativity – indeed, informing it at every step – was the production of knowledge and the means to transmit it. Activism around 1968 must in this respect be understood as a form of communicative action, one that asserted the right to break silence, to challenge authority's monopoly on truth.

1968 East and West

Whether expressed in a common commitment to American popular culture (blue jeans, rock 'n' roll, fashions, movies); in border-crossing exchanges in the form of tourism, youth festivals, and so on; in participation in transnational reading, listening, and style-publics; in a self-consciously world-embracing orientation connecting the global to the local; in opposition to imperialist aggression, above all the American war in Vietnam; or in the intellectual commitments of student organizations or avant-garde groups

---

[42] Horn, *The Spirit of '68*.

like the Surrealists and Situationists, contemporaries understood that they were participants in a common struggle against a common enemy: a "repressive system" operative in both capitalist and state socialist guises.[43] As a joint declaration of French and Czech Surrealists put it in 1968: "[A] new phenomenon ... leads the youth in most countries to rise against all forms of repression. Whatever the openly declared objectives of these movements and their differences in different contexts, they have ... the intransigent refusal of institutions in common."[44]

This refusal of institutions was part of a worldwide revolt against bureaucratic and technocratic domination, a rebellion of "idealism" and utopian possibility against the straitjacket of "realism" imposed by elites.[45] This revolt ranged itself against habits of deference and submission to elites claiming authority on the basis of histories and received social conditions, the Cold War, etc., as well as more generally against the instrumental rationality of both capitalist and Communist society. This revolt was related to a second factor, a widespread disillusionment with the results of systems of rule arising out of a comparison of the democratic claims of Communist and capitalist societies against their actual deeds. This disjuncture between words and deeds produced a sort of cognitive dissonance. The US war in Vietnam and the crushing of the Prague Spring by the USSR and its satellites became the twin poles of this disillusion, not only within the two blocs but across them. Everywhere, 1968 was rooted in a sense of disillusionment brought on by the failure of ruling elites to act in accordance with their societies' proclaimed values. The Czechoslovakian art theorist and critic Jindrich Chalupecky, a vocal advocate of grassroots workers' democracy in the Prague Spring, put the matter as follows: "There comes a time for all governments when they have to put into practice the programs which they have presented to the people."[46]

That Communism wore out its welcome in Eastern Europe during the four decades it was in power there is entirely unsurprising in the light of Bolshevism's history of suppressing democratizing alternatives to its rule, dating back to the beginning of the Russian Revolution.[47] As the Czech

[43] "The Platform of Prague," reprinted in Michael Richardson and Krzysztof Fijalkowski (eds.), *Surrealism against the Current: Tracts and Declarations* (London: Pluto, 2001).

[44] "The Platform of Prague."

[45] Karol Edward Soltan, "The Divided Spirit of the Sixties," in Vladimir Tismaneanu (ed.), *Promises of 1968: Crisis, Illusion and Utopia* (New York: Central European University Press, 2011), 135.

[46] "Workers' Councils – or Directors' Councils? Remarks of a by no means impartial observer," in Vladimir Fišera (ed.), *Workers' Councils in Czechoslovakia 1968–69: Documents and Essays* (New York: St. Martin's, 1978), 108–113, 109.

[47] See Emma Goldman, *My Disillusionment in Russia* (New York: Doubleday, Page & Company, 1923); Maurice Brinton, *The Bolsheviks and Workers' Control, 1917–1921: The State and Counter-Revolution* (London: Solidarity, 1970); see also Voline, *The*

Communist dissident Ludvík Vaculík put it in his famous 1968 manifesto "Two Thousand Words": "Most of the people of Czechoslovakia optimistically accepted the socialist program, but its direction got into the wrong people's hands."[48] The problem with the leadership of the Communist Party of Czechoslovakia from this perspective was precisely that, under the influence of Stalinism, it had thrown away the emancipatory gains of the bourgeois revolution in the service of the goal of a socialist revolution, destroying both in the process. This irony was central to the analysis of the Czechoslovakian philosopher Ivan Sviták, a major voice for workers' control during the Prague Spring. "Socialist democracy," he wrote, "must fulfill at least the elementary functions of existing democracies; otherwise it becomes a deceptive and misleading slogan, an ideological fraud."[49] A similar point was made by the student radical Jan Kavan, who argued that "in bourgeois society, the 'bourgeois freedoms' are in practice useless, for they cannot be transformed into effective social action. In a socialist society these freedoms can be the foundation for direct democracy."[50] The "bourgeois freedoms" were not an end in themselves in any case, as Jindrich Chalupecky observed, but merely a necessary prerequisite to a form of democracy *greater* than that available under capitalism.[51]

It is important to note that these freedoms, moreover, far from being historically guaranteed under capitalism, had to be fought for and won in Western societies as well.[52] In 1960s Europe, one only need look at the

Unknown Revolution (London: Freedom, 1955); Bertrand Russell, *Theory and Practice of Bolshevism* (London: George Allen & Unwin, 1920).

[48] Ludvík Vaculík, "Two Thousand Words for Workers, Farmers, Scientists, Artists, and Everyone" (June 27, 1968), in Jeremi Suri (ed.), *The Global Revolutions of 1968: A Norton Casebook in History* (New York: Norton, 2007), 158–165, 159.

[49] Ivan Sviták, "Heads Against the Wall," in Ivan Sviták, *The Czechoslovak Experiment: 1968–1969* (New York: Columbia University Press, 1971), 24–42, 34–35. "[It] must," he continued, "as a first step toward its realization, organize elections and abolish the basic institutions conflicting with the fulfillment of civil rights, that is, with freedom of speech, of the press, of assembly, and of conscience."

[50] Jan Kavan, "Testament of a Prague Radical," *Ramparts Magazine* (September 28, 1968), 53–60, 58. "The working class can play its political role only when it has freedom of speech and information, and freedom to organize," he continued. "Only then can workers' control of industry be possible."

[51] "The restitution of human freedom cannot be reduced to what is known as the 'classic' type of democracy, to an egalitarian universal suffrage with a choice among several candidates and several parties. This type of democracy was created by the Third Estate to meet its own needs – by merchants, businessmen and artisans, when they had gained freedom for their own actions." Jindrich Chalupecky, "All Power to the Workers' Councils," in Fišera, *Workers' Councils in Czechoslovakia 1968–69*, 146–154, 151.

[52] Writing in 1968, Petr Cerny made the point as follows: "It is frequently forgotten by the traditional left that 'bourgeois freedoms' were not generously handed down by the bourgeoisie. They were often the result of years of struggle. British history illustrates this well enough. The right to free assembly, universal suffrage, freedom of movement and above all the freedom to disseminate information, would have been unthinkable

dictatorships in Spain, Portugal, and Greece to reinforce the point. Freedoms of expression and assembly did not exist in an either/or relationship with other more utopian freedoms for which 1968 radicals fought; rather, the presence of the former was a condition of the latter. This is why, for many of the radicals of 1968 on both sides of the Iron Curtain, struggles against communism and against capitalism represented two sides of the same coin.

An important trend in the recent scholarship emphasizes that 1968 in the Eastern Bloc must be understood on its own terms; that is, that emancipatory impulses in state socialist countries should not be thought of as deficient against a normative Western model.[53] Here it is critical, as Anna Krylova has argued, to avoid "project[ing] ... liberal subjectivity onto non-liberal subjects."[54] It is possible to go a step further, moreover, by observing that what was "socialist" about the "socialist sixties" was not just an alternative, nonliberal modernity; it was the persistence of classical dilemmas of social organization passed down across the nineteenth century, deformed by Stalinism, but still being worked out in the second half of the twentieth century. Crucially, this work took place on both sides of the Cold War divide, meaning that what 1968 in East and West had in common was not just a set of globalizing commitments but a set of revolutionary problems that had yet to be resolved in either location.[55]

Activists in state socialist societies were dealing with the consequences of one particular answer to these problems, the state socialist tradition passed down from Bolshevism. Those in the authoritarian capitalist societies of Southern Europe were in a similar position, inasmuch as the fascist or fascizoid regimes in place there were precisely a result of struggles against the revolutionary left unfolding in the decades after 1917. In the liberal democracies of Western Europe, activists faced demands to conform to Cold War categories and priorities that forced them to

without the courage and sacrifice of the anonymous men and women who made up the Chartist and early trade union movements. In that sense, bourgeois freedoms are workers' freedoms, the very minimum starting point for the construction of socialist freedom"; Petr Cerny, *Czechoslovakia 1968: What "Socialism"? What "Human Face"?* (London: Solidarity), pamphlet no. 55.

[53] For example, Katherine White, "East Germany's red Woodstock: The 1973 Festival between the 'Carnivalesque' and the Everyday," *Central European History*, 51(4) (December 2018).

[54] Anna Krylova, 'The Tenacious Liberal Subject in Soviet Studies," *Kritika: Explorations in Russian and Eurasian History*, 1 (2000), 119–146. See also Andrew Zimmerman, "Foucault in Berkeley and Magnitogorsk: Totalitarianism and the Limits of Liberal Critique," *Contemporary European History*, 23(2) (May 2014), 225–236.

[55] In this context, Joachim C. Häberlen and Mark Keck-Szajbel are correct to emphasize that the existing scholarship often serves to reify Cold War divisions rather than think across them; Häberlen and Keck-Szajbel, "Introduction," in Häberlen, Keck-Szajbel, and Mahoney, *The Politics of Authenticity*, 3.

experience the consequences of this struggle as well. Nevertheless, from the perspective of many activists in both East and West, Eastern Europe was ahead of the curve where socialism was concerned. It is thus important, apropos of current attempts to deprovincialize Eastern Europe, to think less in terms of a sixties cultural revolution in which state socialist societies only imperfectly took part than of a border-crossing conversation about exit strategies from capitalism that took place across the three zones of Europe in the different political contexts created by earlier attempts to discover that strategy.

It was precisely the nature of these contexts that determined the prospects of radical action. As observed above, the possibility of pursuing any sort of democratic-emancipatory politics was decisively influenced by the amount of space allowed for political and cultural nonconformity under different types of regimes. The situation varied from country to country, but in general, state socialist and capitalist-authoritarian rule placed severe limitations on the extent to which it was possible for protest to unfold in the public sphere. It is important not to overemphasize the limitations placed on radicals under dictatorships as compared with those in liberal democracies, however; as the editors of an important volume of oral history on 1968 have pointed out, violating public space was risky in the latter, too.[56] Nevertheless, in the state-socialist East and the capitalist-authoritarian South, the boundaries of possibility were circumscribed by the more or less totalizing claims of regimes.

Local contexts also helped determine the extent to which a quintessential feature of 1968 – the fusion of cultural and political forms of radicalism – could take place. Where regimes denied the possibility of open political engagement, political longings were frequently sublimated into cultural activity, expressed in artistic production or countercultural lifestyle. Everywhere across the three zones of Europe, the local reception of global influences synergized social conflicts. Local actors understood themselves as part of a global phenomenon, partaking of ideas and practices in general circulation. The shapes of local histories arose precisely out of the way the global manifested in a local setting or, put differently, out of the intersection of local and global influences over a given terrain.

If everywhere in Europe young people sought to participate in the global youth rebellion, their ability to *enact* that rebellion was largely determined by the degree of control a local establishment claimed over political discourse and cultural expression. In the state socialist dictatorships of the East and the right-wing authoritarian dictatorships of the South, public expressions of nonconformity were extremely dangerous

---

[56] Von der Goltz and Mark, "Encounters," 164.

both to their protagonists and – to the extent that they hoped for total control – to the authorities. Even in the more permissive societies of Western Europe, the behavior of New Left and countercultural insurgents was heavily policed through drug raids, obscenity prosecutions, and campaigns of defamation in the mainstream media (e.g. the official campaign against the UK's flagship subcultural publication, the *International Times*). It thus makes little sense to think in terms of a "closed East" and an "open West" around 1968; rather, it is better to understand the possibilities of political action in the 1960s as a matter of degree.

The totalizing aspirations of dictatorships, however, made the stakes in the more closed societies correspondingly higher. In Eastern Europe, for example, many of the key caesurae having to do with the possibility of an emancipatory breakout related precisely to state socialist regimes' attempts to come to terms with the impact of Western popular culture and the political ideas of the New Left. This reinforces the extent to which the problem of "1968" in Eastern Europe – no less than in Western or in Southern Europe – was a transnational-historical one, for it was around the issue of reception that some of the most salient political conflicts around 1968 were organized.[57]

In Eastern Europe, moreover, the fact that regimes were formally left wing changed the context of many of 1968's main claims. The meaning of Marxism, operating variously as an ideological pretext for one party rule and a set of still-emancipatory political and philosophical ideas, differed drastically on the two sides of the Cold War divide. Opposition to the Vietnam War, for example, as part of a broader resistance to American imperialism, was a position shared by both young radicals and regimes. This meant that in some cases it could represent a site of convergence between the aims of regimes and those of young radicals. Similarly, support for Third World liberation projects produced ambiguous and contradictory situations in the Eastern Bloc. The writings of Mao, Castro, and Guevara, as well as that of Western figures like Marcuse, could meet variously with official approval or censure, changing the playing field for activists. To cite one striking example, Fidel Castro's support for the Soviet invasion of Czechoslovakia in August 1968 cut the ground out from underneath the feet of East German radicals who imagined that the projects of humanist socialism and Third World liberation were natural bedfellows, producing something approaching a spiritual crisis for many activists.[58]

---

[57] See Timothy S. Brown, "East Germany," in Klimke and Scharloth, *1968 in Europe*.

[58] "It is useless to say that Czech sovereignty has not been violated," said Castro in a radio and television address, "but there is no doubt that the Czechs were returning toward capitalism and would inexorably go into the arms of capitalism"; "'Violation but justified'

Ultimately, the extent to which the emancipatory impulses of the 1960s could articulate with an emancipatory local politics was in very large part a function of the degree to which the state was willing and able to use force to suppress alternative politics. This is one important reason why "the sixties" manifested themselves differently in different locations. Local conditions, again, not only determined the prospects for the development of political movements but, as we will see in subsequent chapters, shaped the sorts of claims they could make. This was true even when, or especially when, those claims represented, as they frequently did in Eastern Europe, a demand for a new and more authentic brand of socialism.

Logics of Revolt

Recent scholarship has highlighted both the prominence and the limitations of the concrete and imaginative bloc-spanning solidarities that characterized sixties Europe. Much has been made, for example, of the supposed incomprehension of Czechoslovakian students when Rudi Dutschke traveled to Prague in April 1968.[59] A Scottish exchange student who saw Dutschke speak in Prague remarked on the disconnect between Dutschke's ideas and those of his hosts, lamenting the "lack of any ideology whatsoever" on the part of the latter.[60] He acknowledged that the Czechoslovakian students' relative lack of political organization might have to do not just with cynicism born of the Stalinist perversion of the Marxist language used by Dutschke, however, but with the fact that the students saw their ideas of humanistic reform to state socialism already being borne by reform currents within the Communist Party. Dutschke's wife Gretchen, together with Rudi in Prague, recalls that the primary feeling among the Czechoslovakian students with whom

says Castro," *Morning Star* (August 28, 1968). "With outstanding cynicism," wrote the Situationists, "Castro has fully justified the military intervention, which, according to him, became necessary as a consequence of the threats to reestablish capitalism. In these words he reveals the truth about his own 'socialism'"; "Reform and Counter-Reform in Bureaucratic Power," *Internationale Situationniste*, 12 (September 1969), 35–43. "[I]t should be emphasized again and again," argued a writer in the British anarchist newspaper *Freedom*, "that two of the very few Communist Parties which approved of the invasion of Czechoslovakia were those of North Vietnam and Cuba – that Ho Chi Minh and Fidel Castro, those glorious bearded heroes of the Marxist left, of the armchair guerrilleros in the university common rooms, of the screaming street-fighters in Grosvenor Square, have publically supported the destruction of free socialism by the Russian Communist regime. If this doesn't teach them, nothing can"; N. W., "Czechoslovakia 1968," *Freedom*, 29(33) (October 26, 1968).

[59] Von der Goltz and Mark, "Encounters," 150–152.

[60] Stephen Morrison, "Students against Rudi," *The Spectator* (April 19, 1968).

Dutschke met was not skepticism about Rudi's ideas per se but about whether the Soviets would allow the experiment of socialism with a human face to continue.[61]

Leaving aside the danger of letting (overwhelmingly male) student celebrities stand in for broader radical forces for whom they supposedly speak, it is fair to say that if transnational exchange predominated, ideas and actions could have different valences in different settings. In assessing bloc-spanning connections, it is therefore useful to think in terms of key internal logics that help us think both comparatively and globally. The first of these, as mentioned earlier, has to do with what we referred to earlier in this chapter as a set of classical revolutionary dilemmas that functioned on both sides of the Cold War divide. It makes sense to speak of a "1968" on both sides of the Iron Curtain, again, not just because of the salience of transnational exchanges and global vision, but because of how activists were forced to grapple with diffuse revolutionary legacies and central revolutionary questions that were operative everywhere.

A second internal logic has to do with psychology. On both sides of the East-West divide, as mentioned earlier, 1968 emerged from that moment when the claims of a regime (of democracy, freedom, equality) could no longer be squared with the lived reality of that regime. As the Czechoslovakian student radical Jan Kavan put it, "we tend to compare socialist *practice* to socialist *theory*."[62] The genesis of 1968's movements lay, in other words, in a moment of transition from belief to skepticism. In the East, the question was how to square the promise of a workers' state with the reality of states in which workers made up the bottom rung of a new class society ruled over by a self-appointed bureaucracy. In the West, it was a question of how countries that claimed to represent freedom and democracy – a claim aimed precisely against state socialist regimes on the other side of the Iron Curtain – could support, for example, the US war in Vietnam.

Despite the differing context, the movements of 1968 on both sides of the Iron Curtain shared something fundamental: they were revolts against the hypocrisy of existing systems that quickly became a search for alternatives to those systems. The American socialist and participant in the Berkeley Free Speech movement Hal Draper, in a reflection that applies as much to Europe as to the United States, argued that the revolt against hypocrisy was a product not of ideological preparation but of its opposite: a naive expectation that there

---

[61] Gretchen Dutschke-Klotz, interview with the author (February 1, 2018).
[62] Kavan, "Testament of a Prague Radical," 58.

was a correlation between the words and deeds of systems of power. For Draper, it was precisely the *lack* of ideology that made the student revolt so potent. "This was the explosiveness of uncalculated indignation," he wrote, "not the slow boil of planned revolt ... the first discovery of the chasm between the rhetoric of Ideals and the cynicism of Power among the pillars of society."[63]

The important of cognitive dissonance helps account for why, as we will see in Chapter 4, individual national "1968s" tended to be organized around "moments of truth" – conjunctures in which the disjuncture between a society's words and its deeds became especially visible and existing crises suddenly exacerbated. These moments of truth fell into a set of more-or-less standard scenarios: conflict between a youth organization and its mother party (West Germany, Czechoslovakia, Poland);[64] hamfisted attempts to police youth sexuality and appearance (Czechoslovakia, France, East and West Germany);[65] the writers' conference issuing calls for cultural liberalization that bled over into regime-challenging political demands (Czechoslovakia, Poland);[66] the musical event galvanizing oppositional sentiment (West Germany, Greece, Yugoslavia);[67] the banning or restriction of access to theatrical or other artistic performances that helped crystalize antigovernment opposition (Poland, Yugoslavia, West Germany, Switzerland);[68] the martyr's funeral turned solidarity-building demonstration (West Germany; Czechoslovakia);[69] and – especially in the East, where simple truth-telling was the most explosive – the open letter or manifesto formulated in the form of a loyal appeal.[70]

---

[63] Quoted in Chris Harman, *The Fire Last Time: 1968 and After* (London: Bookmarks, 1995), 44.

[64] Zdeněk Nebřenský, "Early voices of dissent," 33.

[65] Zdenek Nebrensky, "Early Voices of Dissent," 34.

[66] See Jan Pauer, "Czechoslovakia," in Klimke and Scharloth, *1968 in Europe*, 163–177, 165; von der Goltz and Mark, "Encounters," 131–163, 138; Stefan Garsztecki, "Poland," in Klimke and Scharloth, *1968 in Europe*, 179–197.

[67] Kornetis, "Spain and Greece," 260.

[68] March 1968 in Poland kicked off by the banning of Adam Mickiewicz's play *Forefather's Eve* at the Warsaw National Theater and the subsequent heavy police action. The June events in Yugoslavia began with a concert riot; see Želimir Žilnik, "Yugoslavia: 'Down with the Red Bourgeoisie,'" in Philipp Gassert and Martin Klimke (eds.), *1968: Memories and Legacies of a Global Revolt* (Washington, DC: Bulletin of the German Historical Institute, 2009), 181.

[69] See Jan Pauer, "Czechoslovakia," in Martin Klimke and Joachim Scharloth (eds.), *1968 in Europe: A Handbook on National Perspectives and Transnational Dimensions of 1960/70s European Protest Movements*. Transnational History Series (London: Palgrave Macmillan, 2008), 163–177, 172.

[70] Jacek Kuron and Karol Modzelewski, "Open Letter" in Poland, or Vaculik's "Two Thousand Words" in Czechoslovakia; see Stefan Garsztecki, "Poland," 182; "Open Letter: Promises of 1968," 3.

These scenarios in turn spawned a set of action forms or protest repertories that achieved wide purchase both inside and outside of Europe: strikes, occupations, and sit-ins; battles with police; mass marches and other intrusions into public space; and the creation of alternative information and avenues of its dissemination. In every case, these action forms were a response to the perception of unjust authority. And behind them, in every case, lay the desire to escape from a stifling Cold War situation in which everything had already been decided for young people coming of age and in which their aspirations for change were unwelcome for reasons that were at once different and also the same. In every case, the search for new ideas and new forms was paramount, but in every case, as we will see in Chapter 2, that search for the new took place in settings heavily laden with the old.

2   Cold War(s) and Hot

In the autumn of 1956, an essay entitled "What Is Socialism?" was pinned to a bulletin board at Warsaw University. Its author was the dissident Marxist Leszek Kołakowski, later to play an important role in the Polish 1968 and achieve notoriety in the international New Left.[1] The essay offered no answers, only a list of negations. "What socialism is not," it argued, was

a society in which someone who has committed no crime sits at home waiting for the police; a society in which it is a crime to be the brother, sister, son, or wife of a criminal; . . . a society in which some people are unhappy because they say what they think and others are unhappy because they do not; . . . a society in which some people are unhappy because they are Jews and others are happier because they are not; . . . a state where people are better off because they praise their leaders; a state where one can be condemned without trial; a society whose leaders appoint themselves; a society in which ten people live in one room; . . . a state where the number of bureaucrats increases more quickly than that of workers; a state where people are compelled to lie; . . . a tyranny, an oligarchy, a bureaucracy; . . . a state with private ownership of the means of production; . . . a state that considers itself socialist solely because it has abolished private ownership of the means of production.[2]

Written against the backdrop of the "Polish October" of 1956, Kołakowski's essay crystalized the unease of dissident Marxist intellectuals in Poland as they groped for an exit from Stalinism.[3] Deliberately provocative, it captured the contradictions of life in a society "where political debate amounted to a dull, uniform reiteration of platitudes that were patently untrue; and . . . cultural life became a deadening apology for those same platitudes."[4] In avoiding giving an answer to its titular question, it touched on the central dilemma confronting the anti-Stalinist left not only in Poland and Eastern

[1] See Carl Oglesby (ed.), *The New Left Reader* (New York: Grove, 1969), 157. Originally published in Leszek Kołakowski, *Toward a Marxist Humanism: Essays on the Left Today* (New York: Grove, 1968).
[2] See Leopold Labedz, *The Use and Abuse of Sovietology* (Livingston: Transaction, 1988).
[3] Chris Harman, *Bureaucracy and Revolution in Eastern Europe* (London: Pluto, 1974), 114.
[4] Harman, *Bureaucracy and Revolution*, 64.

Europe generally but in Western Europe as well. If "state socialism" was false, then what was *real* socialism? The entire radical process that came to expression behind the Iron Curtain in 1956 – and that would rise again across Europe and around the world in 1968 – centered on discovering the answer to this question.[5]

Radical ferment around this issue was by no means only of concern to intellectuals but an expression of multi-class discontent throughout the Eastern Bloc after the death of Soviet dictator Joseph Stalin in March 1953. Across Eastern Europe, restive subjects of the Soviet empire signaled that they were at breaking point.[6] Protests ranged themselves in the first instance against the difficulties of daily life expressed in issues like wages, work norms, and other bread-and-butter issues. Behind these, however, was an implicit (and often explicit) political critique of the shortcomings of state socialism, in terms of both its material conditions and its refusal of rights of free expression and self-determination. In June 1953, 100,000 workers at the ZISPO works in Poznań, Poland took part in a violent uprising against the government under the slogans "We Want Freedom" and "Down with False Communism."[7] In East Germany that same month, a workers' uprising saw 25,000 protestors in the streets and hundreds killed.[8] In July, unrest rocked the Soviet Gulag, with a half-a-million-strong prisoner revolt at the Vorkuta slave labor camp in the Arctic.[9] By February 1956, when Nikita Khrushchev's "secret speech" before the 20th Congress of the CCCP revealed in shocking detail the extent of Stalin's crimes, the stage was set for further rebellion. The speech sent shockwaves through the international left and prepared the ground for a post-Stalinist "thaw" in the East in which liberalizing trends developed alongside continued nervous repression on the part of state socialist bureaucracies.

Aside from Tito's Yugoslavia, which had broken with the USSR in 1948, Poland was, along with Hungary, the most precocious of the Eastern Bloc

---

[5] Kołakowski later adopted a very different political standpoint; see John Connelly, "Jester and Priest: On Leszek Kołakowski." *The Nation*, September 23, 2013.

[6] Zdenek Nebrensky, "Early voices of dissent," 33.

[7] Mauricio Borrero, "Spring Thaw, Summer Frost: Eastern Europe in 1968," in Elaine Carey and Alfred J. Andrea (eds.), *Protests in the Streets: 1968 across the Globe* (Indianapolis: Hackett, 2016), 65. See also Johanna Granville, "Poland and Hungary 1956: A Comparative Essay," in Kevin McDermott and Matthew Stibbe (eds.), *Revolution and Resistance in Eastern Europe: Challenges to Communist Rule* (Oxford: Berg, 2006), 57–77.

[8] Borrero, "Spring Thaw, Summer Frost," 65. On the June 1953 uprising, see also Matthew Stibbe, "The SED, German communism and the June 1953 Uprising: New Trends and New Research," in McDermott and Stibbe, *Revolution and Resistance in Eastern Europe*, 37–55.

[9] Harman, *Bureaucracy and Revolution*, 82.

countries in demanding a turn away from Stalinism. Dissident energies in Poland coalesced in 1955–1956, finding expression in the "Polish October" of 1956, which saw Władysław Gomułka swept to power on a wave of enthusiasm for reform. Demands for change were expressed by a so-called October Left centered on the journal *Pro Postu*, which counted Leszek Kołakowski among its prominent contributors. The character of *Pro Postu*'s reformism was captured in the manifesto of the short-lived Union of Revolutionary Youth (URY), drawn from different youth groups and the Revolutionary Youth Councils. The URY, read the statement in *Pro Postu*, sought "to preserve the line of the Marxist party of the working class in our actions, reserving for ourselves the right to interpret the line of the party and influence the decision on this line. We recognize the political role and importance of the leadership of the party [... but we] are also opposed to our organization receiving orders from the party."[10] The limitations of this approach were quickly revealed. Under the "reformer" Gomułka, formations like the URY were subsumed back into the party apparatus and strict limitations placed on the activity of the intellectuals around *Pro Postu*. Kołakowski's "What Is Socialism?" essay was banned by Gomułka personally as a "profound slander about the idea of socialism."[11]

The Polish October took place against the backdrop of the reform process in Hungary, which reached a bloody culmination in the Hungarian uprising of October–November 1956. There, the Communist Party had tried to steer a "New Course" away from Stalinism under the leadership of Imre Nagy. As would happen in Czechoslovakia a decade later, but in a more thoroughgoing way, demands for reform quickly developed a dynamic of their own. In the wake of Khrushchev's secret speech, the Young Communists (DISZ) in Hungary organized the "Petőfi Circle," named after the poet Sándor Petőfi, a key figure of the revolution of 1848 in Hungary. Dedicated to the discussion of Stalinism, the problems of revolution, and the history of the workers' movement, the group played a key role in creating the intellectual atmosphere culminating in the Hungarian uprising.[12] Its members were strongly influenced by events in Poland, both the repression and trials following the Poznań riots of 1953 and the ongoing mobilizations that resulted in the Polish October.[13] Like the reformers in Poland, they spoke a language of socialism that personified its demands in the figures of leader and party. Demonstrators in the October 22 march that precipitated the Hungarian rebellion bore massive portraits of Lenin and Nagy, the latter having been called to head the government by the Russians only days before.[14]

[10] Quoted in Harman, *Bureaucracy and Revolution*, 117.
[11] Harman, *Bureaucracy and Revolution*.   [12] Harman, *Bureaucracy and Revolution*, 125.
[13] Harman, *Bureaucracy and Revolution*, 127.
[14] Harman, *Bureaucracy and Revolution*, 129.

At stake was not simply the replacement of one leader by another, however; the discussion centered, again, on the content of "socialism" – that is, on the question of how to achieve a society that left not only capitalism but Stalinism behind. It is no surprise that the signature action form of the revolts in Poland and Hungary was the workers' council or "Soviet"; in reaching back to the rank-and-file council as an expression of mass workers' democracy, rebels planted their flag at a place on the revolutionary timeline prior to the institution of Bolshevik party dictatorship, reviving what in the early days of the Bolshevik revolution been called "nonparty" militancy – political struggle rooted in the radical rank and file, plebiscitary and participatory, scornful of pious orthodoxy, leaning toward direct action and skeptical of self-appointed "vanguards."[15] Demands like those of the Hungarian Writers' Union for "workers' control" and "socialist democracy" did more than put forward the hopes of a minority of Marxist intellectuals – they expressed the reality on the ground, where ongoing rank-and-file mobilizations created institutions like the Central Workers' Council of Greater Budapest, "the first real Soviet to be seen in Europe for nearly forty years."[16]

This was the context in which Kołakowski's "What Is Socialism?" essay criticized the traditions established in the Russian Revolution and passed down through Stalinism to the Eastern Bloc People's Democracies. Some of the items on his list – arbitrary police power, the taking of hostages, guilt by social and family association – were little more than the practices of Bolshevik "war Communism," developed in 1918–1921 and extended and systematized under Stalin.[17] Others – the sycophantic worship of infallible leaders, the paranoid closing off to the world, the perversion of truth and knowledge, show trials – were developments of Stalinism itself. One item in particular – the reference to the perils of Jewish identity – was a reference to the late-Stalinist brand of anti-Semitic account-settling

---

[15] See Brinton, *The Bolsheviks and Workers' Control, 1917–1921* (London: Solidarity, 1970).

[16] Harman, *Bureaucracy and Revolution*, 182–183. On the Central Workers' Council of Greater Budapest, see Bill Lomax, *Hungary 1956* (London: Allison & Busby, 1976). What can be said of the potential of the Workers' Councils in 1956 Hungary is the same that Eric Weitz said about the ones in post–World War I Germany: "By all accounts, the workers councils were the key institutions that emerged in the German Revolution, as they had been in the Bolshevik Revolution. Much of the historical debate has centered on the question of just how radical were the councils .... [It is] correct, it seems to me, to emphasize the potential of the councils, and not just their immediate conservatism. Certainly, there is evidence enough of efforts to turn them into effective agencies of power, if not in the immediate weeks and months of the Revolution, then during the socialization strikes in spring 1919 and the general strike that defeated the Kapp Putsch in spring 1920"; Eric D. Weitz, "Foreword to the English edition," in Pierre Broué, *The German Revolution: 1917–1923* (Berlin: Historical Materialism, 2006), xi–xxi.

[17] See Grigori Maximov, *The Guillotine at Work in Russia* (Chicago: Berkman Fund, 1940); see also Paul Avrich, *The Russian Anarchists* (Princeton: Princeton University Press, 1967).

2.1 Young married couple in revolutionary Budapest shortly before the Soviet attack on the capital, November 1956 (Bishopsgate Institute Archives).

exemplified by the Doctors' Plot in the USSR and the Slansky trial in Czechoslovakia, a phenomenon that would play a key role in the government's campaign against the Polish student movement a decade later.

Critically, Kołakowski's theses as a whole were rooted in the idea that the "bourgeois freedoms" of free expression and assembly were a necessary prerequisite for socialism. It was precisely in stripping these away, and in undermining the Soviet as an organ of mass democracy, that Bolshevism had robbed the revolutionary movement of its emancipatory content.

To be sure, the idea of "workers' control" was subject to multiple interpretations, many of them more reformist than revolutionary. Not everyone in the streets in the Hungarian revolution was a committed socialist revolutionary, or even necessarily a leftist, and demands for socialist renewal were intimately bound up with demands for national self-determination. Equally important, in the context of formally "socialist" societies, the ideological charge of particular symbols and terms was inverted. On the shop floor, the language of Marxism might not be the most effective in conveying dissatisfaction with the formally "Marxist" system. As the British New Left writer Chris Harman observed, "[m]any of the best and most militant workers completely rejected the normal terminology of socialist revolutions . . . . After all, why should they wave a red flag they had seen flying over concentration camps? . . . And yet their slogan – the factories are ours – summed up the essence of Marxism."[18]

The stakes were clearly understood by the party leadership in Poland, where, as Gomułka was being forced to reject calls to open a revolutionary second front against the Russians engaged against the rebels in Budapest, the October Left was arguing in favor of a "system of councils" that would represent an actual workers' self-management as opposed to a self-management via party proxy.[19] *Pro Prostu* saw in calls for workers' self-management, indeed, precisely an attempt "to give the dictatorship of the proletariat its real content."[20] One of the reasons for the eventual suppression of the journal was its temerity in raising the slogan "All Power to the Councils."[21] Gomułka himself identified the central issue when he bitterly denounced ideas of a "system of workers' councils from low to high in all branches of the economy" as representing an "anarchist utopia" that would render the government "superfluous."[22] This was an astute observation, for it was precisely anarchism and those doctrines whose content was explicitly or implicitly anarchist – not only the Soviet as an institution, but traditions like anarcho-syndicalism and

---

[18] Harman, *Bureaucracy and Revolution*, 153.
[19] These efforts were subordinated to the party by April, 1958 but were essentially dead earlier; see Harman, *Bureaucracy and Revolution*, 109, 121.
[20] Quoted in Harman, *Bureaucracy and Revolution*, 119.
[21] Harman, *Bureaucracy and Revolution*, 122.
[22] Quoted in Harman, *Bureaucracy and Revolution*, 118.

council communism – that had historically posed the counterweight to the Bolshevik model of socialism being challenged in Poland and Hungary in 1956.

This is why, in analytical terms, there can be no "1968" in which "1956" does not figure prominently, nor a "European Sixties" in which Western Europe appears merely as a normative model for Eastern European imitation. The uprising of 1968 in Eastern Europe represented far more than cultural-intellectual overspill from the West taking place against a backdrop of political stultification. To be sure, Marcuse was read in Hungary and LSD consumed in East Germany, even as regimes tried to quarantine the unwanted political effects of such cultural activity; more important is that in the East, attempts were being made, again, to come to grips with the same classical revolutionary dilemmas that were central to the long 1960s in the capitalist countries of Western and Southern Europe. Around 1968, in other words, the two halves of the Iron Curtain existed in a dialectical relationship.

Nor were the Eastern European activists of 1956 and 1968 fighting for "1989" – that is, for an abandonment of socialism and the heedless embrace of capitalism as an unproblematic model for individual and social freedom.[23] Here, the oft-repeated interpretation that holds Eastern Bloc rebels to be authentic freedom fighters against Communist tyranny and those in the West to be spoiled children ungrateful for the benefits of capitalism and liberal democracy can hold little scholarly interest.[24] Leaving aside its obvious political intention, the argument ignores the reality that millions of people in the Eastern Bloc opposed capitalism and aspired to a democratic socialism denied them by Stalinism.[25] As a Czechoslovakian student radical put it in 1968: "To those in Russia and America who imagine that we Czechs hungered for

---

[23] On this theme, see the essays in Kevin McDermott and Matthew Stibbe (eds.), *Eastern Europe in 1968: Responses to the Prague Spring and Warsaw Pact Invasion* (Basingstoke: Palgrave Macmillan, 2018).

[24] The dismissive liberal line is exemplified in Tony Judt, *Postwar: A History of Europe since 1945* (New York: Penguin, 2005). For a cogent takedown of the "spoiled children" claim, see Irena Grudzinska-Gross, "1968 in Poland: Spoiled children, Marxists, Jews," in Vladimir Tismaneanu (ed.), *Promises of 1968: Crisis, Illusion and Utopia* (New York: Central European University Press, 2011), 43–53.

[25] "In Eastern Europe," write Joachim C. Häberlen and Mark Keck-Szajbel, "critics opposed Stalinist regimes in all their iterations, yet without embracing Western-style parliamentary democracy; on the contrary: reformers ... consistently called for a different form of socialism"; Joachim C. Häberlen and Mark Keck-Szajbel, "Introduction," in Joachim C. Häberlen, Mark Keck-Szajbel, and Kate Mahoney (eds.), *The Politics of Authenticity: Countercultures and Radical Movements across the Iron Curtain, 1968–1989* (New York: Berghahn, 2018), 1–23, 5.

capitalism as the forbidden fruit, I must say frankly that such a regression does not interest us in the least."[26]

Far from taking for granted the superiority of Western liberal democracy – a system that had failed spectacularly in preventing the rise of fascism, even if it ultimately succeeded (in alliance with the Soviet Union) in defeating it – their goal was to uncover the democratic content of socialism itself. Ivan Sviták was one of only many to make this point. "[T]he great problem of modern industrial society of the East as well as of the West," he wrote, was "the problem of how to bring the elite under democratic control."[27] This was a problem for which neither Western parliamentary democracy nor Eastern state socialism had an answer. And to find that answer would involve, in both East and West, a search for theoretical perspectives and action forms, radical source material, and – above all – the identity of the social forces that would make the revolution.

The Past inside the Present

This search took place in radically changed circumstances from those that had determined the context of radical activism in the interwar period. The year 1945 was a major caesura in Europe. On the ruins of defeated Nazi Germany, a four-power system of occupation laid the groundwork for what would become a four-decade division of Europe into opposing camps. Communist Russia and the Western capitalist allies of Britain and America had cooperated to defeat Nazi Germany, but with Adolf Hitler's death in April 1945, latent divisions came to the fore. Stalin, bolstered by agreements made at the Yalta Conference of February 1945, continued the process of remaking Eastern Europe in the Soviet Union's image that had begun in the final year of the war. This involved purges, show trials, forced collectivization, and all the other hallmarks of Stalinist rule. The so-called Peoples' Democracies founded in Bulgaria (1944), Yugoslavia (1945), Poland (1945), Albania (1946), Romania (1947), Czechoslovakia (1948), East Germany (1949), and Hungary (1949) formed an anticapitalist bloc codified in the formation of the Warsaw Pact alliance in May 1955, itself a response to the integration of West Germany into the Western North Atlantic Treaty Organization (NATO) alliance founded in April 1949. Winston Churchill's reference in a 1946 speech to an "Iron Curtain" that had fallen across Europe supplied an enduring metaphor for the seemingly impenetrable barrier between the "socialist" and "free" worlds.

---

[26] Jan Kavan, "Testament of a Prague Radical," *Ramparts Magazine* (September 28, 1968), 53–60, 54.

[27] Ivan Sviták, "Prologue to Intervention," in Ivan Sviták, *The Czechoslovak Experiment: 1968–1969* (New York: Columbia University Press, 1971), 131–146, 135.

In Eastern Europe, the horizons of democratic possibility were circumscribed even before the wave of Stalinization swept over the region from mid-1947. Sharing "a common experience of military repression, ruthless exploitation, forced labor, mass deportations, and genocide," the countries of what would become the Soviet Bloc had little to draw on in terms of democratic traditions.[28] The scale of physical destruction and human suffering was staggering. Alongside the war's legacy of mass death (six million Poles alone were killed), there was a massive postwar wave of migration and dislocation in which "armies, prisoners, deportees, forced laborers, and refugees roamed across Eastern Europe's brutalized landscape."[29] The strength of the left in Eastern Europe had been seriously reduced by interwar authoritarian regimes and especially by Nazism and Stalinism. Prewar purges had decimated the Soviet Union's own Communist Party as well as those of Poland, Yugoslavia, and Hungary.[30]

Yet Communism's role in the wartime antifascist coalition placed it in a strong postwar position, strengthening democratizing trends within Communist parties. Even as it transformed the social and political landscape, the war prepared the ground for a utopian longing rooted in the antifascist coalitions of the war years.[31] A major effect of the war was to reinvoke the broad-based political alliances that had characterized the Popular Front era of the 1930s. These provided the basis for a short-lived but powerful postwar antifascist surge that saw Communist parties, as key bulwarks of the wartime resistance, achieve a previously unheard-of level of respectability and influence. Communist parties became the preeminent organizations of the left both in Western countries like Greece, Italy, and France and Eastern countries such as Czechoslovakia, Yugoslavia, Albania, and Bulgaria.[32] The postwar antifascist moment meanwhile created the space for the temporary ascendance of individual "national roads" to Communism, as opposed to those dictated by Moscow.[33] The postwar left-populist resurgence and the antifascist consensus with which it was joined briefly signaled the possibility of a different sort of Europe than the one which in fact arose, but the postwar antifascist moment was short-lived, with coalitions based on the wartime resistance going defunct by 1947.[34]

In that year, the enunciation of the Truman Doctrine and the Marshall Plan, the founding of the Cominform as a successor to the Comintern,

---

[28] Geoff Eley, *Forging Democracy: The History of the Left in Europe, 1850–2000* (Oxford: Oxford University Press, 2002), 304.
[29] Eley, *Forging Democracy*, 304–305.   [30] Eley, *Forging Democracy*, 305.
[31] Eley, *Forging Democracy*, 287.   [32] Eley, *Forging Democracy*, 287.
[33] Eley, *Forging Democracy*, 306.   [34] Eley, *Forging Democracy*, 301.

dissolved in June 1943, and the expulsion from government of Communist parties in Italy and France signaled a hardening of Cold War battle lines.[35] That process saw erstwhile Western allies now recast by the Soviets as a new danger on a par with fascism and Soviet Communism repositioned by the West as a new totalitarian threat as or more dangerous than that represented by the defeated Nazis. The Western NATO alliance was organized around the new superpower status of the United States of America, its signatories pledging to defend each other in the event of a Soviet invasion. In the East, the members of the Warsaw Pact similarly pledged to defend the Peoples' Democracies from attack by the West. In practice, these signatories – Poland, Hungary, Romania, Czechoslovakia, East Germany, Bulgaria, and (until 1968) Albania – were effectively satellite states of the Soviet superpower. NATO operational doctrine was hereafter based on the threat of massive Soviet and Warsaw Pact tank armies surging into West Germany across the plains of the Fulda Gap. It was understood that in such a conflict tactical nuclear weapons would be deployed, that Germany would be reduced to a radioactive wasteland, and that the rest of the world might follow along with it. The threat of nuclear destruction accordingly became an early leitmotif of the peace movement and the New Left.

Simultaneously, the bipolar division of the world came to provide the conceptual framework for all social conflict, wherein challenges to the status quo on both sides of the Iron Curtain were interpreted through the language and concepts of the Cold War. Thus, for example, peace campaigns could be instrumentalized by Eastern Bloc governments for their anti-Western content or demonized by Western governments for giving aid and comfort to the Communist enemy. Similarly, cultural innovations like rock 'n' roll could be seen not merely as an annoyance to the older generation but interpreted as a serious political threat, either of Communist subversion in the West or of capitalist intrusion in the East. Processes of "Americanization" and "Sovietization" occurred, partly as a natural result of the economic dependencies created by aid programs like the American "Marshall Plan" and the Soviet "Molotov Plan," partly as a consequence of dedicated programs of cultural influence. In creating physical destruction, World War II laid the groundwork for political and cultural transformation.[36]

For the new left-wing social movements of the 1950s and 1960s, the question was one of how to find breathing room within the "new system of

---

[35] Eley, *Forging Democracy*, 307.
[36] See Manuel Bragança and Peter Tame, *The Long Aftermath: Cultural Legacies of Europe at War, 1936–2016* (New York: Berghahn, 2015).

disciplinary power" represented by the Cold War.[37] In Yugoslavia, Tito steered a course independent of Stalin, although ultimately, as the events of 1968 would show, not in a way that protected the democratic potential of socialism. One of the New Left's biggest achievements would be to identify precisely the Cold War system as *the* problem facing the world, simultaneously identifying the left wing of the bipolar arrangement – Soviet Communism – as a false one that had little to do with the long-standing socialist goal of human emancipation. Thus if, as a leading historian puts it, "'1968' challenged the hegemony of '1945,'" it also engaged and called into question the legacy of "1917."[38]

Spain in the Heart

In assessing that legacy, another critical revolutionary moment was placed on the historiographical agenda of the New Left: the Spanish Revolution and Civil War of 1936–1939. The war to defend a left-liberal Spanish Republic against a military insurgency of right-wing generals had become a *cause célèbre* for the international left while providing a military proving ground for international fascism. Troops and materiel from fascist Italy and Nazi Germany helped turn the tide in favor of the insurgents and, in case of the Germans, allowed them to practice the techniques of terror-bombing civilian populations that they would use on Rotterdam, Warsaw, and London a little over a decade later. The war symbolized the great ideological divisions of the interwar period, recalling a world caught up in the struggle of competing fascist and Stalinist totalitarianisms. It was for precisely this reason that it maintained its relevance in the postwar period, for if the combatants had changed after 1945, the Manichean division of societies into warring camps had not.

Yet the either/or ideological decision posed by the Spanish Civil War – and, in a different form, by the post–World War II settlement – concealed a third alternative, one inimical to fascist, Stalinist, and bourgeois-democratic regimes alike: that presented by revolutionary anarchism. The Spanish Civil War had proceeded apace with the Spanish Revolution, which was marked by a grassroots uprising of anarchist militants in industry and agriculture. This was not the bomb-throwing anarchism of popular imagination but an anarchism rooted in the collectivist ethos of workers' self-management, signified by the close collaboration between the anarcho-syndicalist CNT (Confederación Nacional del Trabajo or National Confederation of Labour) and the anarchist affinity

---

[37] Eley, *Forging Democracy*, 301.   [38] Eley, *Forging Democracy*.

group FAI (Federación Anarquista Ibérica or Iberian Anarchist Federation).

While anarchist militias faced Franco's troops at the front and anarchist miners in Asturias fought fascist troops with dynamite liberated from the work site, the CNT-FAI collectivized factories in Barcelona. Peasants meanwhile established agricultural collectives in Aragon, Catalonia, and Valencia. The revolution was resisted bitterly by the Republican government but even more bitterly by the Spanish Communist Party and its Russian secret police advisers.[39] These tried at all costs to put the brakes on the grassroots rebellion, even to the extent of sabotaging the anarchist war effort behind the line with arrests, withholding of supplies, and other forms of chicanery.[40] The ghost of Spain after 1945 was thus not just the ghost of a lost opportunity to smash fascism before it gathered enough force to start a world war; it was the ghost of a social revolution independent of parties or Marxist ideology, a revolution owing less to the Bolshevik seizure of power in Russia in 1917 than to the Paris Commune of 1871.[41]

Outside of Spain, the Revolution and the Civil War provided a rich source of myth and inspiration. As early as 1964, the Situationists placed the lost Spanish Revolution at the center of a striking *détournement* in which a nude bathing beauty declared, with haughty self-assurance, "There's nothing better than fucking an Asturian miner!"[42] The playful reference to the revolutionary "potency" of these anarchist miners signaled the extent to which the ghosts of the Spanish Revolution still haunted the radical imagination of the 1960s. Spain remained "in the heart" of the revolutionary, as the title of the Situationist pamphlet had it, because the issues underpinning the Revolution and Civil War remained very much unresolved in the 1960s.

Spain held a mythological quality in the 1960s, in particular for inspiring radicals seeking a Third Way between capitalism and communism. But it was also linked to fierce debates in the 1960s about the proper direction of radical activity. Student activists mesmerized by the struggle of Third World countries against Western imperialism often enthusiastically embraced anticolonial leaders with little consideration of the actual content of their

---

[39] On internecine conflict in the Spanish Revolution and Civil War, see Franz Borkenau, *The Spanish Cockpit: An Eye-Witness Account of the Political and Social Conflicts of the Spanish Civil War* (London: Faber & Faber, 1937).

[40] George Orwell, a fighter with the Trotskyist POUM, documented the Comintern's sabotage of the war effort in his famous memoir of the Spanish Civil War; George Orwell, *Homage to Catalonia* (New York: Harcourt, 1969).

[41] On the impact of the latter, see Julia Nicholls, *Revolutionary Thought after the Paris Commune, 1871–1885* (Cambridge: Cambridge University Press, 2019).

[42] "España en el corazón" (Spain in the Heart), tract (July 1964).

politics. This failure of ideological vision was not lost on those militants, many of them older, who continued to take inspiration from the struggle against fascism in Spain. "One of the most profound lessons of the Spanish Civil War," wrote the American militant Russell Blackwell, a veteran of the war who served time in a Russian prison,

is that in the fight for social justice we must fully comprehend the difference between freedom and dictatorship. That this lesson is lost on some of our non-ideological and ahistorical new leftists, who think of themselves as revolutionaries, is evidenced by the ease, sometimes fervor, with which they hail Fidel Castro, Che Guevara, Mao Tse Tung and Ho Chi Minh. It was the Fidels, the Hos and Maos of the Thirties who betrayed the Spanish Revolution, and to confuse these dictators of one-party states with anarchism is the most arrant nonsense.[43]

The anarchist group Nanterre, writing in May 1968, argued similarly: "We want to see whether the FNL of Vietnam is a revolutionary organization. It is clear that the fact of its struggle against US Imperialism alone says nothing about its revolutionary position."[44] A Maoist militant interviewed years later picked up on the same theme, remembering: "We organized a lot of demonstrations and our Maoist-led group tried to prove it was more radical than the others. The Maoists were the only ones who sold and distributed newspapers printed by the North Vietnamese and the NLF in South Vietnam. We thought we were the only 'true defenders' of what was, in fact, Vietnamese Stalinism and state capitalism."[45]

This line of analysis was similar to that of the Situationists, who regarded the Third World liberation movements as but another face of the spectacle.[46] Their skepticism, and its relationship to the ongoing question of the nature of the Soviet Union, has been aptly summarized by Guy Debord's biographer Anselm Jappe:

[D]espite widespread condemnation of Stalinism and defection from the French Communist Party, virtually no Left thinkers dared so much as describe the Soviet Union in plain language as a class society, much less renounce their allegiance to the Leninist tradition. At most, their hopes would simply be shifted to some other *state* or other – to Yugoslavia or Cuba, to Vietnam or Algeria, or, and above all, to China.[47]

[43] Russell Blackwell, "The Spanish Revolution Revisited," *New Politics*, 7(3) (Summer 1968), 84–89.
[44] Anarchistische Gruppe Nanterre, "Nationale Befreiung oder Klassenkampf?, in Lutz Schulenburg (ed.), *Das Leben ändern, die Welt verändern! 1968 – Dokumente und Berichte* (Hamburg: Edition Nautilus, 1998), 85–92.
[45] Mitchell Abidor, *More May Made Me: Additional Elements of an Oral History of the 1968 Uprising in France* (Oakland: AK, 2018), 117.
[46] Anselm Jappe, *Guy Debord* (Oakland: PM, 2018), 97.   [47] Jappe, *Guy Debord*, 88–89.

It was precisely these states, and the Western Communist parties who owed them their allegiance, that had, for the Situationist International, "[t]he task of illusorily representing the revolutionary option in the world."[48] Against this illusory revolution, Spain represented for the Situationists and many others, alongside the Hungarian Revolution of 1956, one of the last significant attempts at the real thing in Europe.

Spanish anarchism was by no means merely a ghost of revolutions past, moreover; opposition from anarchists and other militants continued in clandestine form throughout the 1950s and 1960s. Exiles from the Spanish Civil War, active as far abroad as Mexico City and New York City, were particularly prominent in Great Britain. London was home not only to tenacious indigenous anarchist groups like "Freedom" and "Solidarity" (the latter the English wing of the French group "Socialism or Barbarism") but also played host to a vigorous Spanish exile presence made up of former militants from the CNT and its affiliated Iberian Federation of Libertarian Youth (FIJL). One of the young radicals inspired by contacts with Spanish expatriates was the young Scottish anarchist Stuart Christie who, in August 1964, traveled to Spain and attempted to assassinate dictator Francisco Franco.[49]

Anarchism was extremely important in France as well, not only in the persons of Daniel Cohn-Bendit and his brother Gabriel, or in the Situationist influence on the March 22 Movement that jump-started the Paris May, but in tendencies like the anarcho-Marxist group Noir et Rouge and the Anarchist Students' Liaison at Nanterre.[50] The latter, tellingly, was founded at the Parisian headquarters of the Spanish CNT in exile ("an anarchist local worthy of the literary imagination," in the remembrance of one activist), over which stood guard two anarchist veterans of the Spanish Civil War.[51] The group did support work for Spanish revolutionaries, organized events such as a forum on "Sexuality and Revolution," and distributed André Bertrand's détourned comic strip, "Return of the Durutti Column," which reimagined the famous anarchist fighting column of the Spanish Civil War.[52] An activist in Lille recalls belonging to a radical circle that enjoyed a close relationship "with

[48] Jappe, *Guy Debord*, 89.
[49] Released from prison in September 1967 after an international campaign, Christie returned to London to take part in various radical initiatives, including the refounding of the Anarchist Black Cross; Stuart Christie, *Granny Made Me an Anarchist: General Franco, the Angry Brigade, and Me* (Oakland: AK, 2007).
[50] See the interviews with Daniel and Gabriel Cohn-Bendit in "Anarchism in the May Movement in France" (SRAFPRINT CO-OP, Union Shop IU 620, IWW, no date).
[51] Jean-Pierre Duteuil, *Nanterre 1968: Notes on the Background to the 22 March Group* (ChristieBooks, electronic edition, 2014).
[52] Duteuil, *Nanterre 1968*.

Spanish anarchists who had fled Francoism. I remember that one of them gave me his library of anarchist pamphlets, works by Kropotkin, Voline, Bakunin, and this was how I discovered the anarchist movement. This was around 1967. So the basis for my ideas came from all these anarchist theoreticians. With this came knowledge of Leninist and Stalinist repression, so my ideas were impregnated with a profound rejection of communism."[53]

The Persistence of Fascism

The ongoing struggle against Franco was part of a broader complex of popular struggles against fascism in wartime or postwar Yugoslavia, Poland, France, and Greece. In the latter, the National Liberation Front/Greek People's Liberation Army (EAM-ELAS), made up of Communist and various pro-socialist groups, helped harry Nazi forces out of the country, only to be set upon immediately afterward by pro-fascist militias armed and abetted by the British, who were concerned enough about left-wing influence in Greece to divert troops from the Italian front in order to crush an insurrection in Athens at the end of 1944/beginning of 1945. The task of keeping Greece within the Western orbit was taken over by the Americans with the onset of the Truman Doctrine from the beginning of 1947, with the USA playing a decisive role in helping to crush left-wing forces in the Greek Civil War of 1946–1949, a war that continued in more or less uninterrupted, if attenuated, form until the fall of the Colonels' dictatorship in 1974.

In the 1960s, fascism was by no means merely a historical phenomenon. Remnants of fascism proved difficult to fully root out in both Italy and Germany, in no small part because of the persistence of fascist attitudes, personnel, structures, and laws. Another major reason was the haste of the victorious Western powers to incorporate former enemies into the Cold War alliance and the attendant willingness to turn a blind eye to the provenance of potential allies against the perceived greater good of limiting Communist influence by any means necessary. In Italy, many Mussolini-era laws remained in place, as did fascist regional administrators and chiefs of police. The early postwar years saw the emergence of a neo-fascist party, the Front dell'Uomo Qualunque (The Common Man's Front), which was subsequently absorbed into Movimento Sociale Italiano (MSI), the first

---

[53] Abidor, *More May Made Me*, 159–160. Sheila Rowbotham, similarly, recalled the presence of Spanish CNT exiles in her local pub, along with a Mau Mau fugitive of the colonial struggle in Kenya, a "despairing Portuguese revolutionary," American GIs, bums and criminals, artists and musicians; Sheila Rowbotham, *Promise of a Dream: Remembering the Sixties* (London: Penguin, 2001), 32.

major neo-fascist party to emerge in Western Europe. Numerous Italian fascists were recruited to the secret CIA stay-behind army, codenamed "Gladio" (Sword). Founded in 1956 with branches across Western Europe, the program was organized to undermine communism by any means necessary, up to and including terror attacks on civilian targets and, in a notable instance, played a role in the Greek coup of April 1967.[54]

The fascist past supplied an enduring metaphor in the present, and not only in countries where, like Greece or Spain, actual fascist and/or authoritarian regimes were in power. In West Germany, for obvious reasons, the persistence of fascist personnel and attitudes became a central lens through which the escalation of conflict with the authorities was viewed by the activist left. Nor was this concern based on a fantasy. Former Hitler supporters similarly remained lodged in important positions in government and the professions. An abortive early neo-Nazi movement, the Socialist Reich Party (SRP), was banned by the government in 1952. The refounded Communist Party (KPD) was banned four years later, on the basis of the (in the event, correct) idea that it served as a front organization for East Germany.[55] West Germany's most important neo-fascist party, the National Democratic Party of Germany (NPD), was established in 1964 and allowed to continue its existence. Former Nazis continued to occupy positions in West German law, academia, and government, while a younger generation of neo-Nazis trained in terror tactics. Josef Bachmann, the attempted assassin of student leader Rudi Dutschke, had active ties to some of these.[56]

The creation of far-right groups was spurred in part by increased immigration in the 1960s. In England, the National Front, founded in 1967, became a focus of working-class recruiting efforts and was associated with street gangs involved in anti-immigrant attacks.[57] In France, the same period saw the rise of small right-wing terror groups with names like Delta Commandos, Christian West, and Youth Front. The far-right group Occident was a threatening force on university campuses in 1968. A more significant and long-lasting group, Jean-Marie Le Pen's National

---

[54] Daniele Ganser, *NATO's Secret Armies: Operation Gladio and Terrorism in Western Europe* (London: Routledge, 2005).

[55] See Patrick Major, *The Death of the KPD: Communism and Anti-Communism in West Germany, 1945–1956* (New York: Clarendon, 1997); see also Timothy S. Brown, "Richard Scheringer, the KPD and the politics of class and nation in Germany: 1922–1969," *Contemporary European History*, 14(1) (August 2005), 317–346.

[56] See "Enthüllung durch Stasi-Akte: Dutschke-Attentäter hatte Kontakt zu Neonazis," *Der Spiegel* (December 5, 2009), available at www.spiegel.de/politik/deutschland/enthuel lung-durch-stasi-akte-dutschke-attentaeter-hatte-kontakt-zu-neonazis-a-665334.html.

[57] For a lucid treatment of the National Front milieu, see David Renton, *Never Again: Rock against Racism and the Anti-Nazi League, 1976–1982* (London: Routledge, 2018), 20–19.

Front, was founded in 1972. In Spain, even under the Franco dictatorship, fascist violence resurged in the 1970s under groups like Guerillas of Christ the King, Commandos of the Anti-Marxist Struggle, Fuerza Nueva, and the Spanish National Socialist Party.

Along with the rise of a stability under governments led by patriarchal male leaders, the postwar period saw a hardening of gender roles that forced women out of the workplace and back into the home. Whereas the Popular Front era had seen a new prominence for women in the public sphere, and World War II had massively unsettled gender roles by disrupting the certainties of home and family, the early Cold War years saw a pronounced patriarchal retrenchment. Although there was a relatively greater participation of women in the workforce in Communist Eastern Europe, in Europe generally women were forced back into a subordinate role by the beginning of the 1950s.[58] The development of peace movements provided one key locus of women's mobilization, especially after 1956 in the rise of the Campaign for Nuclear Disarmament (CND).[59] But even with the development of New Left organizations in the 1960s, the subordinate status of women remained ubiquitous. In the year 1968, in De Gaulle's France, women still needed permission from their husbands to open a checking account. As in West Germany, both abortion and homosexuality were illegal, part of a broader pattern of heteronormative oppression. Transnational campaigns around abortion rights and gay liberation would become hallmarks of the post-1968 wave of activism. In and after the crisis year of 1968 itself, however, conflicts around the attempts of women and homosexuals to end their subordinate status within emancipatory movements would become flashpoints in many New Left organizations.

Everywhere, the specific radical interests of 1968, whether rooted in theories like those of the Situationists, in attempts to reclaim lost traditions of the revolutionary left, or in efforts to import from abroad the source material(s) of cultural-political revolution, took place against a backdrop of widespread social conservatism that left the young generation feeling suffocated.[60] From this perspective, the proximal cause of one of the most striking and explosive revolts of 1968, the French May, is instructive. The strict segregation of young men and women in the dormitories at Nanterre was more than just a mere rebellion against a social inconvenience facing university students; it was a rebellion against the whole edifice of social conservatism in France. This is why, in general

---

[58] Eley, *Forging Democracy*, 321.   [59] Eley, *Forging Democracy*, 325–326.
[60] See, for example, the voices in Ronald Fraser (ed.), *1968: A Student Generation in Revolt* (New York: Pantheon, 1988).

no less than in France, the revolt of 1968 took place on the terrain of everyday life.

A World in Revolt

The settling of political disputes left over from Europe's own history of war, fascism, and revolution took place amidst a new revolutionary surge in which Europe was no longer center stage. The upsurge of radicalism in sixties Europe had many causes, but the crucial context for it lay outside Europe, in Europe's former colonies. Alongside the Cold War and nuclear arms race, decolonization was the most important large-scale process of the postwar period. The scale of change was momentous. In 1945 there were only four independent countries in Africa. By the end of 1960 there were twenty-six. India and Pakistan gained independence from Great Britain in 1947, while France was forced to relinquish its colonies in two bitter wars in Vietnam and Algeria. The American and Soviet superpowers very quickly moved to impose their own interpretations on the independence movements, fueling a series of proxy wars across Africa, Asia, and Latin America that were reflected back to the European continent in a number of ways.

The most consequential of these for the movements of 1968 was without a doubt the American war in Vietnam. This Second Indochina War (the first being the French war of 1946–1954) was perhaps the single most widely shared issue uniting protests across the globe. There was no place in Europe on either side of the Iron Curtain where outrage against the war was not a central focus of youth protest and a burning concern of New Left intellectuals. The war became a key site of intergenerational contact expressed in alliances between young radicals and older intellectuals. It made up a source of widely disseminated visual tropes depicting the consequences of state violence, from napalm attacks on peasant villages to the self-immolation of protesting Buddhist monks. And it became a symbolic point of moral opposition that could function in the capitalist West as well as in the Communist East. In providing a focal point for protest against unjust authority, the war synergized protests against a host of local issues, becoming a key site of the global-local intersections characteristic of 1968.

Individual European nations had their own colonial conflicts to deal with. In France, the war in Algeria (1954–1962) intensified social and political divisions that continued to fester throughout the 1960s. Algeria was unique in the French empire in that there were around one million colonists ("pieds-noirs") out of a population of ten million, significantly higher than European populations in Vietnam or the British Raj. This meant that the war in Algeria reflected back into metropolitan France more strongly than it otherwise might have. The war became a signature issue for the generation of French students coming of age at the beginning of the 1960s, organized in the National Union of French Students (UNEF). That same war also fueled the development of far-right forces and contributed to the political polarization of French society, not least because of the military putsch of May 1958.[61] More generally, the Algerian War strengthened the French state, increased tendencies toward authoritarianism, and fueled the rise of the radical right in France.

The experience of opposition to the war, in turn, influenced a generation of activists who would be prominent in the French May. In France, it was not untypical for older militants around 1968 to have been socialized into political struggle by the war in Algeria, in some cases being involved in transporting Vietnamese National Liberation Front (FLN) documents or otherwise supporting the war effort. In the case of the so-called *pieds rouges*, this meant actually moving to Algeria to support postwar reconstruction efforts.[62] Many French activists gained their first political experience in the national liberation support groups founded to aid the anticolonial movements in Algeria and Vietnam. The formation of the small Trotskyist and Maoist "groupuscules" was accelerated by the failure of the French Communist Party (PCF) to support the FLN.[63] Repressed knowledge of episodes of colonial violence in the metropole, such as the murder of Algerian demonstrators in Paris in October 1961, continued to simmer below the surface.[64]

The continuing presence of colonial subjects in the metropole, meanwhile, was a crucial component of the broader internationalism of European student movements. "Our internationalism was implicit and simply taken for granted," recalls the British activist Sheila Rowbotham. "It did not occur to us to justify or explain why we were connected to King or to Dutschke .... One influence on us had been CND, which had always included peace protestors from other countries. There had also been the anticolonial movements and the connection to southern Africa. Then came the war in Vietnam, along with opposition to the regime of the right-wing Greek Colonels."[65] The living presence of foreign radicals, she continued, made "internationalism ... much more than an abstract

---

[61] Richard Wolin, *The Wind from the East: French Intellectuals, the Cultural Revolution, and the Legacy of the 1960s* (Princeton: Princeton University Press, 2010), 41.

[62] Abidor, *More May Made Me*, 32.

[63] George Katsiaficas, *The Imagination of the New Left: A Global Analysis of 1968* (Boston, MA: South End, 1987), 58.

[64] See Jim House and Neil MacMaster, *Paris 1961: Algerians, State Terror and Memory* (Oxford: Oxford University Press, 2006).

[65] Rowbotham, *Promise of a Dream*, 172.

political idea, because the students who came from South Africa, Rhodesia, Latin America, the United States, Greece, Italy and Ireland brought information and radical ideas from their own milieux."[66]

International student umbrella organizations, such as the Communist-funded International Student Union in Prague and the International Student Conference based in Leiden, The Netherlands, were an important vehicle of these exchanges. The latter was partly funded by the US government, which infiltrated the organization in order to sway student agendas. The Prague-based International Student Union became a central node for disseminating information about local affiliate unions across the globe, and also a center for language translation to help keep local unions abreast of key developments among its members. Equally important was the emergence of the Tricontinental Conference – Organization of Solidarity with the People of Asia, Africa and Latin America (OSPAAAL) – which began publishing a leftist quarterly *Tricontinental* out of Havana. The publication linked sympathetic groups in Europe to the Third World through its readership and funding sources.[67]

The emergence of transnational activist networks was heavily influenced by First World–Third World exchanges for which colonialism had supplied the basis.[68] One of the earliest of these was the Jeanson network, led by the French intellectual Francis Jeanson during the Algerian war. Taking advantage of the fact that white people could move more freely than Algerians between France and Algeria, the network supplied couriers – "valise carriers" – to smuggle arms, money, and documents for the FLN. The network involved figures like the anticolonial activist Henri Curiel, and it was supported notably by Simone de Beauvoir and Jean Paul Sartre.[69] The work of this group took place in the context of pan-Islamist and pan-African networks, of which the FLN was a part.[70]

In West Germany, the presence of African and Middle Eastern students in West German universities placed distant events on local agendas, synergizing student protests in West German cities like Berlin and

---

[66] Rowbotham, *Promise of a Dream*.

[67] See Andy Stafford, "Senegal: May 1968, Africa's Revolt," in Philipp Gassert and Martin Klimke (eds.), *1968: Memories and Legacies of a Global Revolt* (Washington, DC: Bulletin of the German Historical Institute, 2009), 129–136.

[68] See Burleigh Hendrickson, "March 1968: Practicing Transnational Activism from Tunis to Paris," *International Journal of Middle East Studies*, 44(4) (2012), 755–774.

[69] On the Jeanson network, see Jim House and Neil MacMaster, *Paris 1961: Algerians, State Terror, and Memory* (Oxford: Oxford University Press, 2006).

[70] See also Jeffrey James Byrne, *The Mecca of Revolution: Algeria, Decolonization, and the Third World Order* (Oxford: Oxford University Press, 2016).

Munich. One of the first public actions of the antiauthoritarian faction of the SDS targeted the visit to West Germany of the Congolese strongman Moïse Tshombe, implicated in the killing of Congolese Prime Minister Patrice Lumumba and seen as a willing tool of imperialist interests. Characteristically, the single most important event in the West German 1968 – the police killing of the student Benno Ohnesorg during the visit to West Berlin of Shah Mohammad Reza Pahlavi – took place during a protest instigated by Iranian expatriates.

If the Third World made up a living, physical presence in the First World, Third World ideas held an equal if not greater importance. The concept of a "Third World," first elaborated by the French anthropologist Alfred Sauvy in the early 1950s, quickly developed an explicitly political valence.[71] Newly liberated countries in Africa and Asia sought to establish a third position between the rigid worlds defined by the Communist and capitalist superpowers. In this they were joined by Tito's Yugoslavia, which sought to elaborate a non-Stalinist model of Communism on the European continent. This goal was codified at the end of the 1950s by the establishment of the Non-Aligned Movement. Founded on the initiative of the heads of state of Yugoslavia, Indonesia, India, Egypt, and Ghana, the movement condemned both Western and Soviet imperialism while pledging to remain neutral in the Cold War. This position was congenial not just to Yugoslavia's Tito, as he tried to steer his country on a course independent of the Soviet Union, but to Mao in China, who was vying with the Soviet leadership for control of the world Communist movement during the same period.

By the middle of the 1960s, China, along with Cuba and Vietnam, stood at the forefront of a distinctly "Third Worldist" brand of politics that understood itself in opposition both to capitalist imperialism – exemplified by American support for anti-Communist forces around the world – and Soviet Communism, which had given up its revolutionary dynamism in favor of a *modus vivendi* with the West. Western radicals were inspired by the Third World's militant defiance of Western imperialism, in particular the resistance of Vietnamese peasants against the American military juggernaut. Maoism, especially with the onset of the Cultural Revolution in 1966, allowed militants to believe in revolutionary communism while nevertheless rejecting the ossified and bureaucratic version on offer in the Soviet Union. The dashing figure of the Argentinean doctor-turned-guerrilla Che Guevara seemed to represent for these activists the possibility

---

[71] On the development of the Third World concept, see Christoph Kalter, *The Discovery of the Third World: Decolonization and the Rise of the New Left in France, c. 1950–1976* (Cambridge: Cambridge University Press, 2016).

of a New Man, born out of the slave conditions of imperialism, free of Old World hang-ups and possessing an unprecedented ability to act. Che's writings, along with those of authors like Franz Fanon, Ho Chi Minh, and Carlos Marigella, inspired European militants with the idea that small committed groups could bring about revolutionary change, making the Third World a rich source of inspiration for those hoping to overturn oppressive conditions in the West.

From the circulation of people and texts, to the syncretic borrowing from multiple sources of theory and practice, to the collapsing of space that allowed events in a faraway location to resonate locally with critical consequences, the influence of the Third World on Europe exemplified key dynamics of 1968. Decolonization struggles made up the really existing context of state violence and popular counterviolence against which the revolt of 1968 took place. They did more than supply the violent background noise for European revolts of 1968; in demonstrating that somewhere, at least, a successful struggle against power was taking place, they made the dream of revolution real in a way it never otherwise could have been in the relatively peaceful and prosperous Europe of the 1960s.

A New Left

The New Left emerged from several sources.[72] The term "New Left" has both a specific and a more general meaning. On the one hand it refers to groups of intellectuals in Great Britain and elsewhere who attempted to forge a left-wing alternative to Bolshevik state socialism. On the other, it refers more broadly to the oppositional left-wing coalitions of the 1960s stretching from intellectuals to student movements to countercultures. Some of its most important progenitors were the peace and disarmament movements of the 1950s and early 1960s. The Cold War sparked a terrifying nuclear arms race that threatened the destruction of entire societies and, indeed, human civilization. The Castle Bravo nuclear bomb test of March 1954 saw the United States detonate a hydrogen bomb of 15 megatons, 1,000 times the explosive power of the bomb that destroyed Hiroshima in 1945. This test was followed in October 1961 by the USSR's "Tsar Bomb," at 50 megatons the most powerful nuclear

---

[72] See Holger Nehring, "Out of Apathy: Genealogies of the British 'New Left' in a Transnational Context, 1956–1962," in Klimke, Pekelder, and Scharloth, *Between Prague Spring and French May*, 15–31; Holger Nehring, *Politics of Security: British and West German Protest Movements and the Early Cold War, 1945–1970* (Oxford: Oxford University Press, 2013); Madeleine Davis, "The origins of the British New Left," in Martin Klimke and Joachim Scharloth (eds.), *1968 in Europe: A History of Protest and Activism, 1956–1977* (London: Palgrave Macmillan, 2008), 44–56.

device ever detonated. The following year, the Cuban Missile Crisis signaled in a terrifying way the very real possibility of a nuclear conflagration. As American Defense Secretary Robert McNamara later admitted, "At the end we lucked out. It was luck that prevented nuclear war."[73]

In response to these developments, a powerful international peace movement established itself in the years 1954–1963. One of the most influential of the peace initiatives was the British CND, founded in 1958. An outgrowth of the National Council for the Abolition of Nuclear War Tests, founded in response to planned British H-bomb tests scheduled for the Christmas Islands in May 1957, the CND grew to encompass some 270 local groups by the end of 1958, 800 by 1961.[74] Identified with the now-famous peace symbol designed by the artist Gerald Holtom, the CND became strongly associated with the Easter weekend marches from the nuclear facility at Aldermaston to London. These "Aldermaston marches" attracted tens of thousands of people by the early 1960s, spearheading an Easter March movement that spread to West Germany, Denmark, Italy, Greece, and the Netherlands.[75]

The CND provided an important focal point for the elaboration of alternative youth identities.[76] "As the largest extra-parliamentary organization in post-war Britain, writes Celia Hughes, "the Campaign became the first radical space in which socially-aware youngsters could invest an uncertain teenage identity, at odds with the conservative customs of home, school, and state institutions."[77] A participant remembers: "Once a year the march passed through the streets with great clamor and glamour. People with battered top hats playing the cornet out of tune and girl art students with coloured stockings – the whole parade of infamy came through the town. It was terribly exciting."[78] In his classic 1968 study, Jeff Nuttall writes of a "wild public festival spirit that spread the CND symbol through all the jazz clubs and secondary schools in an incredibly short time. Protest was associated with festivity."[79] In making this connection, wrote Sheila Rowbotham, CND helped "to shift the parameters of 'politics' and lay the basis for a radicalism outside the orbit of both parties and trade unions."[80] More simply, as she put it, "CND enlarged the space to be weird."[81]

---

[73] D. Errol Morris, *The Fog of War* (2003).
[74] Michael Frey, The International Peace Movement," in Klimke and Scharloth, *1968 in Europe*, 33–44, 39.
[75] Frey, "The International Peace Movement," 39.
[76] Celia Hughes, *Young Lives on the Left: Sixties Activism and the Liberation of the Self* (Manchester: Manchester University Press, 2015), 74–81.
[77] Hughes, *Young Lives on the Left*, 74.   [78] David Widgery, quoted in Fraser, *1968*, 31.
[79] Jeff Nuttall, *Bomb Culture* (London: Strange Attractor, 2018), 50th anniversary edition.
[80] Rowbotham, *Promise of a Dream*, 69.   [81] Rowbotham, *Promise of a Dream*, 71.

2.2 Subcultures on parade: Students (Bishopsgate Institute Archives).

The international peace movement not only played a critical role in preparing the way for the protest movements of 1968 but also overlapped with them in significant ways. The peace movement was international in orientation and transnational in makeup. By the early 1960s, some 100 nonaligned (non-Communist) peace groups were in operation in 44 countries.[82] Pacifist internationals like the War Resisters International (WRI) and the International Fellowship of Reconciliation (IFR) served as umbrella organizations for activism across national boundaries. A July 1957 conference in Scotland, the Pugwash Conference on Science and World Affairs, saw the birth of the Pugwash Movement, which sought to unite scientists from both sides of the Iron Curtain in a shared commitment to

[82] Frey, "The international peace movement," 36.

2.3 Subcultures on parade: Folkie (Bishopsgate Institute Archives).

nuclear disarmament and world peace. The British intellectual Bertrand Russell published a manifesto in 1955 calling on world leaders to avert the dangers of nuclear war, a document lent considerable weight by the inclusion of Albert Einstein among its eleven signatories.[83] The Bertrand Russell Peace Foundation founded a few years later became a major vehicle of transnational activist exchange in the burgeoning movements of 1968.

The peace movement's more radical adherents rejected the Cold War bloc system altogether, arguing that the nuclear arms race was a result of the spiritual and political bankruptcy of both sides. In this way, the peace movement prefigured 1968's refusal to take a side in what activists

---

[83] This was the Russell–Einstein Manifesto, issued July 9, 1955.

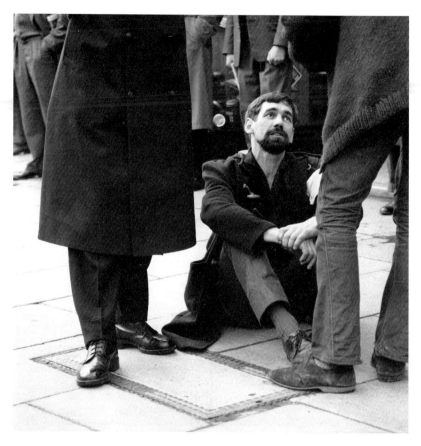

2.4 Subcultures on parade: Beatnik sitting in (Bishopsgate Institute Archives).

regarded as a false choice between capitalism and communism. The peace movement introduced a new informal political sensibility, new tactics of direct action, and new concerns, not least a focus on anti-imperialism that bridged opposition to the French war in Algeria with that against the US war in Vietnam. Finally, the peace movement was itself a major participant in the protests of 1968. As Michael Frey has pointed out, the antiwar protests of the 1960s were by no means a narrow student affair but a movement of concerned citizens from all walks of life.[84]

[84] Frey, "The international peace movement," 42.

2.5 Subcultures on parade: Teddy Boy (Bishopsgate Institute Archives).

The early sixties apogee of the peace movement coincided with the birth of the New Left, which differentiated itself from the old not only by rejecting aspects of the Marxist tradition as they existed in the Stalinist bureaucracies but in its embrace of new issues, tactics, and actors. A major impetus for the birth of this "first New Left" was the revelation of the crimes of Stalinism by Nikita Khrushchev in February 1956. Khrushchev's speech threw a bomb into the international Communist movement, leading to mass defections in some parties (in Italy and Great Britain especially) and denial in others, especially the French. The speech cleared the ground for greater autonomy for some parties but had little effect in others.[85] The

---

[85] Eley, *Forging Democracy*, 333.

Soviet invasion of Hungary furthered the destruction, although again, some Western Communist parties proved remarkably resistant to coming to terms with what Stalinism actually meant. The first wave of New Left intellectuals driven away from Soviet Communism included figures like the historians E. P. Thompson, John Saville, and Perry Anderson, and the dean of British Cultural Studies, Stuart Hall.

New Left intellectuals were spurred into action not only by Khrushchev's speech but by the shock of two key events of 1956: the British and French invasion of the Suez Canal zone at the end of October and the Soviet invasion to crush the Hungarian uprising at the beginning of November.[86] "These two events," wrote Hall, "unmasked the underlying violence and aggression latent in the two systems that dominated political life at the time – Western imperialism and Stalinism . . . . 'Hungary' brought to an end a certain kind of socialist innocence. On the other hand, 'Suez' underlined the enormity of the error in believing that lowering the Union Jack in a few ex-colonies necessarily signaled the 'end of imperialism.'" In this way, wrote Hall, "'Hungary' and 'Suez' . . . symbolized the break-up of the political Ice Age."[87]

The Vietnam Solidarity Committee (VSC), founded in June 1966 by activists connected to the Bertrand Russell Peace Foundation and the International Marxist Group (IMG), was an important early focus of mobilization for the British New Left, becoming a collection point for a range of different nonconformist cultural-political stances and initiatives.[88] In France, the intellectual New Left was centered in groups like Socialism or Barbarism, the Situationist International, and the group around the journal *Arguments*. These groups were, it has been accurately observed, the only ones to have predicted the French May.[89] In West Germany, the New Left inhered in trade unions, churches, and student groups – most importantly, the SDS – and was associated especially with the journal *Kursbuch* under the editorship of the writer Hans Magnus Enzensberger. In each country, the New Left sought to open up a fresh moral terrain in which the socialist project could flourish anew.

An important focal point of New Left organization was the institution of the political club. If not exactly a new organization form – the club was a key feature of the French Revolution of 1789 and its

---

[86] Gerd-Rainer Horn, *The Spirit of '68: Rebellion in Western Europe and North America, 1956–1976* (Oxford: Oxford University Press, 2006).

[87] Stuart Hall, "Life and times of the first New Left," *New Left Review*, 61 (Jan/Feb 2010), 177–196.

[88] Hughes, *Young Lives on the Left*, 62.   [89] Wolin, *The Wind from the East*, 20.

successor revolutions of the nineteenth century – the political club nevertheless counted as a fresh intervention in a political scene dominated by political parties and trade unions, those sites of the industrial worker–centric Old Left politics against which the New Left rebelled. In the UK, even earlier, a network originating in the Universities and Left Review Club and coffeehouse encompassed some fifty groups.[90] Thirty clubs proliferated around the journal *New Left Review* alone. In West Germany, clubs like Ça Ira and the Republican Club, founded in 1967 – their names announcing their inspiration in the French Revolution – became important centers of left-intellectual mobilization.[91] In Poland, clubs such as the Crooked Circle and the Contradiction Seekers were early progenitors of the 1960s rebellion. The student club as a cell of independent politics was flourishing as early as 1963.[92] Clubs played a key role in the Prague Spring as well.[93]

Another early and important feature of New Left activity was represented by political journals like Jean Paul Sartre's *Les Temps Modernes* (*Modern Times*), *New Left Review* (UK), *Quaderni Rossi* (Italy), and *Praxis* (Yugoslavia), which brought student activists together with an older generation of Marxist intellectuals. A leading organ of neo-Marxist critique in the East with international reach, *Praxis* played a particularly important role in helping to forge networks both within and between the respective Cold War blocs. Founded by professors at the University of Zagreb in 1964, it sought to free Marx from the grip of Stalinists, returning to his early writings and insisting on the importance of free speech as a necessary condition for the rigorous social criticism Marx had demanded. Intellectuals from across Europe sat on its editorial board, and from 1965 onward, the journal appeared in an international edition in German, French, and English.[94] The Praxis Group also convened a Summer School on the Croatian island of Korčula, which became an important site of transnational exchange for the international left intelligentsia.[95]

[90] Davis, "The origins of the British New Left," 50.

[91] Timothy S. Brown, *West Germany and the Global Sixties: The Anti-Authoritarian Revolt, 1962–1978* (New York: Cambridge University Press, 2013), 76–78.

[92] Stefan Garsztecki, "Poland," in Klimke and Scharloth, *1968 in Europe*, 179–197, 184; see also Zdenek Nebrensky, "Early voices of dissent," 33.

[93] Kavan, "Testament of a Prague Radical," 58.

[94] Borrero, "Spring thaw, summer frost," 76.

[95] Boris Kanzleiter, "1968 in Yugoslavia: Student revolt between East and West," in Klimke, Pekelder, and Scharloth, *Between Prague Spring and French May*, 84–100, 222, 225. On Praxis, see Gerson Sher, *Praxis: Marxist Criticism and Dissent in Socialist Yugoslavia* (Bloomington: Indiana University Press, 1977). On the darker role played by some Praxis figures during the rise of Serbian nationalism in the 1980s and 1990s, see

The revival of Marxist thought as an ideological-historical recovery project had a strongly bibliographic character. Antonio Gramsci's *Prison Notebooks*, written in secret under the Mussolini dictatorship, were already in publication again as early as the late 1940s.[96] German theorists of the Frankfurt School forced into exile by the Nazis – Theodor Adorno, Max Horkheimer, Herbert Marcuse, Wilhelm Reich – achieved a new prominence in the 1960s, their works reprinted first in bootleg and later in trade editions. Their perspectives on fascism, authoritarianism, mass media, and sexuality were taken as gospel by the 1960s generation of student radicals interested not just in material relations but in the manipulation of consciousness under regimes of misrule. The 1966 *Bibliography of Revolutionary Socialism* published by the West German student radical Rudi Dutschke signaled the intention of recovering suppressed traditions – including not just Marxism but anarchism – and putting them to use in the new conditions of the postwar period.[97]

If one meaning of "New Left" refers to the postwar neo-Marxist project and its intellectual protagonists, a second usage refers to the entire 1968 project, encompassing the student movement(s) and counterculture in Europe and North America. The New Left's concerns included a new focus on personal subjectivity, feelings, emotions; the rediscovery of Marx's early writings on alienation and the writings of the Frankfurt School; the fusion of Marxism with Existentialism and psychoanalysis; a shift in focus from large-scale projects like the nationalization of industry to changing the face of daily life; a new valuation of the importance of the individual, not only in terms of personal subjectivities but in terms of action strategies, which now focused on concepts like participatory democracy and direct action; and a shift in focus away from the industrial proletariat as the proposed revolutionary subject in favor of students, the intelligentsia, and marginal groups from the realm of youth *bohème*. At root, the New Left was based on the idea, as one of the young radicals at the University of Nanterre who helped jump-start the Paris May put it, "that the revolutionary process is not merely a change in the economic means of production."[98]

The above-mentioned Socialism or Barbarism made explicit early on the impulses fueling the antiauthoritarian revolt of 1968. Founded in the

---

Laura Secor, "Testaments betrayed," *Jacobin* (June 14, 2018), www.jacobinmag.com/2018/06/yugoslavia-praxis-journal-tito-marxism-socialism.

[96] Eley, *Forging Democracy*, 293.

[97] Rudi Dutschke, *Ausgewählte und kommentierte Bibliographie des revolutionären Sozialismus von K. Marx bis in die Gegenwart* (Heidelberg: Druck- und Verlagskooperative HFHB, 1969).

[98] Duteuil, *Nanterre 1968*.

late 1940s and existing until 1967, the group staked out territory to the left of Marxism-Leninism, insisting on the importance of workers' self-management and attracting the support of anarchists and council Communists. Initially aligned with Trotsky's Fourth International and its analysis of the Soviet Union as a "degenerated workers' state," the group quickly came around to the view that "the limitations of Soviet Communism, far from being Stalin's work alone, were traceable to Lenin's conception of the party as an authoritarian vanguard responsible for inculcating proletarians with 'class consciousness.'"[99] The group was distinctly ahead of its time, putting forward a fierce critique of Soviet Communism years before the official revelation of Stalin's crimes. A founding member, the Greek-French theorist Cornelius Castoriadis, put the issues thusly in 1949:

Never has there been more talk of "Marxism," of "socialism," of the working class, and of a new historical era. And never has genuine Marxism been so distorted, socialism so abused, and the working class so often sold out and betrayed by those claiming to represent it. "Socialism," we are told, has been achieved in countries numbering four hundred million inhabitants, yet that type of "socialism" appears inseparable from concentration camps, from the most intense social exploitation, from the most atrocious dictatorship, and from the most widespread brutish stupidity.[100]

Socialism or Barbarism's staking out of a revolutionary position to the left of Marxism-Leninism was a powerful influence on the Situationist Guy Debord, who belonged to the group. It was also attractive to young activists of May 1968, who rejected the Cold War settlement and the mainstream left landscape closely tied to it. "I couldn't become Communist," recalled one, "because, after all, I knew what the Stalinist regime was . . . . There were the two Blocs and we saw no way out between them. There were the events in East Berlin in 1953, there was Poland, and then there were the workers' councils in Hungary in 1956." Shown a flyer by a friend at the Sorbonne, he recalls, "I read it and I found it really terrific and I looked to see where it was from and it was Socialisme ou Barbarie."[101] Socialism or Barbarism was seen to be refreshing precisely because it spoke truth about the situation facing sixties activists. As a female activist put it, Socialism or Barbarism was "the only group that said things that didn't come out of the 19th century,

---

[99] Wolin, *The Wind from the East*, 57.
[100] Cornelius Castoriadis, *Political and Social Writings: Volume 1, 1946–1955* (Minneapolis: University of Minnesota, 1988), 76.
[101] Abidor, *More May Made Me*, 9.

that didn't use a classist wooden language and spoke of the problems of the day."[102]

Socialism or Barbarism inspired the formation in 1960 of a sister group in the UK, Solidarity, which published an eponymous newspaper and pursued a similar blend of anarchism and council communism. "East and West," the group wrote, "capitalism remains an inhuman type of society where the vast majority are bossed at work and manipulated in consumption and leisure . . . . The 'Communist' world is not Communist and the 'free' world is not free."[103] The group's goal of a "democratization of society down to its very roots" seemed to find expression in the May 1968 uprising in France, and the group's leading intellectual, Maurice Brinton (né Chris Pallis), published an important early analysis of the events.[104]

The journal *Arguments* was another key repository of the new thinking. Founded in 1956, it rejected political sectarianism and dogma in general and authoritarian Soviet Communism in particular. The *Arguments* group supported the resurgence of Marxist humanism reflected in the works of figures like Karl Korsch and György Lukács. Like Socialism or Barbarism, it was influential for Guy Debord, whose masterwork *Society of the Spectacle* sought to update Marxist analysis to account for the new psychic terrain of consumer capitalism. In the "spectacle," Debord discovered the new location of Marx's "false consciousness," under which individuals were, in Richard Wolin's apt phrase, "reduced to a state of somnambulant compliance."[105]

The 1960s revival of anarchism was important, among other reasons, for bridging the politics of the New Left and the lifestyle radicalism of the international counterculture. One of the things that was new about "neo"-anarchism was the way that traditional anarchist themes dovetailed with the politics of personal lifestyle, drawing as much from popular culture as from shop-floor militancy. At the same time, anarchism provided an avenue of contact between the counterculture and the artistic avant-garde, paving the way for cutting-edge theorists and theories to work their influence on the wider political movement of 1968. Anarchism's centrality in this set of relationships made it a flashpoint in conflicts between the more mainstream and/or dogmatic Marxist left and the antiauthoritarian lifestyle revolt of the radicalized wing of the counterculture. At the same time, in serving as a link between specific political contexts and international currents of popular culture and avant-garde theory, anarchism played a major role in the transnationalism of 1968.

---

[102] Abidor, *More May Made Me*, 7.   [103] *As We See It* (London: Solidarity, 1967).
[104] *As We See It*. See also Maurice Brinton, *Paris: May 1968* (London: Solidarity, 1968).
[105] Wolin, *The Wind from the East*, 60.

Yet even if traditional anarchism kept a low profile in 1968 – in some cases because anarcho-syndicalist organizations historically dedicated to labor militancy were unsure of, or even rejected, what they might interpret as the frivolous aspects of sixties youth militancy – the cultural-political avant-gardes that we will examine in detail in Chapter 3 borrowed explicitly from anarchism, drawing on its history and putting its lessons to use. They did this in the first instance as part of their attempt to codify youth-revolutionary impulses and discover tactical ways forward in their struggle with the establishment, but they also did it as part of an attempt to seize the interpretive high ground in struggles with those portions of the New Left – e.g. Maoists and Trotskyists – which, from the anarchist perspective, lacked coherence in their thinking about the relationship between authority and revolution.

Anarchism was especially central for the Amsterdam Provos, an early and precocious group of activists seeking to break down the boundaries between youth subcultures, radical politics, and daily life. For them, as we will see in Chapter 3, the renewal of anarchism was intimately connected to the need for the emergence of fresh protagonists willing and able to challenge the postwar status quo. In this sense, they shared in a broader preoccupation of the New Left – the assertion of the potential for action in a situation in which action was supposed to be impossible. The assertion was hardly frivolous, for even in the liberal democracies of Western Europe, activists were not operating within societies in which all questions had been settled; rather, they recognized the manifold ways in which the limitation of their horizons, whether in terms of the politically permissible or in terms of their experience of daily life, were part of a broader pattern of oppression. One fundamental act of 1968, in this sense, was to practice empathy – to recognize, to cite only one salient example, how injuries to Third World freedom fighters in Vietnam were also injuries to themselves.

The rebellion was no mere phenomenon of empathic projection, however. It took place not just amidst a punishing Cold War with all its restrictions on belief and behavior but in a world aflame with brutal proxy conflicts and guerrilla insurgencies. The American war in Vietnam raged across the entire period; there was a crisis in the Congo, counterinsurgency warfare in Latin America, colonial conflict in Portuguese Angola, the Arab-Israeli conflict in the Middle East. In these hot wars, postmaterialist concerns rooted in the relative peace and prosperity of continental Europe could be but a distant dream.[106] Even within Europe, the shape of the postwar settlement was highly contingent;

---

[106] Just how "hot" the Cold War became is shown in Paul Thomas Chamberlin, *The Cold War's Killing Fields: Rethinking the Long Peace* (New York: HarperCollins, 2018).

the ghosts of social conflicts past were still a living presence. Activism in Europe took place in a context of war, in other words – not only a Cold War that squeezed individuals between the competing claims of the superpowers but hot wars that had to be on the agenda of activists dedicated to overcoming artificial barriers between people, regions, and ideas. The "sixties," in other words, were a response to problems operative across the three worlds and connecting them. The particular shape of sixties activism grew out of the search for solutions to these problems. And that search took activists not just into the realm of politics but, as we will see in Chapter 3, into the realm of culture.

3   Cultural Revolutions

"What is the Provotariat?" asked the Amsterdam Provos in a 1966 manifesto:

All Provos, beatniks, bums, Halbstarken, teddy-boys; blouson noirs, Gammler, raggare, stiljagi, mangupi, students, artists, criminals, a-socials, anarchists, and the ban-the-bombers. Who don't want a career, don't want to endure a regular life .... Here, in the carbon-monoxide-polluted asphalt jungles of Amsterdam, London, Stockholm, Tokyo, Moscow, Paris, New York, Berlin, Milan; Warsaw, Chicago. The Provotariat is the last insurgent group in the welfare state.[1]

With this passage the young Dutch radicals identified a key social feature of the nascent 1968: an international and transnational scene of "outcasts, dropouts, and provocateurs," young rebels who wore, listened to, and paraded in the street their challenge to the postwar settlement.[2] Invoking youth cults like the "raggare" (Sweden), "stiljagi" (Soviet Union), and "mangupi" (Turkey), the Provos exercised the border-crossing vision characteristic of 1968, but they expressed a key preoccupation of the sixties radical: the search for untapped revolutionary potential. For the Provos, as for many other radicals of the first hour around 1968, workers were no longer a force capable of revolution. "The Proletariat," as they put it, "is the slave of the politicians. Watching TV."[3] Only members of the so-called Provotariat, made up of youth subcultures and juvenile delinquents, still possessed the disruptive power to overturn existing conditions. The very name of Provo emphasized this assertion, being lifted directly from a well-known 1965 Dutch study of the *Nozem* – rough equivalents to the English

---

[1] "Aufruf an das internationale Provotariat," *Provokatie*, 8, reprinted in *Oberbaum Linkeck Almanach 1965–1968*, www.infopartisan.net/archive/1967/266718.html. See the instructive discussion of worried government responses to the very same subcultures in William Jay Risch, "Introduction," in William Jay Risch (ed.), *Youth and Rock in the Soviet Bloc: Youth Cultures, Music, and the State in Russia and Eastern Europe* (Lanham: Lexington, 2015).

[2] See the discussion in Gerd-Rainer Horn, *The Spirit of '68: Rebellion in Western Europe and North America, 1956–1976* (Oxford: Oxford University Press, 2006), 5–53.

[3] "Aufruf an das internationale Provotariat."

Teddy Boys – whom the author dubbed "provos" after the French *provoquer*.[4] The choice of name revealed the goal: Provo sought to channel even the most superficially unpolitical youth rebellion, making explicit its political implications and lending it an analytic background rooted equally in the spirit of the sixties moment and in earlier radical traditions. "PROVO," as they put it, "encourages rebellion wherever it can."[5]

Teenage Riot

In the form of the Provotariat, the Provos identified an essential ingredient in the uprisings of 1968: a semiautonomous international youth culture with its own mores, preoccupations, and style. The existence of this culture had been presaged already in the 1940s and 1950s by the birth of the "teenager" – a social type between childhood and adulthood made

3.1 Seizing the means of cultural production: Amsterdam Provos (photo: Leonard Freed, courtesy of Magnum).

---

[4] Richard Kempton, *Provo: Amsterdam's Anarchist Revolt* (Southport: New Autonomy, 2007), 38.
[5] "Provo magazine leaflet," in Peter Stansill and David Zane Mairowitz (eds.), *BAMN (By Any Means Necessary): Outlaw Manifestos and Ephemera, 1965–1970* (New York: Autonomedia, 1999), 18.

possible by new mass-mediated possibilities of sensibility, mobility, and consumer choice. In the 1960s, this developing youth culture was synergized by new developments in fashion, music, and the arts. By the middle of the decade, it also began to take on a distinctly political coloration. On the one hand, a widespread new "life feeling" encompassing unconventional modes of thought and behavior seemed to fit naturally into a resurgence of left-wing ideas and practices, especially in the second half of the 1960s with the emergence of the American war in Vietnam as the central issue for the international New Left on both sides of the East-West divide. On the other, especially in the East, authorities went out of their way to politicize youth subcultures as a threat to dominant values, forcing young people into a political role whether they wanted to be in one or not.

Popular music played a leading role in the genesis and spread of the new youth culture, as well as in its politicization. From the beginning of the 1960s, politically inspired folk music was an important vehicle of emancipatory youth culture. From the Soviet Union to France, from Italy to East Germany, "guitar poets" drew on older left-wing traditions of political song, updating them with an eye toward the Beat-influenced Anglo-American folk revival.[6] The political import of folk and political song was codified in events like the annual Berg Waldeck festival in West Germany, which brought together East and West German influences in its blending of older traditions of Central European socialist song and new American influences drawing on Civil Rights and militant labor traditions.

By the mid-1960s, rock 'n' roll began to supplant folk and jazz as the music of rebellion. The so-called Beat Wave of the mid-1960s carried the sounds of English groups like the Rolling Stones, the Beatles, the Kinks, and the Small Faces to both sides of the Iron Curtain. With its power "to open up questions of identity, justice, repression, will, and desire," this music became the template *par excellence* for youth rebellion.[7] The example of the English groups inspired the formation of homegrown bands, sometimes possessing a political charge of their own, more frequently forced into an unwished-for political stance by the attitude of the authorities. Groups with an explicit Marxist or anarchist message were few and far between, although they did become more prominent after the year 1968. Instead, as will be seen below, music became political where the aspirations of fans ran up against the trepidation of elites.

---

[6] Rossen Djagalow, "Guitar poetry, democratic socialism, and the limits of 1960s internationalism," in Anne E. Gorsuch and Diane P. Koenker (eds.), *The Socialist Sixties: Crossing Borders in the Second World* (Bloomington: Indiana University Press, 2013).

[7] Greil Marcus, *Lipstick Traces: A Secret History of the Twentieth Century* (Cambridge, MA: Harvard University Press, 2003), 56.

By the mid-1960s, the juvenile delinquents prized by groups like the Provos and feared by regimes on both sides of the Iron Curtain were joined by a new species, the Beat-influenced proto-hippie, who flocked to public gathering places such as Dam Square in Amsterdam, the Kaiser Wilhelm Memorial Church in West Berlin, the Piazza Duomo in Milan, and Mayakovsky Square in Moscow.[8] These public gathering spaces became key sites of transnational exchange in which countercultural denizens mingled with travelers from around Europe and the world. In local terms, they became flashpoints for conflict about where young people had a right to be and what they had a right to do while being there. To congregate in public space – especially public space intended to memorialize the state, tradition, war heroes, and so on – was to challenge dominant values of duty and sobriety, to subvert the rule of the clock that marked time for legitimate activity on both sides of the East-West divide.

On both sides of that divide, the appearance of Beat music threatened established gender roles and stoked fears of social unrest. Because of the totalizing nature of state socialist claims over cultural life, such fears were intensified in Eastern Europe.[9] The Eastern Bloc was far from homogenous in its relationship to popular music, however.[10] Whereas in some countries, such as Bulgaria and Romania (and, for much of its history, East Germany), authorities were known for their particularly negative stance toward Beat music, regimes in Yugoslavia, Poland, and Hungary were characterized by relatively liberal stances. These more flexible attitudes did not preclude attempts to instrumentalize popular music for the regimes' own purposes, however, and indeed, the former was frequently intended to serve the purposes of the latter.[11] In general, Communist elites simultaneously worried about Western influence while hoping to capitalize on new trends to win the affection of the young.

The German Democratic Republic (GDR) exhibited a notably arbitrary stance. After the building of the Berlin Wall in 1961, the GDR saw an explosion of bands inspired by the sounds of the American Forces

---

[8] On hippies and space in the Soviet Union, see Juliane Fürst, *Flowers through Concrete: Explorations in the Soviet Hippieland* (Oxford: Oxford University Press, 2018); Julianne Fürst, "'If you are going to Moscow, be sure to wear some flowers in your hair': The Soviet hippie 'sistema' and its life in, despite, and with 'stagnation'," in Dina Fainberg and Artemy M. Kalinovsky (eds.), *Reconsidering Stagnation in the Brezhnev Era* (Lanham: Rowman & Littlefield, 2016).

[9] They existed on both sides of the Cold War divide, however. See Uta Poiger, *Jazz, Rock, and Rebels: Cold War Politics and American Culture in a Divided Germany* (Berkeley: University of California Press, 2000).

[10] Rüdiger Ritter, "1968 – the emergence of a protest culture in the popular music of the Eastern Bloc?," in Beate Kutschke and Barley Norton (eds.), *Music and Protest in 1968* (Cambridge: Cambridge University Press, 2013), 205–221, 206.

[11] Ritter, "1968."

Network and other Western stations. Making raw and primitive Beat music with the help of smuggled or homemade distortion and delay boxes, they took names – the Beatlers, the Bottles, the Brittles, the Brightles, the Big Beats, the Five Stones – meant to evoke associations with leading British bands.[12] Playing in officially tolerated but youth-run clubs that quickly burst acceptable boundaries, they represented what came to be regarded by the regime as an intolerable intrusion of Western-oriented chaos. This impression was influenced by events in neighboring West Germany, notably the infamous riot at the Rolling Stones concert in West Berlin's Waldbühne in September 1965, which produced a moral panic on both sides of the Wall. It was intensified for East German authorities in October, when, following the regime's banning of a number of popular Beat groups, young fans protested en masse in Leipzig before being brutally suppressed by police.[13] Musical "resistance" against the state's totalizing claims in East Germany thereafter evolved in connection with the "blues" scene of traveling shaggy bands and fans with their semilegal excursions, encampments, and "people's festivals."[14]

In Poland, where half a million guitars per year were being sold by the early 1960s, the regime exhibited a relative openness toward rock music, even if it stood at odds with the nonconformist habitus that formed around it. As elsewhere in Europe, youth delinquency developed in the 1950s, with the subculture of so-called Bikini Boys who sported an image supposedly representing the 1954 American hydrogen bomb test on Bikini Atoll on their neckties.[15] A rock-'n'-roll-oriented hippie commune culture began to develop as early as 1965.[16] Hundreds of Polish Beat groups were formed, among them Czerwone Gitary (Red Guitars) – the

---

[12] Heiner Stahl, "A border-crossing soundscape of pop: The auditory traces of subcultural practices in 1960s Berlin," in Sheila Whiteley and Jedediah Sklower (eds.), *Countercultures and Popular Music* (Abingdon: Taylor and Francis, 2014), 225.

[13] See Dorothee Wierling, "Der Staat, die Jugend und der Westen: Texte zu Konfliktender 1960er Jahre," in Alf Lüdtke and Peter Becker (eds.), *Akten, Eingaben, Schaufenster: Die DDR und ihre Texte. Erkundungen zu Herrschaft und Alltag* (Berlin: De Gruyter, 1997), 223–240, 223; see also Dorothee Wierling, "Beat heißt schlagen: Die Leipziger Beatdemonstration in Oktober 1965 und die Jugendpolitik der SED," in Rolf Geserick (ed.), *Unsere Medien, Unsere Republik 2: 1965: Warten auf den Frühling*, vol. 4 (Marl: Adolf Grimme Institut, 1993).

[14] See Michael Rauhut and Thomas Kochan (eds.), *Bye, Bye Lueben City: Bluesfreaks, Tramps and Hippies in der DDR* (Berlin: Schwarzkopf & Schwarzkopf, 2004). See also Michael Rauhut, *Rock in der DDR, 1964–1989* (Bonn: Bundeszentrale für politische Bildung, 2002).

[15] Tom Junes, "Facing the music: How the foundations of socialism were rocked in Communist Poland," in Risch, *Youth and Rock in the Soviet Bloc*, 229–254.

[16] William Jay Risch, "Only rock 'n' roll? Rock music, hippies, and urban identities in Lviv and Wrocław, 1965–1980," in Risch, *Youth and Rock in the Soviet Bloc*, 81–99.

"Polish Beatles."[17] They performed at the 1966 "Spring Festival of the Teenagers" alongside a number of other indigenous Polish groups. That same year, Western bands like The Hollies and The Animals were allowed to play in Poland. The following year, the potential consequences of this relative openness were demonstrated by the Rolling Stones. As it had done in Western capitals like West Berlin and Zurich, the Stones' appearance precipitated the near-destruction of the venue (the Palace of Culture and Science), followed by two days of riots.[18]

Polish authorities subsequently tried to coopt Beat music by fostering safe groups such as No To Co, which mixed Western Beat influences with nods to Polish folk tradition.[19] Such an approach was seen as an antidote to the key fear of Communist regimes when facing popular music: that the popularity of Anglo-American sounds represented a form of cultural imperialism that would end up bringing with it not only Western sounds and fashions but Western ideas, possibly even capitalism itself. Music scenes in Hungary and Yugoslavia were characterized by the state's attempts to turn popular music and youth culture in regime-friendly directions. Even during the post-1968 period, when the crushing of the Prague Spring cast a pall over the landscape of political liberalization in the Eastern Bloc, the state in these countries continued to seek to use popular music both as a means of coopting youth and achieving national prestige.[20] Indeed, liberalization around popular music made up a key regime strategy for dealing with the political tensions left over from 1968.[21]

In Czechoslovakia, where some 500 rock bands had received state licences to perform in the latter half of the 1960s, the post–Prague Spring repression made popular music a site of intense contestation. Even as state attitudes toward jazz and jazz rock were being liberalized at the beginning of the 1970s, what would become Czechoslovakia's best-known band, the Plastic People of the Universe, was being

[17] Anna Pelka, "Youth fashion in Poland in the 1950s and 1960s: Ideology, resistance, and manipulation," in Kathrin Fahlenbrach, Martin Klimke, Joachim Scharloth, and Laura Wong (eds.), *The Establishment Responds: Power, Politics, and Protest since 1945* (New York: Palgrave, 2012), 197–210, 204.

[18] Europopmusic, "1968 in Poland," www.europopmusic.eu/Newsletters/Features/Protest_68/1968_in_Poland.html.

[19] This style was exemplified by the group No To Co. See Pelka, "Youth fashion in Poland in the 1950s and 1960s," 204.

[20] Ewa Mazierska, "Introduction," in Ewa Mazierska (ed.), *Popular Music in Eastern Europe: Breaking the Cold War Paradigm* (New York: Palgrave MacMillan, 2016), 6. See also Madigan Fichter, "Rock 'n' roll nation: Counterculture and dissent in Romania, 1965–1975," *Nationalities Papers*, 39(4) (2011), 567–585.

[21] See Beate Kutschke, "Anti-authoritarian revolt by musical means on both sides of the Berlin Wall," in Kutschke and Norton, *Music and Protest in 1968*, 188–204.

mercilessly harried. Founded one month after the Soviet invasion of August 1968, taking their name from a song by Frank Zappa, the Plastic People were indelibly linked to Czech underground culture in the post–Prague Spring era.[22] The band's licence to perform was revoked in 1970, and some of its members were sentenced to prison terms over the course of the 1970s. Yet it was the state's repression of the band that helped create the Charter 77 movement led by the playwright Václav Havel and others. The scene formed around the band, meanwhile, made of the so-called *máničky*, became the Czech analog to the East German blues fans who opted out of GDR society over the course of the 1970s and 1980s.

Communist regimes' criminalization of popular music exemplifies the process described by Detlef Siegfried as "politicization from above."[23] As Vratislav Brabenec, a member of the Plastic People of the Universe, put it: "I am one of those whose cultural actions, not political actions, were sufficient to make me a subversive. The politicians made us political, by being offended by what we did and the music we played."[24] Popular music could also be made political "from below" – either through the creation of explicitly political music or through the act of *imputing* a political stance onto existing music. Whatever the intention of the artists, fans themselves frequently understood rock 'n' roll as a call to rebellion that could and did take on a political coloration. The music of the Rolling Stones, especially, was interpreted in such terms, notably in riots in West Berlin (1965), Warsaw (1967), and Zurich (1967, 1968).[25] Tellingly, one of the most militant factions in the West Berlin scene of the late 1960s, the so-called Blues (the "Hash Rebels"), cited the riot at the Stones' 1965 Waldbühne concert as a formative moment in their politicization.[26]

---

[22] See Jonathan Bolton, *Worlds of Dissent: Charter 77, The Plastic People of the Universe, and Czech Culture under Communism* (Cambridge, MA: Harvard University Press, 2012).

[23] Detlef Siegfried, "Unsere Woodstocks: Jugendkultur, Rockmusik und gesellschaftlicher Wandel um 1968," in *Rock!* (1995), 52–61, 53.

[24] Ed Vulliamy, "1989 and all that: Plastic People of the Universe and the Velvet Revolution," *The Guardian* (September 5, 2009), www.theguardian.com/music/2009/s ep/06/plastic-people-velvet-revolution-1989.

[25] On the latter, see Rolf Werenskjold, "A chronology of the global 1968 protest," in Martin Klimke, Jacco Pekelder, and Joachim Scharloth (eds.), *Between Prague Spring and French May: Opposition and Revolt in Europe, 1960–1980* (New York: Berghahn, 2011), 283–307, 299. On the connection between politics and music, see Detlef Siegfried, *Time Is on My Side: Konsum und Politik in der Westdeutschen Jugendkultur der 60er Jahre* (Göttingen: Wallstein, 2006).

[26] Ralf Reinders and Ronald Fritsch, *Die Bewegung 2 Juni: Gespräche über Haschrebellen, Lorenzentführung, Knast* (Berlin: Edition ID-Archiv, 1995), 23. The classic account is Michael Baumann, *How It All Began* (Vancouver: Arsenal Pulp, 1977).

Eastern Europe was not the only place where Communists worried about rock music as a form of American cultural imperialism. In Greece, under a right-wing dictatorship from 1967 to 1974, Communist youth organizations were almost as suspicious of rock music as the Communist regimes in the East. Even as they tried to coopt rock for political purposes, they sought to foster appreciation for indigenous Greek folk music as a more "authentic" and politically salutary alternative.[27] In Italy, similarly, the growing radicalization of the late 1960s saw folk music emerge as a preferred expression of militant working-class consciousness,[28] while in West Germany, debates about the relative artistic-political merit of individual forms (jazz, folk, rock) were central to music criticism in and around the burgeoning New Left.[29]

Meanwhile, a new breed of political agitator had its eye on the Beat-influenced "youth proletariat" as an untapped source of insurrectionary power. As early as 1966, Roel van Duijn proclaimed "Provo is Beat," suggesting a natural affinity between what he saw as two related attempts to upset the status quo.[30] The Dutch alternative journal *Hitweek*, alongside publications like *Heatwave* in the UK and *Song* in West Germany, sought to establish the political legitimacy of popular culture while instrumentalizing it in the service of a wished-for political rebellion.[31] Attempts to will into existence an alliance between "pop and politics" characterized the activity of the more open-minded of political militants as well.[32] Commenting on riots at a Rolling Stones concert in Zurich, Swiss radicals argued that Mick Jagger and the Stones

---

[27] Nikolaos Papadogiannis, "Greek Communist youth identities and rock music in the late 1970s," in Timothy Scott Brown and Lorena Anton (eds.), *Between the Avant-Garde and the Everyday: Subversive Politics in Europe, 1957 to the Present* (New York: Berghahn, 2011), 77–91. See also Nikolaos Papadogiannis, *Militant around the Clock? Youth Politics, Leisure and Sexuality in Post-dictatorship Greece, 1974–1981* (New York: Berghahn, 2015).

[28] Giovanni Vacca, "Music and countercultures in Italy: The Neapolitan scene," in Whiteley and Sklower, *Countercultures and Popular Music*, 238.

[29] See the chapter "Sound," in Timothy Scott Brown, *West Germany and the Global Sixties: The Anti-Authoritarian Revolt, 1962–1978* (New York: Cambridge University Press, 2013). Such debates were by no means strictly or even primarily European phenomena. They were also important in the Global South, where in locations as diverse as Brazil and Bangladesh, ongoing struggles over decolonization made cultural imperialism a particularly sensitive issue; see Christopher Dunn, "Mapping tropicália," in Timothy Scott Brown and Andrew Lison (eds.), *The Global Sixties in Sound and Vision: Media, Counterculture, Revolt* (New York: Palgrave Macmillan, 2014), 29–42; Samantha Christiansen, "From 'Help!' to 'helping out a friend': Imagining South Asia through the Beatles and the Concert for Bangladesh," in *Rock Music Studies*, 1(2) (2014).

[30] Robert Adlington, "Expressive revolutions: '1968' and music in the Netherlands," in Kutschke and Norton, *Music and Protest in 1968*, 12–28, 17.

[31] Adlington, "Expressive Revolutions," 17.   [32] Adlington, "Expressive Revolutions."

have spoken for us all, with: "I can't get no *Satisfaction!*" That we can't find any satisfaction is the fault of those who want to convince us that life consists of nothing other than subordination and striving to get ahead, respect and careers, study and credentials, industry ... peace and order, propriety and laws, VW and Opel, Bratwurst and Rösti .... [A]nd because the bourgeois cannot find any joy in something as useless as Beat, our enthusiasm is a slap to their face.[33]

Here, the rebellious claims of popular music appeared as a weapon aimed at the entire edifice of bourgeois society. Popular music was the site at which resistance to all problems converged, not only capitalist competition, enforced consumption, and the boredom of conformity but "the napalm war against Vietnam, the oppression of colored people in the USA and South Africa, and the discrimination against foreign laborers in Switzerland."[34]

Avant-Gardes

The potential for rock to become political – a transformation sometimes actually achieved, sometimes merely hoped for – was indicative of a broader trend: the tendency, around 1968, for cultural expression to be transformed into political action. The new type of left-wing radical who emerged in the West to channel this upsurge of youth radicalism – not just the Provos in Amsterdam but groups like King Mob in London, Onda Verde in Milan, and the Kommune I in West Berlin – arose out of a characteristic 1960s convergence: the fusion of popular culture, radical politics, and avant-garde art. Growing out of the experiences of daily life and rooted in the relationship of youth to authority in the spaces of the city, this convergence drew on all manner of social and cultural nonconformism linked to new expressions in the popular arts. Its components were not entirely new, however, but arose out of earlier trends.

The new oppositional youth culture was foreshadowed and synergized by a transnational literary avant-garde heavily influenced by the American Beats.[35] The American Beat writers staked out new aesthetic and psychic terrain with immense appeal on both sides of the Atlantic. Books like Allen Ginsberg's *Howl* (1956), Jack Kerouac's *On the Road* (1957), and William S. Burroughs's *Naked Lunch* (1959) probed the boundaries of acceptable speech while celebrating values of nonconformism,

---

[33] Antiautoritäre Junge Sektion der PdA (Partei der Arbeit), "Rebellion is berechtigt," in Lutz Schulenburg (ed.), *Das Leben ändern, die Welt verändern! 1968 – Dokumente und Berichte* (Hamburg: Edition Nautilus, 1998), 206–208, 206–207.
[34] "Rebellion is berechtigt," 208.
[35] See Nancy M. Grace and Jennie Skerl (eds.), *The Transnational Beat Generation* (New York: Palgrave Macmillan, 2012).

spontaneity, and creativity for its own sake. These explorations exercised an outsized influence on the imagination of a young generation of European writers who took the Beats as a starting point for counter-cultural explorations of their own. Figures like the Dutch poet Simon Vinkenoog, the Scottish novelist Alexander Trocchi, the West German poet and novelist Rolf Dieter Brinkmann, and the Italian writer and critic Fernanda Pivano played major roles in infusing the Beat sensibility into Europe.

Already at the beginning of the 1950s, Vinkenoog had published the anthology *Atonaal* ("Atonal," 1951), which brought together a who's-who of the writers of the so-called Fifties Movement. This group was close to the CoBrA (Copenhagen, Brussels, Amsterdam) group, whose members included the Dutch painter, sculptor, and graphic designer Constant Nieuwenhuys ("Constant") and the Danish painter and sculptor Asger Jorn, both of whom were involved with the Situationist International. Vinkenoog's 1965 novel *Liefde* helped prefigure the Dutch youth revolt associated with Provo. Rolf Dieter Brinkmann, famous for his best-selling 1968 "pop novel" *Keiner weiß mehr* ("Nobody knows any-more"), subsequently helped pioneer the importation of American Beat writings into West Germany, publishing them in German translation in his 1969 anthology *Silverscreen*.[36] Trocchi coedited the literary magazine *Merlin* in Paris in the early 1950s, coming into contact there with some of the American Beats as well as with Guy Debord, future founder of the Situationist International. Trocchi, author of the controversial Beat novel *Cain's Book* (1960), became an international countercultural *cause célèbre* in connection with his legal travails around drug and obscenity charges, meanwhile playing a role in the formation of an international counter-cultural network through his Project Sigma.[37]

These networks emerged under the direct influence of visits to Europe by leading Beat figures. Alan Ginsberg and Peter Orlovsky visited Amsterdam in 1957, in search of Gregory Corso, and met and spent time with Simon Vinkenoog. Ginsberg and Vinkenoog establishing a lifelong friendship, and Vinkenoog became Ginsburg's translator into Dutch.[38] Vinkenoog's home subsequently became a key stopover point

[36] Anthony Waine, "Fatal attractions: Rolf Dieter Brinkmann and British life and culture," *The Modern Language Review*, 87(2) (April 1992), 376–392.
[37] On Sigma, see Niek Pas, "In pursuit of the invisible revolution: Sigma in the Netherlands, 1966–1968," in Brown and Anton, *Between the Avant-Garde and the Everyday*, 31–43.
[38] Jaap van der Bent, "'O fellow travelers I write you a poem in Amsterdam': Allen Ginsberg, Simon Vinkenoog, and the Dutch Beat connection," *College Literature*, 27 (1), Teaching Beat Literature (Winter 2000), 199–212.

for Beat poets reading in Amsterdam.[39] Gregory Corso spent significant time in the late 1950s and early 1960s in both West and East Berlin. His collaboration with his West German translator Walter Höllerer yielded an important 1961 anthology of Beat writers in German translation.[40]

Ginsberg's 1965 stay in London helped solidify a UK Beat scene already under development through figures like Donald Allen, Gene Feldman, and Max Gartenberg. In June 1965, along with Lawrence Ferlinghetti and Gregory Corso, Ginsberg performed at the International Poetry Incarnation at the Royal Albert Hall, an early, major event in the development of underground art in England. The

3.2 Allen Ginsburg as King of the May. Prague, May 1, 1965 (Alamy).

[39] Bill Morgan, *The Beats Abroad: A Global Guide to the Beat Generation* (San Francisco: City Lights, 2015), 110.
[40] Morgan, *The Beats Abroad*.

same year, Ginsberg was in Prague, where students celebrating May Day spontaneously elected him King of the May.[41] The mass celebration of the Beat poet, fresh from discomfiting his guests in Communist Cuba by his comments on politics and homosexuality, prompted Czechoslovakian authorities to have him expelled from the country.

In his poem "Kral Majales," penned on his subsequent flight to London, Ginsberg wrote: "and the Communists have nothing to offer but fat cheeks and eyeglasses and lying policemen, and the capitalists proffer Napalm and money ... [and] drink gin and whiskey on airplanes but let Indian brown millions starve."[42] Ginsberg visited Poland on the same trip, meeting with the Russian poet Andrei Voznesensky.[43] Russia at that time already claimed its own Beat collective, the "Youngest Organization of Geniuses" (SMOG, after the Russian acronym). Ginsberg's friend Lawrence Ferlinghetti read in Berlin with Voznesensky at the Berlin Literary Colloquium in February 1967, and on a trip to Russia in the same year he was able to meet with a Russian translator of the Beats, Andrei Sergeev.[44]

The spread of Beat influence had not only a cultural but a political impact. With Beat, as with so much of Europe's 1960s cultural revolution, the transnational was very much an *active* affair. Figures like Vinkenoog in the Netherlands, Brinkmann in West Germany, and Pivano in Italy took it upon themselves to see that Beat and other new writings would find their way to their respective countries. The Beat sensibility helped open the ground for a new life feeling that extended from their novels and poetry to influence the habitus of young nonconformists who were increasingly unwilling to live by old moral codes and strictures. In this way, the Beats foreshadowed, and in many cases directly influenced, the rise of an international counterculture in the latter part of the 1960s.

Simultaneously, Beat opened up new themes of sexuality, homosexuality, drug use, and other transgressive or nonconformist behavior, expanding the boundaries of acceptable expression. The new openness not only pushed against cultural prejudices but also directly against the power of the state, with classic works such as Ginsberg's *Howl* and Trocchi's *Cain's Book* facing high-profile obscenity trials. In this way, the Beats foreshadowed, if inadvertently, the purposeful use of cultural provocation as a way of attacking establishment power, a tactic that was to

---

[41] Petr Blažek, "The deportation of the King of May," in Chris Johnstone (ed.), *BIC: Behind the Iron Curtain: Review of the Institute for the Study of Totalitarian Regimes* (Czech Republic: Institute for the Study of Totalitarian Regimes, 2012), 35–47. See also Petr Kopecký, "Czeching the beat, beating the Czech: Ginsberg and Ferlinghetti in Czechia," *The Sixties*, 3(1) (2010), 97–103.

[42] Morgan, *The Beats Abroad*, 129–30.   [43] Morgan, *The Beats Abroad*, 132.

[44] Morgan, *The Beats Abroad*, 135.

be repeated by many other groups and publications for whom "obscenity" became a terrain of conflict with the authorities.

The influence of Beat did more than help create and channel the pre-political impulses in the first hour of the revolt, however. It also helped prepare the ground for subsequent utopian projects, especially from artists close to the Situationist milieu. One of the most prominent of these was Trocchi's Project Sigma, an initiative prefigured in his 1962 essay "Invisible insurrection of a million minds." Reprinted in the January 1963 issue of *Internationale Situationniste*, the essay called for the establishment of a "spontaneous university" that would revolutionize education and with it human society.[45] The project was subsequently introduced in the Netherlands by Vinkenoog, who in 1966 secured fund-ing for a Sigma Center from Amsterdam's Department of Art Affairs.[46] Another project hatched out of the Situationist milieu, and closely related both to Sigma and to Provo, was Nieuwenhuys' "New Babylon," which envisioned a future free urban utopia in which the human being of the future, "Homo Ludens," would be free to unfold his or her creative potential.[47] These projects had in common a concern with the utopian potential of the city, of play and education and, especially in the case of Sigma, became an influence on the development of international counter-cultural networks.

Sixties utopian projects saw attempts to erase altogether the distinction between art, politics, and daily life. Impulses that began at the avant-garde fringe of the art world – to make art relevant; to free it from the control of museums and other centers of cultural authority; to break down the boundary between artist and audience; to uphold "play" as an anti-dote to the grim instrumental rationality of work/school/family – had an obvious political valence waiting to be realized. Neo-Marxist and/or anarchist-oriented groups like the Surrealists and Situationists were expli-cit about the radical democratic and antiauthoritarian thrust of their projects. In turn, a new class of political provocateur drawn from the world of student *bohème* seized on the art/politics fusion as a fresh avenue for radicalizing postwar societies. These radicals sought to expand the new ideas beyond the atelier and the café, connecting them to the

[45] Alexander Trocchi, "A revolutionary proposal: Invisible insurrection of a million minds," in Andrew Murray Scott (ed.), *Invisible Insurrection of a Million Minds: A Trocchi Reader* (Edinburgh: Polygon, 1991). The piece was originally published in the Scottish journal *New Satire*, and subsequently under the title "Technique du coupe du monde" in *Internationale Situationniste*, 8 (January 1963), 48–54. See also Alexander Trocchi, "Sigma: A tactical blueprint," *City Lights Journal*, 2 (1964).

[46] McKenzie Wark, *The Beach beneath the Street: The Everyday Life and Glorious Times of the Situationist International* (London: Verso, 2015).

[47] Pas, "In pursuit of the invisible revolution."

burgeoning student protest movements and to the wider field of insurrectionary youth subcultures.

Debates about the status of culture were bound up with a thoroughgoing reevaluation of the role of the artist. During the insurrection of May 1968, the activists of the Parisian "People's Studio" posed the question as follows: "What is bourgeois culture?" It was nothing less, they answered, than "the instrument by which the oppressive power of the ruling class separates and isolates artists from other workers by granting them a privileged status."[48] Rejecting the autonomy of the artist, they argued that art must be integrated into the broader liberation struggle. The privileged status granted the artist, they argued, placed him "in a position in which he can do no harm, where he functions like a safety valve in the mechanism of bourgeois society. We are all bourgeois artists. How could it be otherwise? ... This means that we have decided to transform what we are in society."[49]

A decisive development in this self-transformation of artists, one that predated but also prefigured the radicalization of art around 1968, was a shift in focus from an art oriented toward *objects* to one oriented toward *action*. This shift was active already in the 1940s and 1950s in the work of abstract expressionists like Jackson Pollock and Willem de Kooning. Their "action painting" juxtaposed different types of media and introduced a performative element into the process of making art in which artistic production itself became part of the artwork. From here it was but a small step to involving the audience in the performance and exploding the boundaries of the canvas and the gallery altogether. The social content of the active turn in the arts was further realized in the development of the Happening, an event in which actions ranging from the identifiably artistic (playing music) to the mundane (performing everyday actions from printed instructions distributed to the audience) mingled to create a new sort of experience in which the distinction between art and daily life was erased.[50]

The Happening had its origins in New York City, where it was introduced by the painter Allan Kaprow at the Reuben Gallery in October 1959. It quickly spread across the Atlantic to become a staple of avant-garde artistic practice. A chief vehicle of this international exchange was the Fluxus movement. Fluxus first developed in 1950s

---

[48] Andrew Feenberg and Jim Freedman, *When Poetry Ruled the Streets: The French May Events of 1968* (Albany: State University of New York Press, 2001), 143.

[49] Feenberg and Freedman, *When Poetry Ruled the Streets*.

[50] See Stefan Wouters, "The influence of happenings on the performative display of subcultures: Insights into the Beat, mod, Provo, and hipster movements," in Alexander Dhoest, Steven Malliet, Jacques Haers, and Barbara Segaert (eds.), *The Borders of Subculture: Resistance and the Mainstream* (London: Routledge, 2015), 55–69.

New York in the orbit of the experimental composer John Cage. Fluxus retained a strong connection to new music throughout its history, but music was only part of a multimedia approach blending performance and visual art, literature and design. Anticommercial and antiart, Fluxus channeled the spirit of earlier European movements like Dada in striving to produce non-sense that would shatter the sensibilities of bourgeois normality. The feel of these ideas is captured in an interview with the German Fluxus artist Arthur Kopcke:

Q: You were in America. Were you successful there?
A: What is that – success?
Q: Do you earn money with this activity? Do you see it as your profession?
A: What is that – money? I don't need money.
Q: What do you think is the sense of your activity?
A: I am looking for a kind of communication between people. Do you know the man next-door? You probably don't know him. You would not talk to him in a tram or at a Beethoven concert. Here you talk to him . . .
Q: Is that art, what you are doing?
A: What is art?[51]

In his Zen-flavored responses to the interviewer, Kopcke touched implicitly on the political content of the Happening. A chief political innovation of 1968 would be to make the politics inherent in the Happening into an explicitly political act.

Fluxus was a key example of the transnational at work in 1968. It was George Maciunas who helped bring it to West Germany and who helped synergize its transnational effect through his network of personal relationships. During a stint as a civilian employee of the US Air Force in the West German city of Wiesbaden, Maciunas helped found the Fluxus International Festival for the Latest Music. The festival became a center of the international Fluxus movement, attracting a diverse group of artists, including the Korean Nam June Paik and the West Germans Wolf Vostell and Joseph Beuys. Beuys was a pioneer of the Happening in the Federal Republic and later went on to establish contact with the left-wing student movement there. The first festivals in 1962 (in Wiesbaden, London, Copenhagen, and Paris) quickly spread across Europe, reaching a peak in 1966 and continuing into the late 1970s. Fluxus festivals took place in cities like Amsterdam, London, Copenhagen, Paris, Stockholm, and Nice, as well as in Franco's Spain. Festivals took place in Eastern Europe as well, in

---

[51] Petra Stegmann, Jennifer Burkard, and Akademie der Künste (eds.), *"The Lunatics Are on the Loose . . ." European Fluxus Festivals 1962–1977* (Down with Art!, 2012), 349. The mannered "what is this" construction draws on techniques Kopcke laid out in his *reading/work-piece No. 82 and No. 92.*

Prague and Vilnius as early as 1966 and in Budapest and Poznań as late as 1969 and 1977, respectively.[52]

Fluxus penetrated the Iron Curtain by several means. The Lithuanian-born Maciunas had long dreamed of a trans-bloc program of radical art, and although his appeals to Soviet authorities went unanswered, he nevertheless succeeded in spreading Fluxus ideas in Eastern Europe through informal channels. Through his network of personal contacts, Maciunas helped spawn Fluxus initiatives in Lithuania and Poland and maintained ties to Action and Fluxus artists in Czechoslovakia.[53] The book *Happenings* by the West Germans Jürgen Becker and Wolf Vostell made its way to Hungary, where it inspired the artists Gabor Altorjay and Tamas St. Turba to plan a festival, subsequently banned.[54] Altorjay also obtained a copy of Fluxus artist Dick Higgins's book *Intermedia*, subsequently establishing contact with Higgins and receiving a generous flow of Fluxus materials from him through the post.[55] Altorjay and his fellow artist Tamás Szentjóby subsequently staged a Happening sufficiently scandalous that they were called into a police station and forced to sign a statement promising they would never hold another one.[56]

The Danish artist Eric Andersen shared Fluxus editions with the Czechoslovakian art critic Jindrich Chalupecky in 1964, inspiring him to promote the work of the Czech artist Milan Knížák and his group Aktual, which at the time of Anderson's visit was already staging Happenings in Prague.[57] By 1966, information about Fluxus started appearing in Czechoslovak art journals and was disseminated from there to other Eastern Bloc countries.[58] The first and only major Eastern European Fluxus festival on the Rhineland model took place in Prague that same year, producing the same sort of dismay in audiences and critics as had the first West German events four years earlier.[59]

Originally an American form, like so many other aspects of the cultural revolution of the 1960s, the Happening articulated with, and drew on, indigenous European forms of art radicalism. Surrealism and

[52] Stegmann, et al., *"The Lunatics Are on the Loose ..."*
[53] Stegmann, et al., *"The Lunatics Are on the Loose ..."*, 345.
[54] Wolf Vostell and Jürgen Becker, *Happenings: Fluxus, Pop Art, Nouveau réalisme* (Hamburg: Rowohlt, 1965); Stegmann, et al., *"The Lunatics Are on the Loose ..."*, 14.
[55] Amy Brouillette, "Remapping Samizdat: Underground publishing and the Hungarian avant-garde, 1966 to 1975," MA thesis, Central European University (Spring 2009).
[56] Interview with Gábor Altorjay, May 2009, cited in Brouillette, "Remapping Samizdat."
[57] Stegmann, et al., *"The Lunatics Are on the Loose ..."*, 346. See also Peter van der Meijden, "Fluxus, Eric Andersen and the Communist East," in Benedikt Hjartarson, Andrea Kollnitz, Per Stounbjerg, and Tania Ørum (eds.), *A Cultural History of the Avant-Garde in the Nordic Countries 1950–1975* (Leiden: Brill, 2016), 324–335.
[58] Stegmann, et al., *"The Lunatics Are on the Loose ..."*, 345.
[59] Stegmann, et al., *"The Lunatics Are on the Loose ..."*

Situationism were of particular importance. Both drew either directly or indirectly on Dada, a movement launched in Zurich in 1915 as a response to World War I. Dada rejected sense, reason, and morality, perfecting a disconcerting art of refusal and madness. Surrealism in particular was profoundly shaped by Dada's heralding of the irrational and the subconscious, but it nevertheless based itself on moral-political commitments, becoming in the 1920s and 1930s the example *par excellence* of a politically engaged artistic avant-garde. The Surrealist group, based in Paris under the leadership of its most important figure, André Breton, flirted first with Communism, later with Trotskyism, and eventually with anarchism, insisting all along on the autonomy of poetry from the demands of politics. Wholly incompatible with Stalinism, this line was somewhat more amenable to the weakened Trotsky in exile, although for him, too, ultimately inadmissible. Nor was the Surrealists' insistence on their ultimate autonomy from politics always palatable to the anarchists with whom the Surrealists worked, but ultimately anarchism was the tendency with which Surrealism best fit.

Surrealism has aptly been characterized as a "moral community," and it is through this lens that its political commitments must be viewed.[60] In this spirit, Surrealism directed its antagonism against both capitalist democracy and Stalinist Communism, dual systems of domination rooted in instrumental rationality. Against this, Surrealism posited a "romantic anti-capitalism" aimed at the "subversive reenchantment of the world."[61] In this way, it prefigured perhaps the fundamental ideological maneuver of 1968 – the refusal of the categories of opposition and allegiance imposed by the Cold War.

Surrealism temporarily disappeared during World War II, many of its leading figures fighting in the Communist resistance and others going into exile abroad. Reconstituting itself after 1945 in a dramatically changed landscape, Surrealism faced dismissal and scorn from groups like the Existentialists and the Lettrists, who found Surrealism at best old hat and at worst politically reactionary.[62] At a moment when the French Communist Party enjoyed unprecedented prestige for its role in the resistance, allowing Stalinists to cement their control of the party, Surrealism swam resolutely against the tide. In their first postwar manifesto, "Inaugural rupture" of June 1947, the Surrealists wrote:

---

[60] Michael Richardson and Krzysztof Fijalowski (eds.), *Surrealism against the Current: Tracts and Declarations* (London: Pluto, 2001), 5.
[61] Don Lacoss, "Introduction: Surrealism and romantic anticapitalism," in Michael Löwy, *Morning Star: Surrealism, Marxism, Situationism, Utopia* (Austin: University of Texas Press, 2009), vii.
[62] Helena Lewis, *The Politics of Surrealism* (St. Paul: Paragon House, 1988), 166.

"Revolutionary elements opposed to the Communist Party share the common and constant fate of being rejected by it and placed in the reviled category of public offenders ... . [W]e have continuously declared our unshakeable attachment to the revolutionary tradition of the workers' movement, a tradition which the Communist Party further forsakes with each passing day."[63]

The Surrealist critique of the PCF was in the first instance a critique of its accommodation with the bourgeoisie; behind this lay a position not only toward the crimes of Stalinism – not yet fully revealed, but obvious to those who cared to look – but toward the historical role of Communism in suppressing revolutionary movements: "The more recent development of Communist policy is a logical and direct consequence of the Moscow trials and the sabotage (in Spain) of the civil war that served the interests first of the bourgeoisie and later of fascism." With this charge, the Surrealists placed themselves out of step with the postwar moment but prefigured key tendencies that would fuel the events of May 1968.[64]

Likewise, the Surrealist group was notable for its support of the cause of Algerian independence during the war of 1954–1962. In September 1960, André Breton was a signatory to the "Manifesto of the 121," a document that called for the "Right to Insubordination" in the war to defend France's colonial interests.[65] The Surrealists likewise supported the Hungarian Uprising of 1956, characteristically situating the Soviet response as one side of a coin of oppression whose other was capitalist imperialism. "It is in the name of democracy and socialism," they wrote, "that police murder functions in Algeria no less than in Hungary."[66] A brief period of infatuation with Castro's Cuba ended when the dictator expressed his support for the Soviets' crushing of the Prague Spring, underlining again the pernicious nature of the bloc politics the Surrealists rejected. By the time of the May 1968 Paris revolt, André Breton had been dead for two years. The group nevertheless distributed a manifesto to students. A Spring/Summer special issue of their journal *L'Archibras* was banned by the authorities, and the editors were brought up on charges of incitement and offenses against the President of the Republic.[67]

---

[63] "Inaugural rupture," in Richardson and Fijalowski, *Surrealism against the Current*, 42.

[64] Surrealism was active in Greece as well in the form of the avant-garde journal *Pali* founded by the Surrealist poet Nano Valaoritis; Kostis Kornetis, *Children of the Dictatorship: Student Resistance, Cultural Politics, and the "Long 1960s" in Greece* (New York: Berghahn, 2013), 23.

[65] Surrealists played a key role in initiating and gathering signatures for the document; see Penelope Rosemont, *Dreams and Everyday Life: André Breton, Surrealism, Rebel Worker, SDS and the Seven Cities of Cibola* (Chicago: Charles H. Kerr, 2008), 80.

[66] Quoted in Lacoss, "Introduction," xix.   [67] Lacoss, "Introduction," xxi.

It is indicative that the title of the banned issue, published only a month after the Soviet invasion to crush the Prague Spring in August 1968, was "Czech Surrealism."[68] In spring 1968, French and Czechoslovakian Surrealists collaborated on "The Pleasure Principle," an exhibition staged in Bratislava, Brno, and Prague.[69] Under the aegis of the Surrealist theoretician Vratislav Effenberger, they produced a joint declaration known as the Platform of Prague, signed by twenty-eight French and twenty-one Czechoslovakian Surrealists, along with eleven others of various nationalities.[70] Declaring the fundamental unity of the political-cultural rebellion across the East-West divide, the Platform called for "a new human awareness against the repression of right and left." Reaffirming the Surrealist dedication to seeking a revolutionary art "in the most obscure zones of psychic reality," it simultaneously lauded Marx and Engels, Lenin and Trotsky, Che and Marcuse. Praising the radicalism of French, Polish, and German university students, mentioning Rudi Dutschke by name, the Platform lauded the importance of the Cuban Revolution and Black Power in the USA as examples of a revolutionary spirit that Surrealism sought to support and extend.[71]

The Surrealist banner of artistic-political revolt was carried forward by the Situationists, for whom the Surrealists were both predecessors and contemporaries. The Situationist International was a successor to the Lettrist International, infamous for the stunt in which one of its members dressed as a priest to proclaim the death of God from the pulpit of Notre-Dame cathedral during Easter mass, inciting a riot among the parishioners.[72] Using provocation to blur the boundaries between art, politics, and daily life, the Situationist International furthered the Surrealist project of creating an alternative conceptual space between dogmatic state socialism and Western capitalist consumerism. Situationist concepts like the "spectacle" (referring to the consumer capitalist dream world of mediated desires substituted for real life), "unitary urbanism" (with its emphasis on the emancipatory potential of the urban environment), and "détournement" (the practice by which the signs of consumer capitalism are recontextualized to produce the opposite of their intended meaning) proved attractive both to artists seeking to disrupt the staid world of the museum and activists searching for new tactics and avenues of

---

[68] "Czech Surrealism," *L'Archibras*, 5.
[69] Don Lacoss, *Surrealism in '68: Paris, Prague, Chicago* (Chicago: Black Swan, 2008).
[70] The Platform of Prague, reprinted in Richardson and Fijalkowski, *Surrealism against the Current*. The Platform was subsequently translated and published by Surrealist groups as far away as New York City and Chicago, Buenos Aires and Havana. See "Dreams of arson and the arson of dreams: Surrealism in '68," http://criticallegalthinking.com/2011/01/12/dreams-of-arson-the-arson-of-dreams-surrealism-in-68.
[71] The Platform of Prague.   [72] Marcus, *Lipstick Traces*.

political engagement. Equally important, the international network created by Situationism spread these ideas across the capitols of the West, spurring the formation of local avant-garde groups using techniques of direct action to disrupt power relations within the spaces of the city.

Situationism was uniquely suited to the shape of the brewing revolt. The Situationist International invoked in its name the ghosts of earlier socialist workers movements, but, unlike those earlier movements, it sought not to rally the proletarian masses for revolution but to make insurgent strikes against the conditions of false consciousness that increasingly seemed to render revolution impossible. The Situationists had a small but important influence on the "French May" through the activities of students at the University of Strasbourg. More generally, however, they predicted the revolt, and their "critique of everyday life" (Henri Lefebvre) opened up the analytic and tactical terrain for it. This critique, in the words of the historian and theorist Miguel Amorós,

condemned the bureaucracy of parties and trade unions, rejected militancy, sexual repression and sacrifice, it spoke of the right to assemblies, direct action, generalized self-management and workers councils; it criticized Stalinist totalitarianism and Soviet or Chinese state capitalism; it rediscovered the history of the workers movement, its bureaucratic degeneration, the counterrevolutionary role of the Bolsheviks; it revisited anarcho-syndicalism, the Spanish Revolution, the repression of Kronstadt and of the Makhnovist movement, the IWW ...[73]

In this way, like the Surrealists before them, the Situationists were crucial avatars of the rebellion of 1968.

The Situationist critique further prepared the ground for a fusion of antiauthoritarian politics with the new youth culture, becoming the terrain *par excellence* for experiments in directly and forcefully reshaping lived experience. Here they supplied the basis for a characteristic feature of 1968, one that differentiates it from all previous historical moments of radicalism: the rise of the youthful provocateur channeling an eclectic, heavily mediated fusion of odds and ends from revolutionary moments past and present, melding them with anarchist-flavored direct action and DIY ("Do-It-Yourself") cultural production while synthesizing mutant strains of popular culture into an explosive new mixture. The rebellion of 1968 was many things, but one thing it was, especially, was the moment when art pranks became serious political business.

---

[73] Miguel Amorós, "A brief history of the Italian section of the Situationist International," https://libcom.org/history/brief-history-italian-section-situationist-international-miguel-amorós.

Urban Rebels

This was demonstrated in the summer of 1965, when the Provos began to show how an antiauthoritarian project rooted in youth's occupation of public space could turn a seemingly placid society on its ear. In seeking to realize the untapped revolutionary potential of youth, Provo drew on two key sources of inspiration. The first of these was the aforementioned act of the Happening. Amsterdam in the early 1960s was a hotspot for new developments in the arts. As in so much of the European art scene, there was a direct connection to New York City. The Living Theater of Julian Beck and Judith Malina made Amsterdam its home from 1964 to 1968. A fall 1967 tour saw the group in Paris and Belgrade, Dublin and Brussels, Barcelona and Bordeaux.[74] As early as 1962, the Americans Melvin Clay and Frank Stern, along with Simon Vinkenoog, organized Amsterdam's first Happening.[75] The same year, the Amsterdam artist Robert Jasper Grootveld launched a career of provocation that would directly inspire the Provos. The centerpiece was a campaign against cigarette smoking that juxtaposed criminalization of drugs such as cannabis with the acceptance of drugs like alcohol and tobacco that were forcefully advertised despite their known health dangers.

Grootveld's attack on tobacco – simultaneously an attack on advertising, consumerism, environmental pollution, and mainstream values – was crystallized in the summer of 1964 in a legendary series of Saturday night Happenings at the Lieverdje statue in Amsterdam's Spui Square. Grootveld's shamanic midnight performances at the statue – ironically, the statue had been financed by a tobacco company – attracted a mix of young intellectuals and juvenile delinquents ("nozem"). Here, what would become Provo's foundational principles began to come into focus: a politics that was performative, anticonsumerist, and pro-environmental; that tested the limits of authority through a war of nerves with the police; that focused on the possibilities of rebellion within the spaces of the city (prefiguring the squatting movement later launched by Provo's successors, the Kabouters); that sought to outrage established interests, resulting in lawsuits, jail sentences, and publicity; and that possessed a realization of the power of the media to amplify the effect of radical actions, indeed, that understood that the media response to an action had to be factored in as an active component of the action. The resulting explosive mixture became a major influence on groups elsewhere, notably in West Germany and the United Kingdom, establishing

---

[74] *International Times*, 18 (August/September 1967), 20.   [75] Kempton, *Provo*, 19.

a template for a style of provocation that would quickly spread to much of the rest of Europe.

As mentioned in Chapter 2, Provo's second main source of inspiration was anarchism, an influence it inherited from the pacifist movement of the late 1950s/early 1960s. Roel van Duijn, a leading Provo who was twenty-one years old at the time of the group's founding, had belonged while still in high school to the Ban the Bomb movement, the Dutch equivalent to the British CND.[76] Like the peace movement elsewhere in Europe, that group was in decline by the early 1960s. Provo's founding document criticized the ritualized nature of peace marches that failed to produce any real change. Direct action, not symbolic gestures, was the key to effective activism. "When slogans and gestures fail," they argued, "we have to turn to action and attack."[77] Provo's commitment to direct action strengthened a connection with anarchism that already existed in group members' contacts with an older generation of anarchists still active in the Netherlands. Van Duijn wrote briefly for the anarchist newspaper *De Vrije* ("The Free") and was inspired both by the Russian Mikhail Bakunin and the legendary Dutch libertarian socialist Ferdinand Domela Nieuwenhuis ("Domela"). Grootveld, meanwhile, was the son of an anarchist who had taught him a healthy disregard for all types of authority from a young age.[78] For the Provos, anarchism offered an antiauthoritarian solution ideally suited to the Cold War ideological stalemate. "Anarchism," they wrote, "propagates the most direct rebellion against all authority, whether it be democratic or Communist."[79] With the traditional focus in many strains of anarchism on the revolutionary potential of socially marginal groups and nonconformist behavior, furthermore, anarchism articulated nicely with Provo's desire to radicalize juvenile delinquency.[80]

With their founding in July 1965, the Provos embarked on an eclectic program of disruption. The first issue of their magazine *Provo*, containing (nonsensical) bomb-making instructions adapted from a 1910 anarchist journal, was confiscated by police. In the next eight months, the numbers of Provo activists and sympathizers grew from 50 to 5,000.[81] A series of "White Plans" called variously for free bicycles to be made available in order to fight traffic congestion (White Bicycle Plan) and for police to be transformed into white-clad goodwill ambassadors (White Chicken Plan). By turns practical and fanciful, these plans expressed the common

---

[76] Kempton, *Provo*, 38.   [77] Kempton, *Provo*, 40.   [78] Kempton, *Provo*, 14.
[79] Kempton, *Provo*, 41.
[80] The group's explicit intention, indeed, was to "renew anarchism and bring it to the young"; "Provo magazine leaflet," in Stansill and Mairowitz, *BAMN*, 18.
[81] Kempton, *Provo*, 44.

aim of presenting authority with initiatives it could not enact without exposing its ineptness or otherwise undermining itself.

It was one episode, however – the "Day of Anarchy" – that put the Provos on the radical map. On that day in March 1966, a smoke bomb attack on the marriage of Queen Beatrix provoked running street skirmishes, driving the police into a frenzied overreaction that was photographed and subsequently put on display in an exhibit on police violence. When, in a perfect postmodern dénouement, the police assaulted the crowd outside the exhibit, prompting an official inquiry, the effect of the provocation was realized beyond the organizers' wildest dreams.[82] With this act, as the editors of the *International Times* put it, "the spell of 'linear' protest was broken."[83] The door was now open, for better or worse, for a multifaceted youth-cultural antiauthoritarian campaign, unmoored from traditional class interests, parties, and ideologies.

New Provo groups were founded around the Netherlands, as well as in Frankfurt, Brussels, Antwerp, Copenhagen, and Stockholm.[84] These were part of a broader wave of group foundings inspired not only by Provo but by Situationism, the Berkeley Free Speech Movement, and American Beat and pop culture. In Italy, youth groups inspired by Provo and by the American counterculture were established in a number of major cities. In addition to a Provo group founded in Milan in November 1966, there was the scene around the journal *Mondo Beat* ("Movimento Mondo Beat"), an underground newspaper published out of the so-called *cave* in the Porta Romana neighborhood of Milan. Drawing inspiration from the rebellion of Beats and Longhairs ("capelloni") who hung around Milan's Piazza Duomo and Piazzale Cordusion, the Mondo Beat scene developed from 1966 under the more-or-less direct influence of Provo.[85]

One of Mondo Beat's leading lights, the Beat poet Vittorio Di Russo, was expelled from Amsterdam after being caught up in a police raid on the Provos in October 1966. His return to Milan was met with a barrage of hostile media attention, which was in keeping with that directed at the Longhairs, whose tent cities in the "Nuova Barbonia" ("New Bumsville") camp founded by Mondo Beat in April 1967 were the target of frequent police raids.[86] Like Provo, Mondo Beat had direct links to anarchist

---

[82] See Pas, "In pursuit of the invisible revolution."

[83] Stansill and Mairowitz, *BAMN*, 15.   [84] Stansill and Mairowitz, *BAMN*, 15.

[85] On the countercultural preconceptions underpinning Mondo Beat, see Angelo Ventrone, "Revolution as a quest for an authentic life: The 1960s and 1970s in Italy," in Joachim C. Häberlen, Mark Keck-Szajbel, and Kate Mahoney (eds.), *The Politics of Authenticity: Countercultures and Radical Movements across the Iron Curtain, 1968–1989* (New York: Berghahn, 2018), 25–44, 34.

[86] On the moral panic generated by the Beatnik presence in Milan, see Robert Lumley, *States of Emergency: Cultures of Revolt in Italy from 1968 to 1978* (London: Verso, 1990).

militants, in this case the "Sacco and Vanzetti" group, which allowed Mondo Beat the use of its printing machines.[87] The "European Conference of the Anarchist Youth" organized by the Sacco and Vanzetti group over Christmas 1966 was attended by militants from France, Sweden, Holland, Belgium, Italy, Spain, West Germany, and Great Britain.[88]

Another group, Onda Verde ("Green Wave"), was founded in November 1966 out of the milieu around Gruppo 63, a collective of artists and intellectuals who married neo-"avantgardist" literary criticism with a Marxist skepticism of consumer society. Gruppo 63 published the journal *I quindici* beginning in fall 1967, combining literary analysis with political features on themes such as the "lynching of the longhairs."[89] A 1968 issue of the journal contained as a special supplement the founding number of the journal *S*, the first Situationist publication in Italy. Some of the journal's publishers were among the founders of Onda Verde, which sought to extend upon the former's political-countercultural commitments. "Onda Verde only proposes what the young people propose," they wrote. "This can be a little or too much, but it is necessary. Non-violence. Resistance to war. Rejection of meaningless words. Rejection of ideologies that exist only because pre-existing interests support them."[90] The group's methods of action were explicitly based on those of the Provos: "play and desacralize, provoke and propose."[91] Onda Verde merged with Mondo Beat in December 1966, realizing a sort of cross-class alliance between the left-literary intelligentsia and the youth rebellion in Italy's streets and plazas.

The characteristic West European blend of anarchism, Situationism, and youth culture found its resonance across the English Channel in the group around the proto-Situationist newspaper *Heatwave*. Founded in July 1966 by Charles Radcliffe and Diana Shelley, *Heatwave* was a typically transnational affair, emerging out of its founders' contacts with the Surrealist-inspired *Rebel Worker* group in Chicago. Like the Provos, whose "Provotariat" manifesto they republished, the editors of *Heatwave* sought to link a resurgent anarchism with the burgeoning youth culture of the 1960s. *Heatwave* drew on the anarchist strand in the British antinuclear movement. These were significant in the CND, as well in the

---

[87] See Mondo Beat, "Mailand im Belagerungzustand," in Schulenburg, *Das Leben ändern, die Welt verändern!*, 67–72.

[88] "European meeting of young anarchists," *Freedom. Anarchist Weekly*, 27(12) (April 16, 1966).

[89] In issue 2 of the magazine.

[90] Quoted in Amorós, "A brief history of the Italian section of the Situationist International."

[91] Amorós, "A brief history of the Italian section of the Situationist International."

philosopher Bertrand Russell's "Committee of 100" and its offshoot "Spies for Peace," which advocated nonviolent direct action and "sit-downs."[92] *Heatwave* also enjoyed close ties to Freedom Press, a publishing house that had been founded in the nineteenth century by the English anarchist Charlotte Wilson and the Russian anarchist Peter Kropotkin.[93] Simultaneously, it sought to reflect what it called "the countless and varied strands of autonomous post-war youth rebellion – rock'n'roll, the Beats, ban-the-bombers, Surrealism, Dada, existential-ism, avant-garde artists, drugs, 'blues' ..."[94] As Radcliffe put it in a characteristic early passage, "[i]f anarchism has nothing to say [to the new generation of youth rebels], it has nothing to say at all."[95]

At the conclusion of a "revolutionary grand tour" to meet the Provos in Amsterdam and the Situationists in Brussels and Paris, Radcliffe, Shelley, and the English Situationist Chris Gray were admitted as the "English Section" of the Situationist International, only to be expelled a short time later in one of Guy Debord's innumerable excommunications.[96] Gray subsequently founded King Mob, a group that drew equally from the antiart traditions of Dada and Surrealism and the revolutionary violence of nineteenth-century anarchism and nihilism.[97] The group published a magazine, *King Mob Echo*, which first appeared in April 1968, and engaged in a series of public stunts aimed at disrupting the "spectacle." These included a June 1968 incident in which members of the group donned gorilla suits and circus horse outfits to assist a crowd pulling down the fences around Powis Square gardens and an infamous Christmas 1968 stunt in which a members dressed in Santa outfits distributed toys off the shelves to children in Selfridges department store. Prompting employees to alert the police, the insurgents thereby "accomplished a Strasbourg-style détournement [in which] children were forced to wit-ness the shocking sight of one of Santa's helpers placed under arrest."[98]

---

[92] On the cultural impact of the CND and the Committee of 100, see Jeff Nuttall, *Bomb Culture* (London: Strange Attractor, 2018), chapter 2.

[93] Rosemont, *Dreams and Everyday Life*, 131.

[94] Charles Radcliffe, "Pop goes the Beatle," *Freedom* (November 16, 1963), quoted in Charles Radcliffe, "Two fiery flying rolls: The Heatwave story, 1966–1970," in Rosemont and Radcliffe (eds.), *Dancin' in the Streets!*, 327–380, 344.

[95] Radcliffe, "Pop goes the Beatle," 344.   [96] Radcliffe, "Two fiery flying rolls," 361.

[97] See Sam Cooper, *The Situationist International in Britain: Modernism, Surrealism, and the Avant-Garde* (New York: Routledge, 2017).

[98] Marcus, *Lipstick Traces*, 438. "'What are they doing to Santa?,' one little boy asked his mum, clutching the fire engine he had been given. 'Never you mind, dear' she replied, hurriedly stuffing the toy into her bag, 'he's probably forgotten to feed the reindeer'"; Phil Cohen, *Reading Room Only: Memoir of a Radical Bibliophile* (Nottingham: Five Leaves, 2013), 100.

Another key group attempting to bridge the gap between student Marxism and radicalized youth subcultures was the "Kommune I" (Commune One), founded in West Berlin at the beginning of 1967.[99] The communards were inspired by the Provos, whom some of them had come to know, first through a 1964 trip to Amsterdam and subsequently through the December 1965 visit to West Berlin of the Dutch writer Leo Klatzer, a former Left-Communist activist with ties to Provo.[100] Equally important in the genesis of the group was the psychoanalytic approach of Wilhelm Reich, with its emphasis on liberated sexuality as an antidote to fascism and Situationist ideas about disrupting the Spectacle through media scandals, pranks, and play. One of the commune's founders, Dieter Kunzelmann, had earlier belonged to the Munich-based Gruppe Spur, a group of painters briefly serving as the German section of the Situationist International. A successor group involving Kunzelmann and student leader Rudi Dutschke, Subversive Aktion, dumped Spur's artistic aspirations in favor of sharpened political critique.[101] Its brand of public outrage culminated in the signature provocations of the Kommune I, notably the foiled April 1967 "pudding bomb" attack on the motorcade of visiting American vice president Hubert Humphrey. With this and other provocations, the Kommune I almost single-handedly radicalized the West German student movement. The group was kicked out of the SDS, but not before it dragged the organization, to its great discomfort, into a realm of pranks and play.[102]

The Kommune I became a nodal point in the propagation of radical ideas, a mirror in which young people around Germany and beyond could see their own struggles reflected. Locally, the commune helped create the space for a radical politics of lifestyle that found expression in groups like the Hash Rebels, radicalized by the 1966 Rolling Stones riot in West Berlin, self-consciously working-class dope-smokers and rock fans rather than student theorists able to cite chapter and verse from the Marxist classics. Such groups, rather than trying to build a broader movement, heralded subculture as an end in itself and fought to preserve the autonomy of radical enclaves in the urban environment.[103]

---

[99] On the Kommune I, see Timothy Scott Brown, "A tale of two communes: The private and the political in divided Berlin, 1967–1973," in Klimke, Pekelder, and Scharloth, *Between Prague Spring and French May*, 132–140.

[100] See Ulrich Chaussy, *Die drei Leben des Rudi Dutschke* (Berlin: Fischer, 1993), 152–153; Ulrich Enzensberger, *Die Jahre der Kommune I: Berlin 1967–1969* (Cologne: Kiepenheuer & Witsch, 2004), 49–53.

[101] See Frank Böckelmann and Herbert Nagel (eds.), *Subversive Aktion: Der Sinn der Organisation ist ihr Scheitern* (Frankfurt: Neue Kritik, 1976).

[102] Brown, *West Germany and the Global Sixties*, 11.

[103] Reinders and Fritsch, *Die Bewegung 2. Juni* (Edition ID-Archiv), 23. The classic account is Baumann, *How It All Began*.

News of groups such as the Kommune I and the Provos spread across Cold War Europe, the Provos receiving correspondence from as far away as Russia, Poland, Yugoslavia, and Czechoslovakia.[104] Yet Provo's Eastern European interlocutors sometimes expressed doubt about the extent to which they could follow the group's example. As the Czechoslovakian student Boja Christovova wrote in a letter to Roel van Duijn: "It isn't very difficult to get thrown in prison in our country. And here it means rather more than in yours … . Our youth is very afraid!!!!"[105] This comment reinforces a key point that must be taken into account in any reading of the differential reception of pop and underground culture in the three zones of Europe – the amount of political space available profoundly shaped not only the extent to which it could penetrate Cold War boundaries but what it could accomplish in the new settings to which it moved.

Scenes and Publics

Indeed, if we accept that the *global*, in the form of the transnational spread of people, ideas, and cultural products, worked its influence across a host of different *locals* around 1968, we must simultaneously recognize that the latter largely determined the shape of the former. Here the "local" is not necessarily a synonym for the nation state, however, but can represent any site at which the border-crossing impulses of 1968 were received and channeled or created and disseminated. The concept of the local, in addition to making up half of a "global/local" antinomy useful in thinking about the relationship between what we might term a "big" (global) 1968 and the various "small" (national) 1968s, can also be understood to represent the concrete settings in which 1968 took place.[106] This is one reason why, rather than thinking in terms of transnational *movements* around 1968, it can sometimes be more helpful to think in terms of *scenes* – loose aggregations of artists, agitators, and dropouts brought together by shared interests, preoccupations, and social situations.[107] Alliances between artists and hippies, juvenile delinquents and countercultural

---

[104] Anna von der Goltz and James Mark, "Encounters," in Robert Gildea, James Mark, and Anette Warring (eds.), *Europe's 1968: Voices of Revolt* (Oxford: Oxford University Press, 2013), 150.

[105] Quoted in von der Goltz and Mark, "Encounters."

[106] On the "big"/"small" schema, see Timothy Scott Brown, "1968 East and West: Divided Germany as a case study in transnational history," *American Historical Review*, 114 (February 2009), AHR forum on the "International 1968."

[107] See Darcy Leach and Sebastian Haunns, "Scenes and social movements," in Hank Johnston (ed.), *Culture, Social Movements, and Protest* (London: Routledge, 2009), 255–276.

subversives, did of course overlap with the student movements and political organizations that arose in parallel with them, but their memberships were more fluid, their transnational reach established not through formal organizational structures but through informal networks based on personal contacts. In this way, the *scene* not only represents the site of 1968 in its concrete local aspect but can be understood as the local expression of the transnational and global.

In both Eastern and Western Europe, denizens of scenes committed a twofold spatial transgression: on the one hand, they occupied public space; on the other, they gravitated toward interior spaces associated with nonconformist and antiauthoritarian values. Chief among the latter were new clubs and performance spaces that emerged in the 1960s as venues for a self-identification of youth as a social force with its own cultural values and political perspectives. From clubs like Hybrydy in Warsaw to underground art spaces like the Zodiak Free Arts Lab in West Berlin, these spaces became sites of alternative arts and unconventional behavior that provoked authorities on both sides of the Iron Curtain.[108] In Eastern Europe, even private homes and apartments became important venues for artistic and personal experimentation. As early as 1965, the "Dumb Poets," a group inspired by Fluxus and Situationism, were able to hold readings and Happenings in private Budapest apartments and, along with groups like the Zugló Circle and the Kassák Stúdió, to delve deep into cultural experimentation. Elsewhere in the East, private homes became venues for experimental film.[109]

If the scene was a spatial phenomenon, it was also very much a visual one, since membership was established through personal style and comportment. By the mid-1960s, visual markers of countercultural belonging and left-wing political affiliation emerged to form a common symbolic language on both sides of the Iron Curtain. As much as establishments complained about the "shaggy" appearance of youth from at least the late 1950s, young leftists appeared fairly conventional until the mid-1960s, when the adoption of hippie clothing and long hair began to signify political affiliations in a more obvious way. Young music fans had of course for years signaled their alternative allegiances through style, but from roughly 1965/6, visual markers of the international counterculture began to merge with antiauthoritarian political aspirations so as to make the one seem coterminous with the other. Blue jeans and second-hand US Army parkas, long hair and beards on men, became universal symbols of

---

[108] Malgorzata Fidelis, "Red state, golden youth: Student culture and political protest in 1960s Poland," in Brown and Anton, *Between the Avant-Garde and the Everyday*, 145–153, 152.

[109] Von der Goltz and Mark, "Encounters," 162.

rebellion linking Prague and Paris, Swinging London and Soviet Russia.[110] With the widespread adoption of the look and values of American hippie culture in the later 1960s, the arrival of postmaterialist values and lifestyles in Europe was impossible to ignore. Everywhere, hippies gathered in public squares or parks or went "back to the land" to live in accord with nature. In the Soviet Union, they faced arrest for marching barefoot across Red Square in protest against the Vietnam War or, in the interests of their own peace and safety, escaped to rural gatherings, like those in the Baltics, where the demands of Soviet authority were less oppressive.[111]

Scenes were constructed around style and the allegiances it suggested as much as around the spaces they occupied, but, critically, they were based on and spread through the exchange of cultural products. Gravitating around shared images, texts, and ideas, they helped create, and were created by, the emergence of *publics*: transnational communities of affinity that united readers or listeners around key texts or sounds across the boundaries of the nation state.[112] Publics were *receptive*, in the sense that they involved the adoption of globally circulating cultural products that fulfilled local needs, but they were also *active*, not merely because the act of reception was itself active – it was local protagonists, after all, who made decisions about what was important to adopt, import, translate, or imitate – but because they connected local scenes that were themselves key sites of cultural production around 1968.

From radical publishers to underground bands, local scenes were the place where the creative activity central to 1968 took place. The activism of 1968 was not just about disputing the claims of authority in street protests; it was about creating an alternative culture from the bottom up. It is no surprise, for example, that the cultural-productive energies of 1968 were linked to one of its signature action forms: the commune. In almost every case, these highly condensed instantiations of scenes made cultural production a central feature of their group life. Whether organized around theater groups, rock bands, or newspapers, communes

---

[110] On the significance of long hair in Russia, see Victor Yerofeyev in Philipp Gassert and Martin Klimke (eds.), *1968: Memories and Legacies of a Global Revolt* (Washington, DC: Bulletin of the German Historical Institute, 2009), 171.

[111] Rebecca Clifford, Juliane Fürst, Robert Gildea, James Mark, Piotr Osęka, and Chris Reynolds, "Spaces," in Gildea, Mark, and Warring, *Europe's 1968*, 190–192. On "hippie walks," see Sándor Horváth, "The making of the gang: Consumers of the socialist Beat in Hungary," in Risch, *Youth and Rock in the Soviet Bloc*, 100–115, 108.

[112] See Michael Warner, *Publics and Counterpublics* (Brooklyn: Zone, 2005); see also Thomas Olesen, "Transnational publics: New spaces of social movement activism and the problem of global long-sightedness," *Current Sociology*, 53 (2005), 419–440; Laila Abu-Er-Rub, Jennifer Altehenger, and Sebastian Gehrig, "The transcultural travels of trends: An introductory essay," *Transcultural Studies*, 2 (2011), 140–163.

expressed the link between new ways of living and new ways of thinking and feeling. The link was a natural one, indeed, because communes understood themselves not just as alternative living situations but as experiments in communicative action.[113] Scenes actively created themselves, not only through avant-gardes' programs of cultural transfer but through acts of self-theorization and self-organization designed to establish their relevance and propagate their ideas. In this regard, the signature action of 1968 was arguably neither the student protest nor the bohemian insurrection but the *alternative project* – the self-organized initiative designed to transform daily life while laying the groundwork for lasting social change.

The London underground scene of the mid-to-late 1960s represents a prototypical site of the alternative project. From international poetry and film events, to psychedelic light shows at the UFO Club, to underground newspapers like *International Times* and *Oz*, London was the quintessential site of "cultural revolution" in the 1960s, not simply because it sat at the center of a mass-mediated and heavily commodified transformation in values and lifestyle that gave it lasting influence but because it embodied principles of independent creativity and participatory democracy, self-organization and self-theorization. Even when it self-effacingly lamented its own lack of political urgency compared to the open insurrections taking place in Paris and Prague, the London underground was *intensely* political, not only because it sought to rethink the values and practices underpinning modern society but because it openly contested authority on the terrain of truth.[114]

An underlying assumption of the London underground, like all 1960s sites of alternative cultural production, was that the corruption of official media demanded the creation of counter-media. This counter-media would simultaneously challenge official lies and put forward truths relevant to a new generation. This standpoint was aptly laid out by William S. Burroughs, a notable contributor to London's *International Times*. "In Western societies, where a democratic façade is still maintained like an old foam backdrop," he wrote, "the real power rests in the hands of those

---

[113] As early as 1967, the Linkeck Commune in West Berlin published an eponymous newspaper that played an important role in the genesis of the Extra-parliamentary Opposition, while the Kommune I helped pioneer the campaign of bootleg publishing that grew in importance over the next few years. The *Big Flame* newspaper and network in London was similarly associated with a commune, as was the paper *Tout* in France; see Marie Černá, John Davis, Robert Gildea, and Piotr Osęka, "Revolutions," in Gildea, Mark, and Warring, *Europe's 1968*, 107–130, 124–126.

[114] On the political significance of the London Underground, see Geoff Eley, *Forging Democracy: The History of the Left in Europe, 1850–2000* (Oxford: Oxford University Press, 2002), 355.

who manipulate the mass mind through mass media." The underground press, he continued, existed precisely "to counter mis-information put out by the official press ... [and] to play up news that is played down or neglected in the official press."[115]

Underground newspapers like *International Times* and *Oz* played a key role in fusing the disparate strands of the sixties revolt, from the Beats, to drugs, to music, to politics. Under the art direction of Martin Sharp, *Oz* became a primary exemplar of the psychedelic visual style in Great Britain. Both newspapers placed great emphasis on popular music, and both also faced a series of legal challenges, in the case of *Oz*, most notably over the infamous "Schoolkids Issue" of May 1970, which featured a sexually suggestive cover as well as a (more than usually) pornographic adaptation of an R. Crumb cartoon, unsuccessfully defended in a high-profile trial that saw editors Felix Dennis and Jim Anderson sentenced to fifteen months in prison, a sentence later overturned on appeal. The example of *International Times* and *Oz*, alongside that of American publications like the *Oracle* and the *Rat*, inspired countless continental imitators, such as *Linkeck* in West Germany and *Hotcha* in Sweden, which replicated the characteristic fusion of radical politics and counterculture, often in much more aggressively political ways.

The flow of radical publications across national boundaries is part of what gave the revolt of 1968 its global character. Alongside the networks created by New Left journals and countercultural newspapers, transnational reading publics emerged around widely shared texts, from Marcuse's *One-Dimensional Man* to the writings of the Beats, Che, and Mao. Key works supplied a shared theoretical and symbolic repertoire that allowed activists to communicate with each other and, by referencing this shared repertoire, to perform (i.e. read, write, cite) their opposition to the system. It was not necessary in this context to have *read* a particular book in question; rather, books represented "badges" of membership in one or more of the radical transnational publics that helped constitute 1968.[116]

Critically, underground publishing initiatives made available texts that were lost or suppressed. In the West, bootleg publishing operations subverted normal processes of capitalist ownership and production while

---

[115] William S. Burroughs, "The function of the underground press," in Stansill and Mairowitz, *BAMN*, 38.

[116] See (along with the other essays in the volume) Quinn Slobodian, "Badge books and brand books: The Mao Bible in East and West Germany," in Alexander Cook (ed.), *Mao's Little Red Book: A Global History* (New York: Cambridge University Press, 2014), 206–224.

providing access to lost knowledge and perspectives. This development prefigured the emergence in the mainstream publishing world of lines aimed at a student-left readership and, at the grass roots, dedicated left-wing publishing houses. In Italy, for example, the Feltrinelli publishing house produced cheap editions of Che and Castro for the student market. In West Germany, similarly, titles of Third World liberation were produced by a range of presses, alongside the work of Rudi Dutschke and other student leaders. The texts created and circulated in these and other venues shaped the contours of an activist imagination that could be shared on both sides of the Cold War divide. In the East, the creation of Samizdat (literally "self-publishing") served much the same purpose. On both sides of the East-West divide, counter-media provided a means of creating a new oppositional culture from below. Around 1968, both the creation and dissemination of new knowledge and the recovery of lost or suppressed knowledge were the indispensable accompaniments to political action.

Cultural Revolutions

The goal of producing political change was intimately bound up with the idea of creating a change in mentality. In a situation of Cold War stasis in which any challenge to political orthodoxy action was seen as particularly dangerous and destabilizing, to change one's consciousness was to create new possibilities of action. As Rudi Dutschke put it in connection with one of the earliest public interventions of the West German student movement, the protest against the visit to West Berlin in late 1964 of the Congolese strongman Moïse Tshombe: "With the anti-Tshombe demonstration, we have for the first time seized the political initiative in this city. We can see it as the beginning of our cultural revolution, in which ... all prior values and norms are called into question."[117] In this context, "cultural revolution" meant the creation of new subjectivities – that is, of overcoming the programming to be obedient and deferential to authority and as a result remain inactive in the face of injustice.

From the mid-1960s, the term "cultural revolution" began to acquire a more specific valence linked precisely to the need to establish the right to take action in a situation of Cold War ideological deadlock. Mao Zedong's scheme of turning rank-and-file militancy against his enemies in the party and thereby strengthening his own position – the Chinese Cultural Revolution (1966–1977) – came to be widely misinterpreted in

---

[117] Uwe Bergmann, Rudi Dutschke, Wolfgang Lefèvre, and Bernd Rabehl, *Rebellion der Studenten oder die neue Opposition* (Hamburg: Rororo Aktuell, 1968), 63.

the West as an authentic form of rank-and-file antiauthoritarianism that could supply a useful basis for activism.[118] The provocateurs of the Kommune I introduced the West German student movement to Maoism by wearing Mao buttons at protests, donning Red Guard uniforms, and brandishing or reading aloud from Mao's Red Book.[119] Mao's visage appeared in countless artworks, and his Red Book was disseminated far and wide as a totem of revolutionary wisdom. The Red Book served as both "badge" and "brand," symbolizing affiliation with a certain flavor of militancy born through new channels of commercial publishing capitalizing on the youth-radical market.[120]

There was not a little orientalism at play in a reception where Mao could appear, in the words of one West German radical, as "a modern Buddha, an Enlightened one."[121] Nor was the deployment of Maoism free of the recuperative tendencies that so vexed left radicals concerned with the political role of culture, or of the sexism that dogged even countercultural depictions of the left project. The dubious political content of Maoist poesy was not lost on Situationists, anarchists, and others with a fine nose for the stench of authoritarianism. As a Nanterre militant caustically observed, Maoism was a "fallback position, a safety net for intellectuals in search of a religion to follow . . . . In this sense, Maoism caught the overflow from the Stalinists."[122]

Yet, paradoxically, in the wake of 1968's high moments of urban insurrection, Maoism came increasingly to serve as a model for antiauthoritarian action. Deriving from the Third World, where an actual struggle against imperialism and capitalism was undeniably taking place (whatever its actual political content), Maoism appeared to young Western adherents as an heir to the revolutionary tradition of Marxism-Leninism that could be held free of responsibility for the deformations of Soviet Communism and promised the potential for a third way between the Cold War blocs. To be sure, Maoism did not have a uniform reception in Europe. It could be strong in Norway and Sweden but weak in Denmark, crucial in Italy but almost nonexistent in the UK, alluring in

---

[118] See the essays in Cook, *Mao's Little Red Book*.

[119] On Rainer Langhans reading from the Red Book in court, see Joachim Scharloth, "Ritualkritik und Rituale des Protest. Die Entdeckung des Performativen in der Studentenbewegung der 1960er Jahre," in Martin Klimke and Joachim Scharloth (eds.), *1968: Handbuch zur Kultur- und Mediengeschichte der Studentenbewegung* (Stuttgart: J. B. Metzler, 2007), 75–87, 79.

[120] Slobodian, "Badge books and brand books."

[121] Hellmuth Costard, "Das ist die Angst des Tonmanns," in Gerd Conradt, *Starbuck: Holger Meins – Ein Porträt als Zeitbild* (Berlin: Espresso, 2001), 44–49, 45.

[122] Jean-Pierre Duteuil, *Nanterre 1968: Notes on the Background to the 22 March Group* (ChristieBooks, electronic edition, 2014).

Hungary but unnecessary in Yugoslavia.[123] As in the case of all border-crossing appropriations around 1968, local needs determined the nature of Maoism's reception.[124]

Where it was deemed useful, on both sides of the Iron Curtain, Maoism seemed to provide a template for a revolt that targeted bureaucracy and unjust authority whatever their sources. Maoism could be a vehicle for linking European struggles with global anti-imperialist ones, but, equally important, it could offer a vehicle for contesting the conditions of everyday life.[125] Above all, Maoism became important for its emphasis on the primacy of practice over theory and for the way in which, as a foreign doctrine pertaining to a foreign situation of which young activists had no direct experience, it could be deployed in a range of situations.

Yet 1968 was not a "cultural revolution" because Maoism provided a template for some activists to practice antiauthoritarian politics, much less a *mere* cultural revolution in the sense suggested by the historian Arthur Marwick, as an overturning of traditional lifeways linked to changing mores and new possibilities of consumption. Nor was 1968 a cultural revolution simply because, as we have seen in this chapter, artists played such a crucial role in shaping its radicalism. Rather, Maoism owed its impact precisely to the fact that it appeared on the European scene at the moment that two powerful ideas – the fusion of culture and politics and the revolution of everyday life – were coming into their own. And those ideas were powerful precisely because they coincided with a widely perceived need to discover new ways of being political.

Whatever the shape of local political arrangements, culture – in the broad sense not only of a sphere of creative activity but of a sphere encompassing style, habitus, and meaning – was the ground on which it was possible to enact a politics outside of the stifling avenues of bourgeois capitalist parliamentarianism or state socialist dictatorship. This entailed

[123] See Thomas Ekman Jørgensen, "Scandinavia," in Martin Klimke and Joachim Scharloth (eds.), *1968 in Europe: A History of Protest and Activism, 1956–1977* (London: Palgrave Macmillan, 2008), 239–252, 242. On Maoism in Great Britain, see Holger Nehring, "Great Britain," in Klimke and Scharloth, *1968 in Europe*, 130. In Yugoslavia, points out Dominique Kirchner Reill, young militants did not "need" Maoism, first because they were inheritors of a successful antipartisan struggle that not only defeated fascism but established communism, and second because Yugoslavia was already involved in alliances with Third World liberation struggles; Yugoslavian radicals were placing emphasis on the search for a humanist socialism as opposed to one that sacrificed humanist goals as supposedly necessary to achieve greater revolutionary potential; Dominique Kirchner Reill, "Partisan legacies and anti-imperialist ambitions: The Little Red Book in Italy and Yugoslavia," in Cook, *Mao's Little Red Book*, 185–205, 188–192.

[124] Reill, "Partisan legacies," 192.

[125] See Richard Wolin, *The Wind from the East: May '68, French Intellectuals, and the Chinese Cultural Revolution* (Princeton: Princeton University Press, 2010), 10.

not just establishing the possibility of taking action to begin with, in a situation of Cold War stasis in which such action was seen as particularly threatening, but encompassed the possibility of changing one's consciousness to reflect the new possibilities of action. In this way, cultural revolution was a metaphor for the idea of self-liberation through action, a key sixties concept that formed an internal line of consistency linking disparate forms of practice.[126] As Robert Gildea and James Mark have observed, a "cultural revolution" could entail everything from changing the political order to changing the self. It could encompass political militancy as much as lifestyle revolt, revolutionary violence as much as radical art. In its diverse and partly overlapping meanings, it encompassed a range of activities across both sides of the Cold War divide.[127]

The sixties were a cultural revolution, ultimately, because culture made up the ground of a rebellion that was fundamentally *pre-political*. Rejecting pre-packaged ideologies in the same way that it rejected Cold War boundaries, the revolt refused that which was passed down, even from left-wing traditions, that seemed no longer useful. This accounts for the importance of art and as much for the importance of the renewed interest in political traditions like Maoism and Trotskyism that seemed to offer the possibility of actually being able to take action, as opposed to having that possibility curtailed by a predetermined Cold War situation. The revolt sought, in other words, to rebuild possibilities of individual and collective agency anew. This is why it could take place on both sides of the Iron Curtain, whatever the possibilities of its success there, and this is why, as we have seen and as we will see further in Chapters 4 and 5, it was characterized above all by attempts to search out the political content with which to fill the vessel of revolt.[128]

---

[126] Černá, et al., "Revolutions," 108.

[127] Robert Gildea and James Mark, "Conclusion: Europe's 1968," in Gildea, Mark, and Warring, *Europe's 1968*, 330.

[128] Arthur Marwick, *The Sixties: Cultural Revolution in Britain, France, Italy, and the United States, c.1958–c.1974* (Oxford: Oxford University Press, 1998).

4   1968 in Three Europes

May Day 1968 in East Berlin unfolded in a spirit of optimism. Winds of change were blowing through the Eastern Bloc. The "Polish March" of that year heralded a new insurgent spirit of democratic reform, even if it had been temporarily blunted by the hardline response of the authorities. Far more important for East Germans was the democratic-socialist insurgency in Czechoslovakia, where, amidst the resurgence of a free press and lively public sphere, the Communist Party under the leadership of Alexander Dubček pursued a plan of reform aimed at alleviating the worst aspects of Stalinism. In East Germany, politically engaged members of the young intelligentsia, notably a circle around the children of the loyal but critical physicist Robert Havemann, watched with keen expectation Czech attempts to create "socialism with a human face." The slogan on a banner at the May Day demonstration – "A Model for Everyone: CSSR [Czechoslovakian Socialist Republic]" – expressed a generalized view and hope.[1]

Like others around the Eastern Bloc, and to an even greater extent because of their location in the divided city of Berlin, this small group of young dissidents existed at the intersection of East and West. They had been immensely impressed by the publication in Czechoslovakia of Ludvík Vaculik's manifesto of democratic socialist rebirth – the "Two Thousand Words" – which spoke to issues confronted across Eastern Europe.[2] At the same time, they enjoyed contact with the West German student leader Rudi Dutschke and some of the members of West Berlin's Kommune I, who visited East Berlin on repeated occasions. From the communards, they gained an impression of Western countercultural habitus and took on key ideas from the psychoanalytic approach to sexual

---

[1] See the photograph reproduced in Timothy S. Brown, "1968 East and West: Divided Germany as a case study in transnational history," *American Historical Review*, 114 (February 2009), AHR forum on the "International 1968."

[2] Ludvík Vaculík, "2,000 words to workers, farmers, scientists, artists, and everyone," in Salar Mohandesi, Bjarke Skærlund Risager, and Laurence Cox (eds.), *Voices of 1968: Documents from the Global North* (London: Pluto, 2018), 295–299.

emancipation current in West Germany. They were aware of counter-cultural developments in the United States as well, and even more of the May 1968 events in Paris. As one of the group put it: "For us, the Paris May and the Prague Spring were two sides of the same coin – the necessary prerequisite for the end of the [Cold War] Bloc confrontation."[3]

As subsequent events would show, their optimism was misplaced. The Soviet Union's intervention against the Prague Spring at the end of the summer presented a stark rebuff to the belief that, as one young dissident put it, they "were taking part in a Europe-wide, if not worldwide, break-through to a purified and modernized socialism."[4] Tellingly captured in the slogans distributed on flyers in the wake of the invasion – "Long Live Red Prague. Up with Dubček"; "Hands Off Red Prague"; "A Dubček to Berlin"; "Ho-Chi-Minh – Dubček" (it was not just in the West that Third World national liberation struggles held their appeal) – the hope was further crushed by stark punishments that included jail sentences and loss of educational privileges. Subsequently, as relatively privileged chil-dren of regime notables, some of this group were able to retreat into a commune modeled on West Berlin's Kommune I: the "K1 Ost." Their efforts to "revolutionize the self" through psychoanalytic and sex-ual experimentation came to grief, however, under the strain of commu-nal living and the pressure of police surveillance.[5]

The contrast with the situation on the other side of the East-West divide could hardly be more striking. Across the border in West Berlin, and in neighboring West Germany, insurgent left-wing politics and countercultural experimentation achieved wide purchase. What began in the mid-1960s as a movement in favor of university reform strongly inflected by determination to root out vestiges of the Nazi period quickly developed into a thoroughgoing demand for radical-democratic change at all levels of society. Engagement in the worldwide movement against the American war in Vietnam merged with a broader anti-imperialism synergized by contacts with foreign students in the Federal Republic,

[3] Marc-Dietrich Ohse, *Jugend nach dem Mauerbau: Anpassung, Protest und Eigensinn (DDR 1961–1974)* (Berlin: Christoph Links, 2003), 191; see also "Erika Berthold und die Kommune 1/Ost," in Ute Kätzel (ed.), *Die 68erinnen: Porträt einer rebellischen Frauengeneration* (Berlin: Rohwolt, 2002), 220–237, 224–225.

[4] Burkhard Kleinert, quoted in Wolfgang Engler, "Die dritte Generation," in Wolfgang Engler (ed.), *Die Ost-deutschen: Kunde von einem verlorenen Land* (Berlin: atb, 2005), 303–340, 311.

[5] On the K1-Ost, see Timothy S. Brown, "A tale of two communes: The private and the political in divided Berlin, 1967–1973," in Martin Klimke, Jacco Pekelder, and Joachim Scharloth (eds.), *Between Prague Spring and French May 1968: Opposition and Revolt in Europe, 1960–1980* (New York: Berghahn, 2011), 132–140.

while countercultural experimentation and unorthodox Marxism provided the fuel for a range of insurgent strategies aimed at revolutionizing the face of daily life.[6]

Scouring the European revolutionary past and the Third World anti-imperialist present for models of radical action, West German activists reproduced a spectrum of left-wing tendencies ranging from Marxist-Leninism to anarchism, from women's liberation to radical environmentalism. The cultural-political output of these radical movements was then coopted and spread through media and channels of consumer capitalism to an entire new generation, much to the disgust of many radical activists, as we will see in Chapter 5. In West Germany, the revolt of 1968 encompassed a whole host of initiatives that were largely impossible under state socialism in the East. If it would be easy to see in this disparity a simple proof of the closed nature of Eastern as compared with the relative openness of Western societies, there were, despite obvious differences in the degree of space for dissent, some fundamentally similar and often-overlooked dynamics at work on both sides of the Iron Curtain.

Nothing About Us Without Us

The cognitive dissonance that tormented young East Germans confronted by the crushing of the Prague Spring had its analog on both sides of the East-West divide. Across the German-German border, young West Germans forced to come to terms with their government's support for anti-Communist repression and war abroad were especially shocked when, in protesting against those things, they confronted the reality of state violence on their own streets. The role of the United States in laying the groundwork for West German democracy made the shock over the USA's behavior and the support for it by the West German

---

[6] On West Germany, see Ingo Cornils, *Writing the Revolution: The Construction of "1968"* (Rochester: Camden House, 2016); Alexander Sedlmaier, *Consumption and Violence: Radical Protest in Cold-War West Germany* (Ann Arbor: University of Michigan Press, 2014); Timothy Scott Brown, *West Germany and the Global Sixties: The Anti-Authoritarian Revolt, 1962–1978* (New York: Cambridge University Press, 2013; 2015); Quinn Slobodian, *Foreign Front: Third World Politics in Sixties West Germany* (Durham, NC: Duke University Press, 2012); Holger Nehring, *Politics of Security: British and West German Protest Movements and the Early Cold War, 1945–1970* (Oxford: Oxford University Press, 2013); Martin Klimke, *The Other Alliance: Student Protest in West Germany and the United States in the Global Sixties* (Princeton: Princeton University Press, 2010); Detlef Siegfried, *Time Is on My Side: Konsum und Politik in der Westdeutschen Jugendkultur der 60er Jahre* (Göttingen: Wallstein, 2006). See also the essays in Alexander Vazansky and Marco Abel (eds.), "What was politics in '68? A special issue on the West German sixties," *The Sixties: A Journal of History, Politics and Culture*, 7(2) (2014).

government all the more acute. After helping defeat the Nazi regime in World War II, America placed its stamp on West Germany, supplying the basis of its constitution, sustaining a sizable military presence, and integrating West Germany into the NATO alliance. The shock of the Vietnam War, indeed, lay not so much in the fact that a technologically modern state would wage war on a freedom-seeking peasant population – something that had been done by imperial powers for centuries – but that it was the United States, that supposed beacon of freedom and democracy, that was doing it.

Growing politicization in student circles from the middle of the decade coincided with the rise of an independent youth culture whose insurrectionary potential had been evident as early as 1962, when young people in the prosperous Bavarian capital of Munich rioted for three days in response to heavy-handed police action against street musicians.[7] The founding of West Berlin's Kommune I in 1967 signaled one of the first attempts to channel this insurrectionary potential in the direction of lifestyle revolt and cultural provocation. In between, the Socialist German Student League became the flagship of the so-called extra-parliamentary opposition (*Außerparlamentarische Opposition* or APO), an informal coalition dedicated to opening up the authoritarian political culture of the Federal Republic in the 1960s. The SDS placed the war in Vietnam – along with reform of the antiquated structures of the university, coming to grips with adults' relative silence on the Nazi past, and dealing with press monopoly – at the top of an agenda that became increasingly radical over the next several years.

The attempt to come to grips with West Germany's relationship to its American mentor against the backdrop of the Nazi past developed in concert with attempts to come to terms with Germany's historical left-wing traditions. Communism played an equivocal role in West Germany. The so-called traditionalist wing of the SDS held sympathies toward East German state Communism from early on. When the founding of a new German Communist Party (DKP) was permitted by the authorities in 1968 – the previous KPD had been banned in 1956 – many traditionalists joined straight away. By contrast, leaders of SDS's antiauthoritarian wing, like Rudi Dutschke and Bernd Rabehl, themselves political refugees from East Germany, had few illusions about the nature of "real existing socialism" in the East. They nevertheless sought to retrieve as much of Marxism as possible, emphasizing theory and ideology in a way that

---

[7] On these so-called Schwabing Riots, see the essays in Gerhard Fürmetz and Thomas Kleinknecht (eds.), *Schwabinger Krawalle: Protest, Polizei und Öffentlichkeit zu Beginn der 60er Jahre* (Essen: Klartext, 2006).

sometimes left them out of step not only with anarchist-oriented counter-cultural radicals in the Federal Republic but, as we have seen, with Eastern European counterparts chafing under Marxist regimes.

Yet, much in the same way that East German radicals experienced the crushing of the Prague Spring as a betrayal of their idealistic belief in socialism, students in West Germany understood the American war in Vietnam – and their own government's support for it – as a betrayal of the democratic values they had been taught. At every stage, from the Bonn government's unquestioning support for the USA no matter how horrific the Vietnam War became, to the dubious nature of the supposedly democratic country of South Vietnam whose freedom the USA was defending, to the blatant falsehoods propagated in the mass media about students and their claims, the gap between official rhetoric and lived reality loomed large. The sea change in attitudes caused by this perceived betrayal was remarkable. At the beginning of the 1960s, young West Germans could look up to figures like John F. Kennedy and Martin Luther King; by the middle of the 1960s, many had begun to look upon the USA as a terrorist state, an obstacle to the freedom of peoples instead of a support for it; by the beginning of the 1970s, a small minority of activists had declared open war against its troops and installations in West Germany.[8]

These developments would have been much less likely if not for the events of June 2, 1967. On that day, the student Benno Ohnesorg was murdered by police during protests against the visit of Shah Mohammad Reza Pahlavi of Iran to West Berlin. Installed in power by a CIA coup in 1953 that overthrew Prime Minister Mohammad Mossadegh at the behest of Western oil interests, the Shah suppressed freedom of speech and exercised state terror through his brutal secret police the SAVAK. The vicious beatings of student protestors carried out in tandem by his agents and the West German police, followed by the murder of Ohnesorg, gave the lie to the government's humanitarian claims. Followed less than a year later by the attempted assassination of Rudi Dutschke by a right-wing fanatic in April 1968 and the following month by the passage of so-called Emergency Laws, which provided for the suspension of civil liberties in the face of a future unspecified crisis, the stage was set for a radicalization that would shake West German society over the next decade.

---

[8] For a comparative perspective on left-wing violence, see Jeremy Varon, *Bringing the War Home: The Weather Underground, the Red Army Faction, and Revolutionary Violence in the Sixties and Seventies* (Berkeley: University of California Press, 2004).

During the same period that students at the Free University in Berlin were mobilizing in favor of reform, students in Poland began doing the same at Warsaw University. Known as the "Commandos" in honor of their reputation for intellectual combativeness, this group of "courageous heretic Marxists" (as they were dubbed by a visiting British journalist) sought to rekindle the emancipatory energies that had first emerged in Poland in the mid-1950s. Continuing the ideological work of student discussion clubs founded in the 1950s and early 1960s, their goal was nothing less than the creation of a renewed socialism that lived up to its promises.[9] The Commandos were well aware of the latest currents of thought in Berlin and Paris, and they were inspired by ideas of a rejuvenated Marxism based on workers' self-management and participatory democracy.[10] They looked at the development of the reform movement in neighboring Czechoslovakia with a hope captured in the slogan "Poland is awaiting its Dubček."[11] Another slogan, equally apposite, captured their desire to meaningfully participate in the system that claimed to represent them: "Nothing About Us Without Us."

Polish students' brand of questioning had its roots in the period of relative openness after 1956, when emboldened members of the young intelligentsia began to ask how it was that, in a society that proclaimed itself the most free and democratic on earth, a classless society in which workers held all the power, one experienced instead a deadening bureaucracy in which even the most basic "bourgeois" freedoms of speech, assembly, and association were denied, let alone the freedoms of economic and social self-management promised by Marxism. The Gomułka regime that had come to power as a consequence of the revolt of 1956 proved itself closed to such questions. After a period of relative openness, the years 1963–1964 saw a renewed wave of repression. Independent literary journals were suppressed and the main discussion club at the University of Warsaw closed, unleashing an "escalating spiral of repression and dissent" in which attempts to deal honestly with social contradictions met with brute force.[12]

It was in this context that the question on the lips of young Eastern Bloc intellectuals was posed in explosive form by two key figures of the Marxist

---

[9] George Katsiaficas, *The Imagination of the New Left: A Global Analysis of 1968* (Boston, MA: South End, 1987), 36.

[10] Jacek Kuron and Karol Modzelewski, "A socialist manifesto for Poland," *International Socialism*, 28 (Spring 1967), 25–27. The essay was previously published in *Kultura* (Paris: Institut Litteraire, 1966).

[11] Mark Kramer, "The Czechoslovak crisis and the Brezhnev doctrine," in Carole Fink, Philipp Gassert, and Detlef Junker (eds.), *1968: The World Transformed* (Cambridge: Cambridge University Press, 1998), 111–172, 127.

[12] Katsiaficas, *The Imagination of the New Left*.

renaissance in Poland, Jacek Kuron and Karol Modzelewski. Their 1964 "Open Letter to the Party" positioned the emerging New Left in Poland as a fresh iteration of a historical process.[13] To begin with, it was a follow-up to what the authors dubbed "the first anti-bureaucratic revolution" – the workers' uprisings of 1953 in East Germany and 1956–1957 in Poland, Hungary, and the Soviet labor camps. Second, it put forward classical demands of the revolutionary workers' moments of the late nineteenth and early twentieth centuries. The program laid out in the Open Letter included workers' control of factories; the replacement of party control by the control of workers' councils; freedom of speech, assembly, and affiliation; free independent trade unions and the abolition of censorship; and the expansion of the revolution internationally in both East, West, and the developing world.[14] By forcefully arguing that "actually existing socialism" was not actually socialism at all, and thereby demonstrating that Eastern Europeans could demand freedom from the USSR without crawling back to capitalism, the Open Letter appealed strongly to those hoping for a "third way" to socialism.

Unsurprisingly, the Open Letter's claims were rejected by Polish authorities, and Kuron and Modzelewski were sentenced to prison terms. This heavy-handed intervention did not put matters to rest, however. Ferment among reform-minded students continued to grow, the Commandos in particular bearing the direct stamp of Kuron and Modzelewski's influence. The explosive force of escalating demands for reform was exhibited two years later when the Socialist Youth Organization at the University of Warsaw celebrated the tenth anniversary of the Polish uprising of October 1956. Leszek Kołakowski, the main speaker at the event, was expelled from the party the following day.[15]

This rising ferment set the stage for the "Polish March" of 1968.[16] The immediate cause of the March uprisings was the banning in January 1968 of the Adam Mickiewicz play *Dziady* ("Forefathers' Eve"). The play had been scheduled for a lengthy run at the National Theater in Warsaw. Written in 1824, the play had a long association with Polish nationalism but had been performed repeatedly over many decades. Its performance

---

[13] See Matt Killingsworth, *Civil Society in Communist Eastern Europe: Opposition and Dissent in Totalitarian Regimes* (Wivenhoe Park: ECPR, 2012), 121.
[14] The program is summarized in the American New Left journal *International Socialism*, 28 (Spring 1967), 25–27.
[15] Katsiaficas, *The Imagination of the New Left*.
[16] On the Polish 1968, see Stefan Garsztecki, "Poland," in Martin Klimke and Joachim Scharloth (eds.), *1968 in Europe: A History of Protest and Activism, 1956–1977* (London: Palgrave Macmillan, 2008), 179–188; Jerzy Eisler, "March 1968 in Poland," in Fink, Gassert, and Junker, *1968*, 237–252; see also Tom Junes, *Student Politics in Communist Poland: Generations of Consent and Dissent* (Lanham: Lexington, 2015).

at this moment, however, was deemed by the authorities to have a clear anti-Soviet valence. The ban on the play took place at precisely the moment when Alexander Dubček in neighboring Czechoslovakia was beginning his project of reforms based on the idea of "socialism with a human face."[17] The ban prompted a student campaign that included the gathering of 3,000 signatures on a letter of protest.[18] The student leaders Adam Michnik and Henryk Szlajfer were expelled from Warsaw University for speaking about the controversy with the French newspaper *Le Monde*.[19] As was so often the case around 1968, protests around a specific scenario – in this case, the banning of an artistic performance – paved the way for more comprehensive demands. The Warsaw branch of the Polish Writers' Association passed a declaration demanding not only a repeal of the ban on the play but an end to censorship and the right of writers to play a role in the development of cultural policy.[20]

The closing of *Forefathers' Eve* provided a crystalizing moment in which was symbolized a whole range of repressions. As the government responded to a student demonstration on March 8 with vicious beatings, delivered not just by police but by "workers' militias" trucked in especially for the occasion to send the "spoiled brats" a message, the system showed its true face once and for all. The student response to these events came out strongly in posters and pamphlets bearing slogans such as "Long live the student-worker alliance," "Don't let police truncheons rule Poland," and "The whole of Poland awaits her Dubček."[21] The regime used the occasion to settle scores within the party and to purge academia through expulsions and the closing of entire academic departments. The particularly ugly state response, even by Stalinist standards, included an anti-Semitic campaign accusing all dissenting students and intellectuals of being Jews who owed their allegiance not to Poland but to Israel. These claims were repeated throughout state media, further enraging protestors with the extent to which the government was willing to resort to blatant falsehood.

---

[17] Gomułka complained to Dubček about the *Dziady* controversy by way of emphasizing the importance of Czechoslovakia keeping its "rogue elements" in check; see Tony Kemp-Welch, "'To hell with sovereignty!': Poland and the Prague Spring," in Kevin McDermott and Matthew Stibbe (eds.), *Eastern Europe in 1968: Responses to the Prague Spring and Warsaw Pact Invasion* (Basingstoke: Palgrave Macmillan, 2018), 125–141, 127.

[18] Rolf Werenskjold, "A chronology of the global 1968 protest," in Klimke, Pekelder, and Scharloth, *Between Prague Spring and French May*, 283–307, 285.

[19] Radio Free Europe broadcast their account of the events back into Poland; see Kemp-Welch, "'To hell with sovereignty!'," 128.

[20] Werenskjold, "A chronology of the global 1968 protest," 285.

[21] Kemp-Welch, "'To hell with sovereignty!'," 128–129.

A statement of solidarity from students in Yugoslavia captured the general response. "All over the world," they wrote, "students are at the forefront in the struggle to create a human society, and thus we are profoundly surprised by the reactions of the Polish socialist regime. Free critical thought cannot be suppressed by any kind of power, not even by that which superficially leans on socialist ideals."[22] Expressing astonishment at the Polish government's cynical response to the crisis, they continued: "For us, young Marxists, it is incomprehensible that today, in a socialist country, it is possible to tolerate anti-Semitic attacks and to use them for the solution of internal problems. We consider it unacceptable that after Polish socialism experienced so many painful experiences in the past, internal conflicts should be solved by such undemocratic means and that in their solution Marxist thought is persecuted."[23]

In the wake of the events, Jacek Kuron and Karol Modzelewski were given renewed prison sentences for helping to organize a student strike, and leading members of the Commandos were sentenced to prison as well. The reception of Kuron and Modzelewski offers a notable example of international solidarity efforts both within and outside the Communist Bloc.[24] The Yugoslavian journal *Praxis* expressed its support, the Czechoslovakian Writers' Association lodged a protest with Polish authorities, and Charles University in Prague invited them to give guest lectures.[25] The "Open Letter to the Party" was quickly available in print in multiple American and European journals. Translated into French, it became one of the most popular writings at the Sorbonne.[26] In court for his role in the September 1968 protests at the annual Frankfurt Book Fair, to the confusion of the judge, the French-German militant Daniel Cohn-Bendit gave his name as "Kuron-Modzelewski."[27]

---

[22] *Student* (April 23, 1968), 4, quoted in Fredy Perlman, *Birth of a Revolutionary Movement in Yugoslavia* (Kalamazoo: Black & Red, 1969).

[23] *Student* (April 23, 1968), 4, quoted in Perlman, *Birth of a Revolutionary Movement in Yugoslavia*. False reporting in the government press was a key issue for protesting students in Warsaw; see Mauricio Borrero, "Spring Thaw, Summer Frost," 84–85.

[24] See the interview with the American "Third Camp Socialists" Joanne Landy and Tom Harrison: www.huffingtonpost.com/john-feffer/regretting-the-regions-ri_b_3187802.html.

[25] In March 1968; see Werenskjold, "A Chronology of the Global 1968 Protest."

[26] Jerzy Eisler in Philipp Gassert and Martin Klimke (eds.), *1968: Memories and Legacies of a Global Revolt* (Washington, DC: Bulletin of the German Historical Institute, 2009), 167.

[27] On the 1968 Frankfurt Book Fair protests, see Brown, *West Germany and the Global Sixties*, 116–119.

Such examples do more, however, than simply provide more evidence that student radicals on both sides of the Iron Curtain knew each others' names and identified themselves as opponents of a common enemy. Like Cohn-Bendit, who was well known for his criticism both of the PCF and of the original Bolsheviks, Kuron and Modzelewski understood themselves as agents of a historical recovery project aimed at rediscovering socialist traditions that Bolshevism and its successors had repressed and tried to erase from history. Far from aping Western democratic models, Polish students in 1968 were grappling with the longstanding issue of socialist democracy. Their response to the chicanery of the Communist government demonstrates, like West German protestors' response to their government's support for the Vietnam War, the key role played by cognitive dissonance in 1968 – it was often where governments' words failed most visibly to accord with their deeds that the potential for rebellion was greatest.

The Radio Lies

During the events in Poland and West Germany, a more momentous event was brewing in France. There, a revolt of students was developing that would spread into the working class and shake the foundations of the French state. Largely quiescent since its Algerian war heyday, the French student movement by 1968 stood at the brink of a mass uprising unparalleled in Europe. The backdrop for student militancy was a stark rise in the number of students of university age in France, reflected in over a threefold increase in the number of French university students between 1958 and 1967.[28] Attempts to alleviate the attendant overcrowding, such as the building of the overflow campus opened at Nanterre in 1964, only added to the generalized feeling of dissatisfaction. A grim campus of concrete, removed from any urban amenities, Nanterre seemed to exemplify the alienated state of French education.[29] The neoliberal Fouchet reforms, which forced students into an early career track and tied their education more closely to the perceived needs of the French economy, lent support to the argument – being made forcefully not only in France but on college campuses from Berkeley to Berlin – that the main purpose of education was not enlightenment but, in Daniel Cohn-Bendit's words, "to turn people into ever more profitable pack-horses."[30]

---

[28] Ian Birchall, "France 1968," in Colin Barker (ed.), *Revolutionary Rehearsals* (London: Bookmarks, 1987), 5–40, 9.

[29] Andrew Feenberg and Jim Freedman, *When Poetry Ruled the Streets: The French May Events of 1968* (Albany: State University of New York Press, 2001), 5.

[30] Daniel Cohn-Bendit and Gabriel Cohn-Bendit, *Obsolete Communism: The Left-Wing Alternative* (London: AK, 2000), 16.

As in the Netherlands and West Germany, the match to the fuse of student discontent was held in the hand of a small group of provocateurs inspired by avant-garde doctrines emerging from the arts and libertarian-socialist politics. As early as November 1966, activists at the University of Strasbourg contrived to have themselves elected to the student union in order to carry out a Situationist-influenced assault on the university. Founding a "Society for the Rehabilitation of Karl Marx and Ravachol" (the latter a notorious nineteenth-century French anarchist), they used student funds to publish a tract by the Situationist Mustapha Khayati – "On the Poverty of Student Life" – that mocked the subservient status of the student within the university and society.[31] The group subsequently distributed the pamphlet at a campus event in the presence of city and university notables, provoking a storm of outrage in the press against "ultra-revolutionaries" and "Beatniks."[32]

The style of subversion pioneered by the Situationist International group at Strasbourg was subsequently taken up at the Nanterre campus by a tiny band of radical instigators. Styling themselves Les Enragés ("the enraged") after the militants of the French Revolution, they launched a campaign of provocation that would lead directly to the upheaval of the French May.[33] In their very name, the Enragés signaled their intention of restaging the revolutionary moments of the past. Singing the "The Internationale," flying the black flag of anarchism and the red flag of communism, "breaking up lecture courses in the name of Mao Tse-Tung and Che Guevara, [they] created a continual political happening."[34] These performances, like those of the Kommune I in West Germany or the Provos in the Netherlands, had an impact precisely because they cast a laser light onto real problems. In connecting issues of daily life (e.g. student exams) with issues of war and imperialism and the organization and larger aims of

---

[31] Angelo Quattrocchi and Tom Nairn, *The Beginning of the End: France, May 1968* (London: Verso, 1998), 92. See Internationale Situationiste, *On the Poverty of Student Life: A Consideration of Its Economic, Political, Sexual, Psychological and Notably Intellectual Aspects and of a Few Ways to Cure It* (Detroit: Black & Red, 2000). *Poverty* was translated into ten languages; see René Viénet's *Enragés et situationnistes dans le mouvement des occupations* (Paris: Gallimard, 1968).

[32] Richard Wolin, *The Wind from the East: French Intellectuals, the Cultural Revolution, and the Legacy of the 1960s* (Princeton: Princeton University Press, 2010), 77. "Rejecting all morality and restraint," claimed the judge presiding over their trial for misappropriating student union funds, "their cynicism does not hesitate to preach theft, and an end to all studies, the suspension of work, total subversion and world revolution with unlicensed pleasure as its only goal"; Cohn-Bendit and Cohn-Bendit, *Obsolete Communism*, 26.

[33] See Jean-Pierre Duteuil, *Nanterre 1968: Notes on the Background to the 22 March Group* (ChristieBooks, electronic edition, 2014).

[34] Feenberg and Freedman, *When Poetry Ruled the Streets*, 6.

capitalist society, they enacted 1968's signature maneuver: connecting the dots on the basis of the position that all struggles were connected.

The Enragés were part of a broader scene at Nanterre that included anarchists, Maoists, and Trotskyists. These groups disagreed ideologically but were united in a common commitment to action. Occupying the faculty lounge, boycotting exams, and organizing an exhibit of photos of undercover police spies on campus, they placed themselves directly in opposition to the power structure on campus.[35] In February, there was a sit-in against curfews and in favor of coed dorm visitation rights, followed by dorm invasions. In March, an attack on the American Express office led to the arrest of six activists belonging to the National Committee for Vietnam. In cooperation with Maoist and other student radicals, they seized administration buildings, leading to a police invasion and the shutting down of campus. From that day hence, the Nanterre militants became the "March 22 Movement," and the stage for the French May was set.[36]

The closure of the Nanterre campus moved the action to the Sorbonne, where disciplinary proceedings were planned against key militants of the March 22 Movement. The Dean of the Sorbonne authorized police to clear the campus, which resulted in running battles with students in the surrounding Latin Quarter. Hundreds were arrested and many injured. A week of protests of increasing scope and violence culminated on May 10, 1968 in the so-called Night of the Barricades. Students and other militants faced off against truncheon-wielding riot police of the CRS (Compagnies Républicaines de Sécurité) with paving stones and Molotov cocktails, while residents threw food to the militants fighting below and dumped water from apartment windows onto the streets to dampen the tear gas.[37] The fighting had less the character of a student riot than of an urban insurrection. Barricades, some sixty of them, were built by "women, workers, bystanders, people in pajamas, human chains to carry rocks, wood, iron."[38] During an attack of the CRS, recalled an activist, a "man on the fifth floor of a building on that street shouted at them, 'You bastards' and tossed his TV onto their heads .... I saw this with my own eyes."[39]

---

[35] Feenberg and Freedman, *When Poetry Ruled the Streets*, 8; see also Duteuil, *Nanterre 1968*.

[36] On the March 22 Movement, see Jean-Pierre Duteuil, *Nanterre 1965–66–67–68: Vers le mouvement du 22 mars* (Mauléon: Acratie, 1988); see also Daniel Cohn-Bendit and Gabriel Cohn-Bendit, *Linksradikalismus: Gewaltkur gegen die Alterskrankheit des Kommunismus* (Hamburg: Rowohlt, 1968).

[37] "People throw water from windows," wrote the sympathetic eyewitness Tom Nairn, "broken water pipes flood the street, people scream from windows, shout frightened obscenities at the advancing live tentacles. *Flics* ("cops") shoot grenades through windows." Quattrocchi and Nairn, *The Beginning of the End*, 31.

[38] Jean-Jaques Lebel, "The Night of May 10," *Black Dwarf*, 13(1) (June 1, 1968), 3.

[39] Mitchell Abidor, *More May Made Me: Additional Elements of an Oral History of the 1968 Uprising in France* (Oakland: AK, 2018), 43–44.

4.1 The Night of the Barricades, Paris, May 10–11, 1968 (photo: Philippe Vermès, courtesy of Johan Kugelberg/Boo-Hooray).

4.2 Paris street demonstration, May 27, 1968 (photo: Bruno Barbey, courtesy of Magnum).

4.3 Students passing cobblestones during the street-fighting in Paris (photo: Bruno Barbey, courtesy of Magnum).

Police overreaction made state violence concrete in a way that could not be ignored. It was one thing to be aware of how authority operated in far-away colonial locations; it was another to experience firsthand the reality of tear gas or a police baton. The CRS quickly earned a reputation for disproportionate violence, prompting the chant "CRS-SS," which, in a way similar to the student movement in West Germany, drew an explicit connection between current police violence and the violence of the fascist past.

The past was also present in the historical recovery project that was central to the movement. Placing revolutionary history and theory in the service of present struggles, the March 22 Movement organized lectures on the Spanish Civil War and Wilhelm Reich, on sexuality and the problems of daily life. "During May, in a *tour de force* of revolutionary theatricality," writes the historian Richard Wolin of this gesture of historical recapitulation, "the students reenacted the entire gamut of insurrectionary possibilities and options: the revolutions of 1848, the Paris Commune, Berlin 1918, and the Kronstadt naval mutiny. Trotskyists, anarchists, Maoists, and Situationists vied – for the most part, fraternally – to endow the unfolding events with meaning and direction." All revolutionary scenarios were not created equal, however.

"The one historical scenario they unanimously rejected," writes Wolin, "was the Bolshevik-orchestrated storming of the Winter Palace of October 1917."[40]

Indeed, the new style of activism was heavily influenced by the negative example of Russian Bolshevism and its successors in the Eastern Bloc Stalinist regimes. As the Revolutionary Action Committee at the Sorbonne put it: "It is for all revolutionaries to take [power] and destroy it immediately. Because, we do not want a state capitalism and a bureaucratic and criminal red bourgeoisie. The revolution of 1917 has taught us how a few 'professional revolutionaries' can completely pervert a social revolution in a few months time: we will try to keep this in mind."[41] It is important to recognize, however, that by "power" these groups meant state power – "political" power – as opposed to *social power*, the power of workers and others self-organized from below.

This impulse was distinctly out of step with the ethos of the French Communist Party. The PCF bitterly denounced the student movement, trying at every juncture to put the brakes on a radical development it did not control and therefore feared. "The French Communists were," it has been pointed out, "among the most loyal supporters of the Soviet Union outside Russia."[42] Their situation was equivocal, however, since they were a reformist party that sought merely to achieve "an advanced democracy as a step toward socialism."[43] Even though it was no longer a revolutionary party – or perhaps because of it – the PCF saw its main goal in May 1968 as to prevent any challenge to its left. In this sense, it was an inheritor of the Bolshevik tradition. From the earliest days of the Russian Revolution, the Bolsheviks acted vigorously to squelch the initiatives of Social Revolutionaries, anarchists, and other nonparty radicals, even to the point of prison and execution.[44]

Radicals were well aware of the nature of the Communist Party, both in history and in the present. "A Communist couldn't speak in public," one activist recalled. "He'd be booed and thrown out. It was impossible for a known Communist .... Someone who'd have begun a speech with 'comrade' .... The word 'comrade' was tainted by the Communists, it was outlawed."[45] Such attitudes were backed

[40] Wolin, *The Wind from the East*, 355–356.
[41] Quoted in Feenberg and Freedman, *When Poetry Ruled the Streets*, 154.
[42] Feenberg and Freedman, *When Poetry Ruled the Streets*, 148.
[43] Feenberg and Freedman, *When Poetry Ruled the Streets*.
[44] See Grigori Maximov, *The Guillotine at Work in Russia* (Chicago: Berkman Fund, 1940).
[45] Abidor, *More May Made Me*, 62–63.

by historically-based political analysis. Daniel and Gabriel Cohn-Bendit wrote about the counterrevolutionary role of the Communist Party in France when the revolt had barely cooled. The title of their book, *Obsolete Communism: The Left-Wing Alternative*, was a play on Lenin's *Left-Wing Communism: An Infantile Disorder*, an attack on the Bolsheviks' left-wing critics published in 1920. Writing the history of little-known events like the Bolsheviks' destruction of the left-wing Kronstadt Uprising of 1921, they argued that the vanguard-party model of Bolshevism had been flawed from the start. The contemporary Soviet Union did not represent a Stalinist "deformation" – as the Trotskyists would have it – but had its roots in the earliest actions of Lenin. The basic argument of *Left-Wing Communism* had been foreshadowed in the Situationist pamphlet *On the Poverty of Student Life*: "The Bolsheviks are wrong because it is no longer 1920, and even in 1920 they were wrong."[46]

From this perspective, the fact that the PCF had played a counterrevolutionary role in the May events was no surprise – it was a continuation of the counterrevolutionary role that many left-wing militants claimed the Bolsheviks had played from the very beginning. The PCF had attempted at every juncture to smear student protestors as bourgeois dilettantes and to steer workers organized in Communist-affiliated trade unions away from the course of open confrontation with the state.[47] The actual rebellion in the universities adhered more closely to the spirit of the Situationists, whose (implicitly anarchist) writings influenced the so-called Enragés of the Nanterre campus who helped kick off the revolt, while the wildcat strikes by workers at Renault, Sud-Aviation, and other concerns took place in spite of, not because of, the leadership of the Communist and Socialist parties. In the French May, the Cohn-Bendits argued, the Communist Party and trade unions had lagged consistently behind the masses, just as they had done in Russia a half-decade earlier.[48] "The Party of Revolution, wrote Tom Nairn while the events were still hot, "is revealed as the Party of Order."[49]

Some militants adopted Maoism in response to this impasse, although as a poorly understood foreign import, itself an outgrowth of a conflict between competing brands of authoritarian Marxism (Mao's conflict with

---

[46] Cohn-Bendit and Cohn-Bendit, *Obsolete Communism*, 222.
[47] Wolin, *The Wind from the East*.
[48] Cohn-Bendit and his brother Gabriel took up this theme in Cohn-Bendit and Cohn-Bendit, *Obsolete Communism*.
[49] Quattrocchi and Nairn, *The Beginning of the End*, 107.

Stalin and the Sino-Soviet split), Maoism was of limited usefulness in the struggles developing in France. The Union of Marxist-Leninist Communist Youth, founded at the École Normale in December 1966, sat out the events of May 1968 entirely, convinced that students in the streets could not make the revolution that theory dictated could only be made by the workers. The "masochistic self-criticism" resulting from this "missed appointment" resulted in the dissolution of the group in the fall.[50] In October of the same year, remnants of that group joined together with elements of the May student rebellion to form the Proletarian Left, whose militants participated in a great "going to the people" that saw work in rural and urban areas, with immigrants, and the creation of "divisions dedicated to high schools, universities, the media, propaganda, the military, women, cinema, health, abortion, international leftism, prisons, and, of course, factories."[51] In this way, Maoism served not just as an object of orientalist projection for French intellectuals but as a template for voluntarist rank-and-file militancy aimed at revitalizing a moribund mainstream left.

Other militants relied on living traditions of the European workers' movement in which the distinction between authoritarianism and antiauthoritarianism, top-down and bottom-up, were more clear. These activists gravitated toward what they regarded as the core and only legitimate expression of working-class power: a system of direct democracy rooted in workers' councils. "The proletarian revolution has spontaneously outlined its adequate forms in the councils," declared the Council for Maintaining the Occupations, a revolutionary committee composed of members of the Enragés and the Situationist International, "in St. Petersburg in 1905, as well as in Turin in 1920, in Catalonia in 1936, in Budapest in 1956. Each time, the survival of the old society or the formation of new exploiting classes has required the suppression of the councils. The working class now knows its enemies."[52] The power of the council as a revolutionary-organizational form was defined by "[t]he dissolution of all external power; direct and total democracy; practical unification of decision-making and implementation; delegates who can be recalled at any time by their electors; the abolition of hierarchy and independent specializations; conscious management and trans-formation of all the conditions of liberated life; permanent creative

---

[50] Julian Bourg, "Principally Contradiction: The flourishing of French Maoism," in Alexander Cook (ed.), *Mao's Little Red Book: A Global History* (New York: Cambridge University Press, 2014), 225–244, 227.

[51] Bourg, "Principally Contradiction."

[52] "Address to all Workers," in Feenberg and Freedman, *When Poetry Ruled the Streets*, 89.

participation of the masses; internationalist extension and coordination."[53]

The emphasis on self-management became one reason why the dominant form of organization in the May events was the "Action Committee," an organ of popular democracy oriented toward direct action in the school, workplace, and neighborhood.[54] "Every workers' revolution in Europe since 1905," point out Andrew Feenberg and Jim Freedman, "had proceeded from a general strike to the formation of 'soviets,' workers' councils poised to seize power from the state."[55] This action and organization form is – alongside the small avant-garde group – the Ur-form of radical organization in the modern era. It is no surprise, then, that this was the form valorized by militants and adopted by strikers. By June 1968, there were some 450 action committees in operation in France. Seeking to link rank-and-file radicalism in the schools and workplaces, neighborhoods and cultural institutions, the action committees demonstrated the attractive power of a form of organization developed in accord with the demands of local struggles.[56]

Even as it focused on proximate issues, the French movement gained strength and inspiration from transnational exchanges. The West German radical K. D. Wolff visited the campus in April 1968 as a representative of the Socialist German Students League. That same month, French students protested in solidarity with German students against the Springer Press monopoly and again after the assassination attempt against Rudi Dutschke.[57] It was only a small exaggeration for Daniel Cohn-Bendit to claim, as he did in *Obsolete Communism*, that the March 22 Movement owed its birth to events in West Germany.[58] Two

---

[53] "Address to all Workers," 88. Distributed in leaflet form during the events, the "Address to all Workers" was published in Viénet's *Enragés et situationnistes dans le mouvement des occupations*, which was translated into English as *Enragés and Situationists in the Occupation Movement* (Brooklyn: Autonomedia, 1992). It is also available in Ken Knabb, *The Situationist International Anthology* (Oakland: AK, 2006, revised and expanded edition), as well as on the website Bureau of Public Secrets: www .bopsecrets.org/SI/May68docs.htm#Address. This depiction of self-management as both tactic and goal, write Andrew Feenberg and Jim Freedman, "was precisely a radical return to the idea of social revolution, a revolution that displaces the state from the center of the stage to allow maximum initiative from below to substitute itself for political domination from a fixed center"; Feenberg and Freedman, *When Poetry Ruled the Streets*, 150.

[54] See Roger Gregoire and Fredy Perlman, *Worker-Student Action Committees: France May '68* (Kalamazoo: Black & Red, 1969).

[55] Feenberg and Freedman, *When Poetry Ruled the Streets*, 147.

[56] Geoff Eley, *Forging Democracy: The History of the Left in Europe, 1850–2000* (Oxford: Oxford University Press, 2002), 351.

[57] Cohn-Bendit and Cohn-Bendit, *Obsolete Communism*, 48–49.

[58] Cohn-Bendit and Cohn-Bendit, *Obsolete Communism*, 49.

days later, Daniel Cohn-Bendit was expelled home to Germany from France, prompting a mass demonstration of students chanting "We are all German Jews." When an official of the PCF denounced him (not inaccurately) as a "German anarchist," thousands marched through Parisian streets chanting "we are all German Jews" in an elemental – and for obvious reasons highly loaded – affirmation of border-crossing solidarity.[59]

The movement also took part in the acts of the globalizing imagination that characterized 1968 everywhere. A member of the March 22 Movement interviewed in London's *International Times* explained: "American youth has been polarized by the Vietnam War but there must be consciousness of the unity of struggle between the youth of all Europe and the youth of America ... . This is not a dream; there are already radical and dynamic student movements in Germany, Holland, France, Belgium, in fact, in all the countries of Europe. This is a common struggle."[60] This struggle was not confined to Western Europe and North America. The March 22 Movement organized a series of "Anti-Imperialist Days" dedicated to discussing Third World struggles in general and the issue of Vietnam in particular. They also expressed a keen interest in Eastern Europe. Far from ignoring what was happening on the other side of the Iron Curtain, as the Western protagonists of 1968 have often been accused of doing, they insisted that revolutionaries must attack the "crushing bureaucracies" on both sides of the Cold War divide.[61]

As Maud Bracke points out, not all elements on the French left understood the fundamental, as opposed to reformist, implications of the struggles in Czechoslovakia and elsewhere in the East.[62] Nevertheless, the militants who best reflected the direct-democratic, councilist ethos of May 1968 understood the critical common issues at stake on both sides of the Cold War divide. And for the student movement more generally, labor provided a "dominant metaphor," not only because students wanted to enlist the aid of workers but because they wanted to pour their radicalism into the mold of the historical struggles borne by the working class in France and elsewhere.[63] In this connection, radicals refused to accept the distinction held up by the

---

[59] Katsiaficas, *The Imagination of the New Left*, 104.

[60] Jacques Tarnero, interviewed in "Alternative Society Now," *International Times*, 32 (May/June 1968).

[61] Alongside themes such as "University and Anti-University" and the "The Anti-Imperialist Struggle," they sought to foster discussion on "The Workers' and Students' Struggle in the East and the West"; Cohn-Bendit and Cohn-Bendit, *Obsolete Communism*, 47; see also Duteuil, *Nanterre 1968*.

[62] Maud Bracke, *Which Socialism, Whose Détente? West European Communism and the Czechoslovak Crisis of 1968* (Budapest: Central European University Press, 2007).

[63] Feenberg and Freedman, *When Poetry Ruled the Streets*, 124.

dominant bureaucratic organs of the Old Left, the Communist and Socialist parties and their affiliated trade unions, between students and a monolithic and separate "working class." The whole point of May 1968 was that shop-floor workers and the managerial elites to which students trained to belong were all, together, part of a class exploited by the capitalist system. Both intellectual labor and physical labor were alienated, and only in a common struggle could they find their common liberation.[64]

Worker-student militancy found particular expression in the realm of cultural production, above all in the revolt's production of coun-ter-media. Mass media in France was controlled by the government in a more thoroughgoing way than in most other Western democ-racies, to the extent that, in Antigoni Memou's words, "public broadcasting equated with state broadcasting."[65] International radio was one of the main ways that French people learned about what was going on in the protests.[66] Activists quickly founded pub-lications to track and theorize the revolt in real time. These included *Barricades*, *Cahiers de Mai*, and *Action*, the latter representing UNEF, SNEsup (National Union of Higher Education), and the March 22 Movement.[67] Tellingly, the very first issue of *Action* was dedicated to criticizing press coverage of the events and reproduced photographs of students being beaten by police.[68] As in Italy and West Germany, left-wing media practice encompassed the twin goals of critiquing official lies and developing the means of presenting the movement's own truths. Characteristic was the cover of an issue of *Action* depicting a supine figure smoking a marijuana joint made out of the newspaper *France Soir*, with the caption "Drug yourself!"

These activities took place against the backdrop of widespread protest against censorship. An episode of the news program *Panorama* dealing with the demonstrations and street battles was banned by the Ministry of Information.[69] Journalists, producers, and technicians went on strike

---

[64] As a characteristic flyer of May 1968 put it: "Workers, you too are forced to struggle to defend your gains against government attacks. You too have encountered the CRS and the Mobile Guards, come to break your resistance. You too have been slandered by the Boss's press and by the government Radio. You know that violence is in the nature of the existing order. You know that it strikes down those who dare to challenge it"; Feenberg and Freedman, *When Poetry Ruled the Streets*, 124.

[65] Antigoni Memou, "Revolt in photos: The French May '68 in the Student and Mainstream Press," in Kathrin Fahlenbrach, Erling Sivertsen, and Rolf Werenskjold (eds.), *Media and Revolt: Strategies and Performances from the 1960s to the Present* (New York: Berghahn, 2014), 147–164, 150.

[66] Memou, "Revolt in Photos."

[67] Feenberg and Freedman, *When Poetry Ruled the Streets*, 33.

[68] Memou, "Revolt in Photos," 152.

[69] Feenberg and Freedman, *When Poetry Ruled the Streets*, 42.

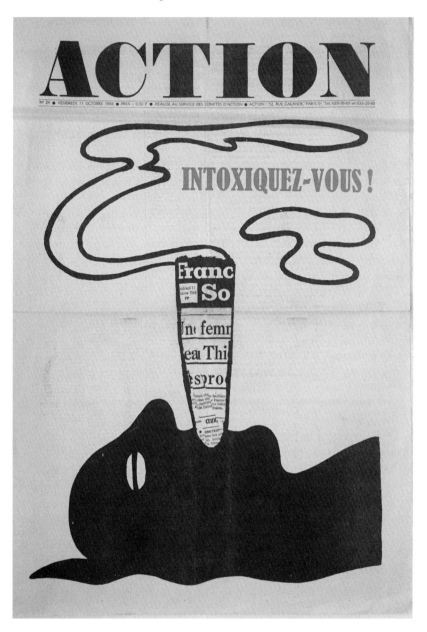

4.4 "Drug yourself!" *Action*, 29, October 11, 1968 (Houghton Library, Harvard University).

demanding more objective reporting.[70] Demands for more even-handed news coverage were echoed by the Parisian transport workers' union. The director of French radio and television, ORTF, was replaced by General de Gaulle, and in some cases, the army took control over striking television and radio stations.[71] A Revolutionary Committee for Cultural Agitation (CRAC) was founded to act in solidarity with striking radio and television personnel and to dispute the cooptation of cultural production to reinforce the needs of capitalism.[72]

The most well-known and striking of all the information-political interventions of May 1968 was the so-called Atelier Populaire (People's Studio/Popular Studio). Founded by students at the École des Beaux Arts, the Atelier Populaire produced a series of posters that retain their iconic stature to the present day.[73] The lithography studios at the École des Beaux-Arts had been on strike since May 8. On May 14, students and artists occupied the studios and began to turn out a series of iconic posters expressing the ideas of the revolt in simple but powerful graphic imagery. During the 50 days of the occupation, the studio created some 350 different posters, producing over half a million copies.[74] The action was in perfect accord with its moment. "[T]he idea was to bring [the posters] to a supporting gallery for sale," recalls one of the artists, "[b]ut we didn't make it ten meters in the street before the students snatched them and pasted them in the street themselves. We understood immediately: there was the idea!"[75] Teams formed from Neighborhood Action Committees and the strike committees of occupied factories were dispatched to paste up the flyers.[76]

The artistic practice of the Atelier Populaire mirrored the direct democratic character of the revolt. "Striking workers, students, artists, intellectuals and hangers-on contributed to a festive atmosphere driven alternately by Rolling Stones records or North Vietnamese revolutionary chants"; their actions were "run by general assemblies, which enforced

---

[70] Kristin Ross, *May '68 and Its Afterlives* (Chicago: University of Chicago Press, 2002), 15.

[71] Rolf Werenskjold, "A Chronology of the Global 1968 Protest," *Report No. 13* (Volda: Volda University College, 2010), 177, 186, 225.

[72] Feenberg and Freedman, *When Poetry Ruled the Streets*, 89.

[73] A collection of posters from the Atelier Populaire was published in paperback as early as a year after the revolt; see *Atelier Populaire: Posters from the Revolution* (London: Dobson, November 1969). More recently, they have appeared in Johan Kugelberg and Philippe Vermès (eds.), *Beauty Is in the Street: A Visual Record of the May '68 Paris Uprising* (London: Four Corners, 2011).

[74] Feenberg and Freedman, *When Poetry Ruled the Streets*, 139.

[75] Quoted in Liam Considine, "Screen politics: Pop art and the Atelier Populaire," Tate Papers No. 24, Global Pop, www.tate.org.uk/research/publications/tate-papers/24/scre en-politics-pop-art-and-the-atelier-populaire.

[76] Feenberg and Freedman, *When Poetry Ruled the Streets*, 144.

4.5 The People's Studio in action (photos: Philippe Vermès, courtesy of Johan Kugelberg/Boo-Hooray).

collectivity and anonymity to keep police scrutiny at bay. Each night poster designs were submitted anonymously for debate and were voted on according to the questions 'Is the political message correct?' and 'Does the poster transmit this idea well?' The debates ranged in duration from ten minutes to several hours, with some extending through the night."[77] The model was subsequently copied in workshops established in other occupied establishments, aided by screen-printing instructions distributed by the Atelier Populaire.[78] The posters reflected the libertarian-socialist content of the revolt, emphasizing themes of solidarity, workers' self-management, and the role of truth as an antidote to the lies of the system. The latter was captured in the laconic legend accompanying a silhouette of a radio microphone: "The Radio Lies."

The Atelier Populaire was notable for the participation of young workers, who came to suggest topics for the posters and were heavily responsible for the posters' foregrounding of workers' issues.[79] All of the posters, indeed, reflected the workers' struggles, since these were the ones on which the students placed the greatest importance. As a sign at the entry of the studio read: "To work in the people's studio is to offer concrete support to the great movement of striking workers who occupy their factories against the anti-popular Gaullist government. In placing all

[77] Considine, "Screen politics."   [78] Considine, "Screen politics."
[79] Memou, "Revolt in Photos," 156.

4.6 The People's Studio in action (photos: Philippe Vermès, courtesy of Johan Kugelberg/Boo-Hooray).

4.7 The People's Studio in action (photos: Philippe Vermès, courtesy of Johan Kugelberg/Boo-Hooray).

his capacities in the service of the worker's struggle, each in this studio also works for himself, because he opens himself practically to the educational power of the masses."[80] It is no surprise, given this orientation, that the first poster produced by the People's Studio bore the caption "Factory, University, Unity"; the Atelier Populaire represented a key site of student-worker solidarity in May 1968.[81]

Workers were open to the possibilities presented by the outbreak of radicalism. The trade unions were initially supportive but cautious. On May 13, the day that students occupied the Sorbonne, the unions called a one-day general strike and demonstration. Rank-and-file radicalism quickly pushed the situation far beyond the unions' initial intentions. In Paris, masses of workers participated in marches and demands for de Gaulle's resignation. Sympathy demonstrations took place throughout the country. The day after the general strike, workers at Sud-Aviation near Nantes launched a sit-down strike and locked managers in their offices. Factory occupations followed, and strikes spread to the Renault plants at Flins and Boulogne-Billancourt outside Paris. By May 18, two million French workers were on strike, by May 22, over nine million

[80] Feenberg and Freedman, *When Poetry Ruled the Streets*, 144.
[81] Feenberg and Freedman, *When Poetry Ruled the Streets*, 142.

4.8 The fascist past in the authoritarian present. Adolf Hitler holding
a mask of Charles de Gaulle (poster of the Atelier Populaire, courtesy of
Houghton Library, Harvard University).

4.9 "The Radio Lies" (poster of the Atelier Populaire, courtesy of Johan Kugelberg/Boo-Hooray).

workers, or roughly two-thirds of the entire French workforce.[82] Thousands of farmers joined in a few days later.[83] All public transportation

[82] Birchall, "France 1968," 14.
[83] Rolf Werenskjold, "A Chronology of the Global 1968 Protest," *Report No. 13* (Volda, Norway: Volda University College, 2010), 165.

in Paris and over 120 factories were shut down, while the strike wave
spread to encompass the communication, culture, and service industries.[84]
Students tried to link up with striking workers at Renault only to have the
union officials lock the factory gates. In the event, the trade unions put the
brakes on continued radicalization, even as a police crackdown took its toll,
and public opinion began to shift from supporting the students to a more
pro-government stance.[85]

In an analysis whose authors included Cornelius Castoriadis, writing
under the pseudonym Jean-Marc Coudray, the May revolt represented
a repudiation of capitalist technocracy, a movement of democratic collectives, spontaneously organized, which modeled a vision of the new
society within the shell of the old. Not Lenin and Bolshevism, still less
Trotsky or Mao, were to be the touchstones of this emerging new society
but the great communes of history – Paris and Kronstadt – and the
moments of workers' self-management in the Spanish Civil War of
1936–1939 and the Hungarian uprising of 1956.[86] The massive strikes
of workers, the efforts of militant youth to connect with them, and the
attempts of trade unions and the Communist Party to keep students and
workers apart showed that once the illusion of normalcy was shattered,
unexpectedly and without warning, the door to social revolution was
opened. Then, the ghosts of revolutions past reared their heads and
classical issues of revolutionary strategy and tactics were again placed
on the table. And here, there was no one revolution but several. As a key
document of the Paris May put it: "Let's always ask *which* revolution is at
stake."[87]

All Power to the Workers' Councils

That question burned just as brightly in the other great insurrectionary
moment of 1968: the Prague Spring. Kristin Ross has argued that the
French May's combination of "intellectual refusal of the reigning ideology and worker insurrection" made it a special case among national
1968s.[88] Yet, in the broader context of bloc-spanning efforts to deal
with the classical dilemmas of revolutionary theory and practice, developments in France can only be considered in parallel with those in

---

[84] Ross, *May '68 and Its Afterlives*, 4.
[85] Arthur Marwick, *The Sixties: Cultural Revolution in Britain, France, Italy, and the United States, c.1958–c.1974* (Oxford: Oxford University Press, 1998), 617.
[86] Wolin, *The Wind from the East*, 104.
[87] "The Amnesty of Blinded Eyes," in Feenberg and Freedman, *When Poetry Ruled the Streets*, 85.
[88] Ross, *May '68 and Its Afterlives*, 4.

Czechoslovakia. Indeed, the question of "which revolution?" that drove events in France was absolutely central to the Prague Spring. At stake was the question of whether, in the words of the Marxist Humanist philosopher Ivan Sviták, socialism would be controlled "from above by the ruling elite (Stalin, Mao, Castro) or whether socialism is regarded as a social framework established through a struggle by the working class – from below."[89] For the Czech Marxist-Humanist dissident Stephen Steiger, the CSSR lay "at the crossroads of two worlds" – one foot in a West that had rejected autocracy and established democracy, however imperfect, and one in an East that had attempted (and failed) to overcome the problem of inequality.[90] The significance of the Prague Spring lay precisely in its attempt to create a synthesis of the two. Reinserting "liberty" into the Marxist equation,[91] in Maude Bracke's phrase, it sought to achieve "a successful combination of equality and freedom" that would serve as an alternative both to capitalism and to state socialism.[92]

This attempted synthesis was by no means merely an effort to link up with emancipatory impulses around 1968 in the West, however; it was above all an attempt to fulfill the promises of 1956 in the East – that is, it was an effort to establish a socialist democracy rooted in intellectual freedom and the control of production by the workers themselves.[93] As had been the case in Poland and Hungary a decade earlier, its goal was to realize the humanist potential of anticapitalism. Here, form was intimately linked to content. "An authentic conception of socialism," wrote Ivan Sviták, "is only the one in which the decisive role is played by the people, the working class, the majority of modern industrial society – not by some sort of elite or by individuals who speak in the name of the working class or the majority, without acknowledging its fundamental civil and human rights."[94] Only through a true socialist democracy would it be possible to achieve what the writer Milan Kundera characterized as a "socialism without omnipotent secret police, with freedom of speech (spoken and written), with public opinion that is heard, and with politics

---

[89] Ivan Sviták, "Prologue to Intervention," in Ivan Sviták, *The Czechoslovak Experiment: 1968–1969* (New York: Columbia University Press, 1971), 131–146, 134.

[90] X, "At the Crossroads of Two Worlds," in The News & Letter Committees, Detroit, and the Marxist Humanist Group, Glasgow, *Czechoslovakia: Revolution and Counterrevolution* (1968), 20–21.

[91] Maude Bracke, "French responses to the Prague Spring: Connections, (mis)perception and appropriation," *Europe-Asia Studies*, 60(110) (2008), 1735–1747.

[92] Jiří Suk, "The Utopian Rationalism of the Prague Spring of 1968," *The American Historical Review*, 123(3) (June 1, 2018), 764–768.

[93] See the sections on Poland and Hungary in Ian H. Birchall, *Workers against the Monolith: The Communist Parties since 1943* (London: Pluto, 1974).

[94] Ivan Sviták, "Prologue to Intervention," 135.

based on it, with a freely developing modern culture, and with people who have ceased to be afraid."[95]

In many ways further along the path of accomplishing this fusion than its Eastern European neighbors, Czechoslovakia was an early and robust contender in postwar efforts to find an alternative to capitalism. The country was unique not only in having a greater reservoir of democratic tradition than any other state socialist country but in having a highly developed pre-war socialist tradition. The Communist Party in Czechoslovakia had been able to work legally for years before its accession to power, building alliances and legitimacy. The soil was more fertile for communism in Czechoslovakia than elsewhere in Eastern Europe. One reason was the brutality of the Nazi occupation. Another was the equivocal role played by the liberal democracies in giving over control of the country to the Nazis to begin with. Communists played a major role in the wartime resistance, and it was the Soviet Union, not the liberal democracies, that ultimately delivered the country from the grip of fascism.[96]

Soviet Communism was but one version of socialist modernity, however. When it squandered its initial goodwill through vicious repression, critics looked not to capitalism but to alternative sources of left theory and practice.[97] The most important aspect of the Prague Spring – the search for left alternatives – thus did not arise out of thin air but was a continuation of a longstanding indigenous conversation about how to achieve socialist democracy. The events that became known as the Prague Spring are associated with the promotion of Communist reformer Alexander Dubček to first secretary of the Czechoslovakian Communist Party in January 1968 and then subsequently with the party's development of an Action Program designed to accomplish socialist modernization and liberalization. The cultural-political spadework for these developments began, however, at least a decade earlier. The post-Stalinist "thaw" that started in 1956 with Khrushchev's denunciation of Stalin's crimes saw a resurgence of nonconformist cultural activity that became intimately linked with the political aspirations of reform-minded students and intellectuals.

---

[95] Quoted in Suk, "The Utopian Rationalism of the Prague Spring of 1968."

[96] Jerome Karabel, "The Revolt of the Intellectuals: The origins of the Prague Spring and the Politics of Reform Communism," Irle Working Paper 20–90 (May 1990), available at www.irle.berkeley.edu/files/1990/The-Revolt-of-The-Intellectuals.pdf;   Suk,   "The Utopian Rationalism of the Prague Spring of 1968."

[97] "A commitment to Marxism and a dislike and rejection of free-market capitalism," writes Maud Bracke, "were central characteristics of Czechoslovakia's political and intellectual cultures, and had been since the 1930s." Bracke, "French responses to the Prague Spring."

Unsurprisingly, given the restrictions on explicit political activity, not to mention the importance accorded intellectuals under communism in general and the structural position of writers under Czechoslovakian communism in particular, the first cracks in the Stalinist edifice in Czechoslovakia took place in the realm of culture. The Czech Writers' Union became a focal point of the new political-cultural sensibility. The emerging importance of writers and literature was signaled by the May 1963 Kafka Conference at Liblice Castle outside Prague. Organized by the writer Eduard Goldstücker, subsequently chairperson of the Czech Writers' Union, the conference introduced Kafka to Eastern Europe, claiming the author as a critic of capitalist alienation and implicitly on behalf of a new, humanist socialism.[98]

At the June 1967 Congress of the Czechoslovak Writers' Union, leading literary figures such as Milan Kundera, Václav Havel, and Ludvík Vaculík issued politically charged calls for a relaxation of restrictions on free expression. Vaculík delivered a "speech . . . stunning in the crystalline ferocity of its denunciation of the authorities who ruled over the intellectuals and the nation," foreshadowing claims he was later to make in the explosive "Two thousand words."[99] Vaculík's speech, ignored by the press, was distributed in leaflet form by student radicals at Charles University.[100] A subsequent expulsion of some of the writers who had criticized the party, followed by the banning of the cultural weekly *Literarni Noviny* and its replacement with a pro-government magazine of the same name, met with widespread condemnation.[101]

Communist hardliners were apoplectic at the criticisms of writers and students but powerless to halt the trend toward greater openness. By the time of the Congress, something resembling a liberal democratic public sphere was beginning to emerge in the CSSR, with *Literarni Noviny* and other journals of the intelligentsia enjoying a massive circulation.[102] Film,

---

[98] On the significance of Kafka for socialist attempts to combat alienation, see Martin Schulkze Wessel, *Der Prager Frühling: Aufbruch in eine neue Welt* (Ditzingen: Reclam, 2018), 57–67.

For a comparative perspective, see Veronika Tuckerova, "Reading Kafka in Prague: The Reception of Franz Kafka between the East and the West during the Cold War," PhD dissertation, Columbia University (2012), 3. The proceedings of the conference were published as *Franz Kafka from the Prague Perspective*; Eduard Goldstücker, František Kautman, and Paul Reimann (eds.), *Franz Kafka aus Prager Sicht* (Berlin: Voltaire, 1966).

[99] Karabel, "The Revolt of the Intellectuals."

[100] Jan Kavan, "Testament of a Prague Radical," *Ramparts Magazine* (September 28, 1968), 53–60, 57.

[101] Kavan, "Testament of a Prague Radical."

[102] These journals, observes Jerome Karabel, "had a combined circulation of 300,000 in a nation of only 14,000,000 people"; Karabel, "The Revolt of the Intellectuals."

music, and theater became key sites for the expression of nonconformist values, such that by the middle of the decade, Prague had become the "unofficial capital of cosmopolitanism" in the Eastern Bloc.[103] Amidst an explosion of newspaper production in the spring of 1968, authors and journalists issued repeated appeals for the abolishment of censorship, which was accomplished by the end of March 1968. Demands for the free flow of information took place amidst calls for thoroughgoing democratization, the formation of new parties, and demands for free elections. The lifting of censorship between January and March 1968 created a situation of more or less complete freedom of speech, and it was not long before people began to say things that pushed up to and beyond the boundary of what was permissible under state socialism.

First and foremost came the attempt to reckon with the legacy of Stalinism. The group K231, formed of former political prisoners condemned under Law No. 231 of the postcoup penal code, was founded in March 1968.[104] With a membership that quickly grew to over 100,000, it became a major venue for the airing of grievances by those who had been unjustly persecuted by the regime.[105] The founding in April of the "Club of Engaged Non-Party Members" (KAN) reasserted the possibility of political action outside the Communist Party, as did the creation of a steering committee for the creation of a new Social Democratic Party to carry on the work of the one that had been forcibly integrated into the Communist Party in 1948. The existence of these new formations represented either an implicit or an explicit rejection of the right to a "leading role" asserted by Bolshevism and subsequently reproduced by state socialist regimes. KAN committed itself in a May 1968 manifesto to aiding in the creation of "a new political system, never realized so far, of democratic socialism."[106] Characteristically, the protection of "human and civil rights" was to be paired with "civil equality," understood not as an embrace of bourgeois democracy but as a socialist act of "defense ... against the dehumanizing forces of capitalism, fascism and Stalinism."[107]

Students, who had already begun to demand a more prominent role in public life in the late 1950s, were a critical force behind the new democratic-socialist mobilization. As early as the spring of 1956, in the wake of Khrushchev's denunciation of Stalin's crimes, they began to agitate for an

---

[103] Rachel Appelbaum, "A Test of Friendship: Soviet–Czechoslovak Tourism and the Prague Spring," in Anne E. Gorsuch and Diane P. Koenker (eds.), *The Socialist Sixties: Crossing Borders in the Second World* (Bloomington: Indiana University Press, 2013), 218–219.

[104] Suk, "The utopian rationalism of the Prague Spring of 1968."

[105] Karabel, "The Revolt of the Intellectuals."

[106] Quoted in Bracke, "French Responses to the Prague Spring."

[107] Quoted in Bracke, "French Responses to the Prague Spring."

autonomous student union. By the middle of the next decade, this aspiration became a demand when students at a national conference insisted on their right to social criticism and representation in parliament.[108] Youth unrest found expression in events like the Halloween disturbances of 1967, when students in the Charles University dormitories, exasperated by power outages, marched chanting "We want light!" before being beaten by police.[109] In March 1968, students organized teach-ins and workers engaged in the first strikes in Czechoslovakia since 1948. In May, demonstrations took place outside the Polish embassy against the Polish regime's anti-Semitic campaign against protesting students and intellectuals. In May, participation in the annual May Day parade was made optional, even as students joined workers in a crowd of 400,000 marching to express support for Alexander Dubček and President Ludvík Svoboda.[110]

An important locus of student radicalism was the group of "Prague Radicals," whose leading lights included Jiri Mueller and Jan Kavan. The group had long agitated for a renewed socialism beyond the limitations of Communist control; as early as April 1964, in a document entitled "The Party and Us," it declared its intention of placing into question the leading role of the party.[111] Like their counterparts, these young radicals engaged with events in the Third World, above all the Vietnam War, which entered heavily into the consciousness of Czechoslovakian students in 1966–1967.[112] Far more important for them, however, was the fate of socialism at home. As the Prague Radicals were at pains to point out, their political activism prior to the accession of Dubček to leadership was directed against the Novotny regime from the left.[113] And after Dubček's accession, their support was provisional, insofar as they interpreted his leadership as legitimate to the extent that it enacted a realization of the socialist potential of society. As Jan Kavan put it in a piece written for the American New Left magazine *Ramparts*, "We did not want to be handed a program and a leader from above again."[114]

---

[108] Katsiaficas, *The Imagination of the New Left*.

[109] Katsiaficas, *The Imagination of the New Left*.

[110] Werenskjold, "A Chronology of the global 1968 Protest," 288–292.

[111] International Marxist Group, "The Revolutionary Left in Czechoslovakia," *Communism versus Stalinism*, 3 (1974), 7.

[112] Jiri Mueller contacted the Chinese Embassy to find out about Cultural Revolution, part of the reason for his expulsion in December 1966; International Marxist Group, "The revolutionary left in Czechoslovakia." For a skeptical reading of the influence of the Prague Radicals, see Paulina Bren, "1968 in East and West: Visions of Political Change and Student Protest," in Gerd-Rainer Horn and Padraic Kenney (eds.), *Transnational Moments of Change: Europe 1945, 1968, 1989* (Lanham: Rowman & Littlefield, 2004), 119–135.

[113] Kavan, "Testament of a Prague Radical," 54.

[114] Kavan, "Testament of a Prague Radical," 58.

Some of the key demands of the growing political opposition were reflected in the Action Program of the Communist Party, adopted at the Plenary Session of the Central Committee of the Communist Party of Czechoslovakia on April 5, 1968. It is important not to underestimate its effect. The reforms contained within it, argued Kavan, "almost precisely what our tiny group of 'Prague radicals' had hoped for only in our most optimistic moments just a year earlier, and what thousands of young people had been willing to fight for in March."[115] The Action Program promised freedom of the press, assembly, and religion and provided for the rehabilitation of political prisoners, including victims of the purges of the 1950s and the measures against artists and writers of the 1960s.[116] The newly liberated press did not shrink from denunciations of the Soviet secret police, and victims of the purges resurfaced to become vocal public critics of Stalinism.[117] The party was in an equivocal position in the face of this outpouring of democracy, for if it was hardly possible to silence the liberated voice of the masses, that voice also threatened to jeopardize the reform project that was never intended to rob the Communist Party of its leading role.

Central to that reform project was the need to revitalize the economy, a task to be accomplished by the partial democratization of the factory. Workers' participation in industry was not a new idea. The drive to establish workplace democracy at the level of the shop floor had deep roots in Czechoslovakia, finding powerful expression in the period between the end of World War II and the Communist coup of February 1948.[118] The study of this early drive toward workers' self-management, conducted by a team under the Czech Marxist Radovan Richta, underpinned the Action Program of 1968.[119] The workers' self-management enshrined in the Action Program was not intended to create socialist democracy in its most capacious sense, however; rather, it was meant to reinvigorate the economy without sacrificing Communist Party control. Ota Šik and other technocrats charged with economic renewal appealed to the idea of workers' self-management as a way of circumventing obstruction from the party

[115] Kavan, "Testament of a Prague Radical," 59.
[116] Central Committee of the Communist Party, "The Action Program of the Communist Party of Czechoslovakia," in Robin Alison Remington (ed.), *Winter in Prague: Documents on Czechoslovak Communism in Crisis* (Cambridge, MA: Massachusetts Institute of Technology Press, 1969), 88–136.
[117] See for example the entry for April 30, 1968 amidst day-to-day accounts of these developments in Werenskjold, "A Chronology of the Global 1968 Protest."
[118] Robert Vitak, "Workers Control: The Czechoslovak Experience," *Socialist Register* (1971), 245–264, 248.
[119] Vitak, "Workers Control," 249.

bureaucracy.[120] They did not, however, intend for workers to use control of the industrial process to establish their independence from the party.[121] Instead, they sought to mimic Western capitalist efficiency through the introduction of market reforms.[122] "The economic reform," as a characteristic passage in the Action Program put it, "will increasingly push whole working teams of socialist enterprises into positions in which they will directly feel the consequences of good and bad management."[123]

The limited goals of the reformers may partly explain why workers were cautious about or disinterested in state-sponsored self-management in the spring of 1968. Surveys taken in the previous two years showed that only 10 percent of workers believed that they had any actual right to self-management, despite the existence of organs of nominal workers' participation in some enterprises.[124] With the proclamation of the Action Program, this basic orientation changed only slowly. As Jindrich Chalupecky, a keen observer, put it, the working class "watched what was happening, certainly with growing attention but still with mistrust and a certain reserve. It was still merely a question of political games on the part of the masters."[125] As one worker put it, "We want to see the government's hand. We want to see whether a fair game is being played. And that can't be done without freedom of the press."[126]

Workers' attitudes toward these "games" came out not only in their initial cool attitude toward the councils but in their concern over freedom of the press. In April 1968, at the moment that the first workers' councils stipulated in the Action Program were being formed,[127] they founded "Workers' Committees for the Defense of Press Freedom." Aimed at protecting the emerging public sphere against threats from the People's Militia, an armed formation of the Communist Party, the committees were a key early example of rank-and-file militancy during the Prague Spring. "The suppression of censorship has played a very important part

---

[120] Vladimir Fišera, "Introduction," in Vladimir Fišera (ed.), *Workers' Councils in Czechoslovakia 1968–69: Documents and Essays* (New York: St. Martin's, 1978), 7–19, 11.

[121] Gerd-Rainer Horn, "The Working Class Dimension of 1968," in Horn and Kenney, *Transnational Moments of Change in Europe*, 95–118, 111.

[122] Bracke, *Which Socialism, Whose Détente?*, 134.

[123] "The Action Programme of the Communist Party of Czechoslovakia," [excerpt], in Fišera, *Workers' Councils in Czechoslovakia 1968–69*, 20–22, 20.

[124] Fišera, "Introduction," 11.

[125] Jindrich Chalupecky, "All Power to the Workers' Councils," in Fišera, *Workers' Councils in Czechoslovakia 1968–69*, 146–154, 152–153.

[126] Petr Cerny, "Czechoslovakia 1968: What 'socialism'? What 'human face'?" (London: Solidarity, 1985), pamphlet no. 55.

[127] Fišera, "Introduction," 10.

in the rapid development of the political life of Czechoslovakia in the direction of democracy," declared a statement of the first committee founded at the Ostrava Nitrogen Works. "But there are other voices ... saying that the democratization process has dangerously invaded the frontiers of the [Communist Party]."[128] Noting that censorship had been suspended, rather than abolished altogether, the committee concluded that the "benevolent attitude of Comrade Dubček" was not enough to secure workers' democratic self-expression.[129] Despite a campaign from the party to criminalize the founders of the first committee, the example of the Ostrava Works inspired the creation of "hundreds of voluntary collectives for the defense of press freedom," which "sprung into being within a month as a result of horizontal contacts between workers."[130]

Workers' belief that, in the words of Jindrich Chalupecky, "they could count on no one but themselves" began to shift their attitudes toward the councils.[131] By June 1968, councils began to be formed in the large factories of CKD Prague and Škoda in Pilsen.[132] These foundings were accompanied by a shift in both scope and content of the councils that outstripped the technocrats' original intentions for them.[133] By the end of the summer, perhaps two dozen were in operation, prompting Chalupecky to observe optimistically: "Since July we have been living among a free people."[134]

Workers' movement in the direction of industrial democracy was strongly supported by Ivan Sviták. Regarding the party, he noted: "Neither the progressive faction, which flirts with the efficiency of the West's industrial society, nor the conservative faction, which ogles the arms of the militia, can speak for the working class."[135] It was precisely "the bureaucratic dictatorship of the apparatus," he wrote, that represented "the main obstacle in the unique experiment of our nation with socialist democracy."[136] The success of that experiment, Sviták argued, must be based on effective cooperation between intellectuals and workers, with pride of place given to the latter. Writing in the journal *Student*, he declared: "The end has come for martial law over thoughts and men. Thus, under conditions of the disintegrating power structure of Stalinism, there is no other more important and urgent

---

[128] Cerny, "Czechoslovakia 1968."   [129] Cerny, "Czechoslovakia 1968."
[130] Cerny, "Czechoslovakia 1968."
[131] Chalupecky, "All Power to the Workers' Councils," 152–153.
[132] Fišera, "Introduction," 11. The first workers' councils were formed by June 1968; see Horn, "The Working Class Dimension of 1968," 111.
[133] Horn, "The Working Class Dimension of 1968."
[134] Chalupecky, "All Power to the Workers' Councils," 152–153.
[135] Sviták, "Prologue to Intervention," 136–137.
[136] Quoted in X, "At the Crossroads of Two Worlds."

task of the workers' movement than to renew in full force the trade union movement for defending the workers' fundamental rights."[137] The leading role of the party enshrined in Leninist orthodoxy, argued Sviták, had "no theoretical support in the works of Karl Marx."[138]

The discomfort of the party with the movement toward democratization emerged strongly in its response to the most famous document of the Prague Spring, Ludvík Vaculík's "Two Thousand Words." Published in June, with seventy prominent signatories, the document made the case for democratic renewal with a hitherto unmatched clarity.[139] "The chief sin and deception of these rulers was to have explained their own whims as the 'will of the workers,'" wrote Vaculík ... ; "Every worker knows they had virtually no say in deciding anything."[140] Although Vaculík was careful to avoid saying it, the implication of the document was that the Communist Party, and by extension the leadership of the Soviet Union, need no longer play the vanguard roles they had long assumed for themselves. As this idea was expressed in *Rudé Právo*, the organ of the Czech Communist Party: "The Czechoslovakian people have their own right to define their way to socialism."[141]

Crystalizing the currents that had given rise to the Prague Spring, the manifesto produced a crisis of authority in Czechoslovakia. "[W]ithin around 48 hours," recalls Jan Urban, the manifesto "convinced people that change was really possible after 20 years of Communist power."[142] The document simultaneously "highlighted the growing tensions between the Dubček regime and the radical intellectuals, and once again revealed the differences separating its signatories from the more technocratic intellectuals close to the Party center."[143] Both Alexander Dubček and technocratic reformers like Ota Šik and Zdeněk Mlynář condemned the "Two thousand words" as a danger to the process of reform.[144]

The Soviet-led intervention of August 20, 1968 saw over 500,000 Soviet Bloc troops invade the country against massive popular resistance. The invasion unleashed "a genuine, although short-lived, revolution."[145] In Prague, rebels remonstrated with, and in some cases fought against,

---

[137] Quoted in X, "At the Crossroads of Two Worlds."

[138] Ivan Sviták, "Heads Against the Wall," in Sviták, *The Czechoslovak Experiment*, 45.

[139] See Vaculík, "Two Thousand Words."

[140] Quoted in Bracke, "French Responses to the Prague Spring."

[141] *Rudé Právo* (April 19, 1968).

[142] Jan Urban, interviewed by Dominik Jůn, "The two-thousand words that started the Prague Spring" (June 27, 2008), www.radio.cz/en/section/curraffrs/the-two-thousand-words-that-started-the-prague-spring.

[143] Karabel, "The Revolt of the Intellectuals."

[144] Karabel, "The Revolt of the Intellectuals."

[145] Martin Palous, "Revolutions and Revolutionaries, Lessons of the Years of Crises: Three Czech Encounters with Freedom," in Vladimir Tismaneanu (ed.), *Promises of 1968: Crisis, Illusion and Utopia* (New York: Central European University Press, 2011), 23.

4.10 Greeting the invaders, Prague, August 1968 (Josef Koudelka, courtesy of Magnum).

invading forces. They removed street signs and house numbers, distributed anti-invasion leaflets, and covered walls in slogans calling to mind those of May 1968 in Paris.[146] Graffiti contained slogans like "We Condemn Soviet Fascism," "USSR = SS," and "Make Love, Not War." Swastikas were painted on Warsaw Pact tanks.[147] "People are using Hippie methods," wrote an English journalist, "sticking flowers into the helmets or into the gun barrels. For the Russians it is absolutely weird."[148] Musicians got in on the act as well.[149] Resistance was far from entirely peaceful, however. Ludvík Vaculík called openly for armed struggle against the Soviet Bloc invaders. Protestors formed human chains in front of tanks, threw Molotov cocktails, and in a few cases destroyed tanks and killed their crews. Sit-ins, vigils, demonstrations, and other forms of passive resistance were the order of the day.

---

[146] "I had never witnessed that kind of resistance," recalled a young West German activist in Prague. "No comparison to what had happened in West Berlin in 1968."

[147] Robert V. Daniels, The *Year of the Heroic Guerrilla: World Revolution and Counterrevolution in 1968* (Cambridge, MA: Harvard University Press, 1996), 191.

[148] *Sunday Telegraph* of August 24, 1968, quoted in Katsiaficas, *The Imagination of the New Left.*

[149] See the text to the song "Russians, Go Home!" in Aktual/Milan Knížák, "Russians, go home! (1968)," in Mohandesi, Risager, and Cox, *Voices of 1968*, 303–304.

4.11 Greeting the invaders, Prague, August 1968 (Josef Koudelka, courtesy of Magnum).

4.12 Greeting the invaders, Prague, August 1968 (Josef Koudelka, courtesy of Magnum).

4.13 Greeting the invaders, Prague, August 1968 (Josef Koudelka, courtesy of Magnum).

The rebellion was not led by students but was a generalized phenomenon – 70 percent of the rebels were young workers.[150] Railway workers blocked shipments from the Soviet Union. A one-hour general strike was called in Prague, and other strikes were threatened. Scattered protests – punctuated by the self-immolations of the students Jan Palach and Jan Zajíc in January and February 1969, respectively – continued through August.[151] In the wake of the invasion, no less than half a million reform-minded Communists were purged from the party and state institutions. Over 300,000 party members were expelled, and another 150,000 quit. The rolls of the writing and teaching professions were heavily purged, with some two-thirds of Writers' Union members losing their jobs.[152] Summoned to Moscow, Dubček returned to Prague to oversee the process of "normalization" – that is, a return to the situation of central

---

[150] Philipp Gassert and Elisabeth Piller, "East Germany: 'Solidarity with Red Prague'," in Gassert and Klimke, *1968*, 160.

[151] See "A letter from Jan Palach addressed to the Union of Czechoslovak Writers (1969)," in Mohandesi, Risager, and Cox, *Voices of 1968*, 308.

[152] Barbara Falk, *Dilemmas of Dissidence in East-Central Europe: Citizen Intellectuals and Philosopher Kings* (Budapest: Central European University Press, 2003), 83.

4.14 Lenin weeps on a poster protesting the invasion (photo: Josef Koudelka, courtesy of Magnum).

4.15 A woman passes out flyers in Prague against the Warsaw Pact invasion (photo: Ian Berry, courtesy of Magnum).

control from Moscow that attained before the Prague Spring – before being forced out and replaced by Gustáv Husák in April 1969.[153]

Ironically, it was not until after the invasion that the experiments in workers' self-management fostered by the Action Program and subsequently radicalized at the grassroots came into their own. In September 1968, there existed only nineteen workers' councils. By the end of the year, there were another 260.[154] In June 1969, despite the general atmosphere of repression, there were 500.[155] As these figures make plain, the Soviet invasion initially had, in the words of the editor of an important contemporary document collection on the councils, "little effect on the organic construction of a global alternative to the bureaucratic system."[156] It was precisely in putting a halt to top-down reform efforts, indeed, that it opened up a greater space for bottom-up, rank-and-file politics.[157] After the invasion, workers began retroactively to defend Dubček and other party reformers in a way that they had not previously, and in particular to recognize in the factory councils a vehicle for protection of their interests vis-à-vis the regime. Indeed, as an informed contemporary observer argued, it was not the Prague Spring as such but the period between November 1968 and January 1969 that most closely resembled the uprisings in East Germany in 1953 and Hungary in 1956.[158] Even if it the Prague Spring was quickly pronounced dead, the phenomenon of grassroots democratization had gone too far too quickly to be immediately crushed by the Soviet invasion.[159]

Industrial workers were at the forefront of the new militancy. In January 1969, some 890,000 workers – one-sixth of the country's work force – gathered in Plzeň for a conference on workers' self-management.[160] The Plzeň conference was by no means dedicated to a restrained vision of the potential of workers' councils. "[I]ndustrial self-management," noted a key participant, "is neither new nor peculiar to this country. It is an old proletarian demand, and in this century nearly every great social movement of the working class has sooner or later made a practical attempt to democratize social relations in industry. This is true of all three Russian Revolutions as well as of

---

[153] On "normalization," see Kieran Williams, "The Prague Spring: From Elite Liberalization to Mass Movement," in Kevin McDermott and Matthew Stibbe, *Revolution and Resistance in Eastern Europe: Challenges to Communist Rule* (Oxford: Berg, 2006), 101–117; see also Kieran Williams, *The Prague Spring and Its Aftermath: Czechoslovak Politics, 1968–1970* (Cambridge: Cambridge University Press, 1997).

[154] Fišera, "Introduction," 12. Also Horn, "The Working Class Dimension of 1968," 112.

[155] Fišera, "Introduction," 13.   [156] Fišera, "Introduction," 7.

[157] Fišera, "Introduction."

[158] International Marxist Group, "The Revolutionary Left in Czechoslovakia."

[159] Fišera, "Introduction," 7.

[160] Horn, "The Working Class Dimension of 1968," 112. See excerpts from the congress in "Workers' councils: The guarantee of democratic administration and managerial activity (1969)," in Mohandesi, Risager, and Cox, *Voices of 1968*, 305–308.

the German revolution of 1918–1920, the Spanish Civil War and the resistance against Stalinism in Yugoslavia, and later by the Polish and Hungarian workers."[161] Efforts at workers' self-management in Czechoslovakia, he continued, were "only the latest link in this chain."[162]

This historical perspective on the activity of the workers' councils was shared by Jindrich Chalupecky. "Like the Soviets in February 1917," he observed, "the workers' councils are spontaneously appearing again, prompted by something that looks suspiciously like historical necessity, and which therefore is also located beyond all plans and theories."[163] The institution of the workers' council, he continued, "is revolution in concrete form, opening the path towards a pluralism entirely different than any we can imagine today. It can no longer even be called democracy, or government of the people, because it is no longer a government; there is no one left to govern any more. There is no more room, either, for traditional politics."[164] The pursuit of a revolutionary activity *prior* to party politics, essentially anarcho-syndicalist in nature, was the golden thread of revolutionary history. "It is as if we were once again in a position to open the revolutionary reader at the first pages," wrote Chalupecky, "as if once again we could aspire, after all the disappointments and all the despair, to freedom in this world of ours."[165]

That the revolutionary potential of the councils was by no means an imposition of intellectuals is evident in a statement of workers at the CKD works in Prague: "The workers of the W. Pieck factory (CKD Prague) wish to fulfill one of the fundamental rights of socialist democracy, namely the right of the workers to manage their own factory. They also desire a closer bond between the interests of the whole society and the interests of each individual. To this end, they have decided to establish workers' self-management."[166] At the beginning of 1969, even in the face of the Soviet invasion and the beginning of normalization, workers could situate their struggle in terms of a renewed, antiauthoritarian Marxism, declaring, "we are beginning to solve the problem of alienation."[167] It is testimony to the vibrancy of these efforts that, in the face of strong official discouragement, there were still some 300 workers' councils in existence during the summer of 1969.[168]

---

[161] Milos Barta, "Genealogy of the Workers' Councils," in Fišera, *Workers' Councils in Czechoslovakia 1968–69*, 156–159, 156.

[162] Barta, "Genealogy of the Workers' Councils."

[163] Chalupecky, "All Power to the Workers' Councils," 154.

[164] Chalupecky, "All Power to the Workers' Councils."

[165] Chalupecky, "All Power to the Workers' Councils."

[166] "Draft statutes for workers' self-management in the Wilhelm Pieck factory (CKD Prague)," in Fišera, *Workers' Councils in Czechoslovakia 1968-69*, 39–43, 39–40.

[167] "Workers' councils: the guarantee of democratic administration and managerial activity," in Fišera, *Workers' Councils in Czechoslovakia 1968–69*, 50–72, 55.

[168] Vitak, "Workers Control," 258.

The persistence of industrial militancy after August 1968 was accompanied by a radicalization of student circles, which, having seen the limitations placed on reformism in Czechoslovakia, moved in an explicitly socialist-revolutionary direction. Students had ties to dissident writers as early as the summer of 1967, but their ties to workers began even prior to that.[169] As early as May 1967, through their joint participation in the Czechoslovak Union of Youth (CUY), students came into contact with young workers in ways that defied official efforts to keep them separated.[170] With Dubček's accession to the party leadership, student radicals took as one of their main tasks to explain and defend his actions to skeptical workers. "We spent many long hours in the factories," wrote Jan Kavan, "during which the artificial barriers between workers and intellectuals were gradually broken down."[171] After the Soviet invasion, these informal alliances were made official and extended. November 1968 saw intensified collaboration between students and workers in defense of the reform program.[172] In December, students concluded an agreement with the country's largest union, the Metalworkers' Union, calling for "mutual support and solidarity, consultation, cooperation, and exchange of information [and] defense of the media."[173] Similar agreements were subsequently concluded with a variety of other unions.[174] In seeking out the inner content of Marxism at it pertained to workers' self-management, as Petr Cerny puts it, the "Prague radicals ..., for a brief moment, achieved what the Western left had only dreamed of in 1968: a worker-student alliance."[175]

A key group in the student mobilization was the Movement of Revolutionary Youth, which counted among its members a number of future signers of Charter 77. One of these was Peter Uhl, an activist with contacts in New Left and Trotskyist circles in France.[176] Uhl subsequently founded a "Revolutionary Socialist Party" – the "Uhl Group" – including among others the West German activist Sibylle Plogstedt.[177] The group sought to foster reading and discussion of the Marxist classics

[169] Jan Kavan, "Havel's Biafra of spirit? Prague Spring and the Student Movement," in The Long Run, blog of the Department of Politics and International Studies (POLIS) at the University of Cambridge (May 14, 2018), www.inthelongrun.org/articles/article/havels-biafra-of-spirit-prague-spring-and-the-student-movement.

[170] Kavan, "Testament of a Prague Radical," 56.

[171] Kavan, "Testament of a Prague Radical," 58.   [172] Kavan, "Havel's Biafra of Spirit?"

[173] Cerny, "Czechoslovakia 1968."   [174] Cerny, "Czechoslovakia 1968."

[175] Cerny, "Czechoslovakia 1968," 12.

[176] Jonathan Bolton, Worlds of Dissent: Charter 77, The Plastic People of the Universe, and Czech Culture under Communism (Cambridge, MA: Harvard University Press, 2012), 58.

[177] Vladimir V. Kusin, "Challenge to Normalcy: Political Opposition in Czechoslovakia, 1968–77," in Rudolph L. Tokes (ed.), Opposition in Eastern Europe (London: Palgrave Macmillan, 1979), 26–59. See Sibylle Plogstedt, Im Netz der Gedichte. Gefangen in Prag nach 1968 (Berlin: Christoph Links, 2001).

and contemporary political thought. The group produced a major document collection – "Bureaucracy No – Revolution Yes," published in 1970 after their arrests at the end of 1969, which was distributed clandestinely in a run of 1,000 copies.[178] The collection contained the writings of early Bolsheviks like Bukharin, Kollontai, and Trotsky; Milovan Djilas's insider critique of the Yugoslavian Communist bureaucracy, *The New Class*; the program of Socialism or Barbarism; the demands of the Polish and Hungarian workers' councils; and Kuron and Modzelewski's "Open Letter to the Party."[179]

The Revolutionary Socialist Party represented a further elaboration of the rejection of the "leading role of the party" that had underpinned student and worker militancy since the early to mid-1960s. In recognizing the need to break away from the idea of "pressure groups" acting on the Communist Party – an idea which, in the words of a sympathetic Western Marxist analysis, only "served to confirm the Party in its monopoly of consciously political activity" – it rejected the very logic behind the Action Program.[180] "We no longer believe in a system where the leadership, even when it is as humane as Dubček, decides for the workers without them," read the group's manifesto, "for only the workers themselves have the right to decide their own destiny. We do not believe in socialism in one country, or that the power of the bureaucracy can be broken in a small isolated country like Czechoslovakia, which would from then on have 'gone its own way,' had its own 'socialism with a human face,' for socialism is only one and its face is human, otherwise it is not socialism."[181]

Neither student activism nor mass efforts at workers' self-management could stand against the betrayal of the democratization by the party leadership during the process of normalization. By April 1969, when Dubček was finally removed from power, there were only a few sporadic protests; the project of "normalization" over which he had presided had done its work. The potential threat posed by the student-worker alliance continued to haunt Husák's public speeches, however, which decried the student-worker contact captured in slogans such as "Students and

---

[178] International Marxist Group, "The Revolutionary Left in Czechoslovakia," 18. On the Revolutionary Socialist Party, see Vaclav Havel and John Keane, *The Power of the Powerless: Citizens against the State in Central Eastern Europe* (New York: Routledge, 1985).

[179] Ian Fraser, introduction to the "Manifesto of the Revolutionary Socialist Party, Czechoslovakia," International Marxist Group (February 1970); originally published in *Black Dwarf*, 14(22) (September 16, 1969). The manifesto was originally distributed in 1,000 copies in 1970; International Marxist Group, "The Revolutionary Left in Czechoslovakia," 18.

[180] International Marxist Group, "The Revolutionary Left in Czechoslovakia," 18.

[181] "Manifesto of the Revolutionary Socialist Party, Czechoslovakia," 20.

Workers Together" and "Students, Intelligentsia, Workers, Unite."[182] It was not long before the SRP activists who had advocated them were arrested.[183] The councils themselves were formally banned in July 1970. Even if it was a "stillborn revolution," Gerd-Ranier Horn is correct to call the Prague Spring "the most promising development in the theory and practice of workers' self-management" in 1960s Europe.[184]

Outside Czechoslovakia, the significance of the experiment in "socialism with a human face" was widely recognized.[185] Protests, work stoppages, and vigils greeted the Soviet invasion from Italy to East Germany, from France to Poland, from the Netherlands to the Soviet Union.[186] For New Left radicals in the West, the invasion was a concrete and immediate example of the debased state socialism they were rejecting. As a letter in the journal *Partisan* put it: "Let us show the free democratic comrades in the CSSR that they do not stand alone in their struggles. We declare our solidarity with them in their anti-authoritarian fight for a free and therefore authentic socialism."[187] As far away as Chicago and Berkeley, protestors brutalized by police carried signs reading "Welcome to Czechago" or sprayed graffiti reading "Welcome to Prague."[188] Polish students produced posters and graffiti bearing slogans such as "Long live Dubček and his party!"[189] West German radicals lauded Czechoslovakian insurgents for their "struggle against Soviet imperialism."[190] The Situationist "Occupation Committee of the People's Free Sorbonne University," meanwhile, conveyed "fraternal greetings" to Ivan Sviták in a telegram proclaiming: "Long live the international power of the workers' council."[191]

---

[182] Kavan, "Havel's Biafra of Spirit?"

[183] International Marxist Group, "The Revolutionary Left in Czechoslovakia," 19.

[184] Horn, "The working class dimension of 1968," 111.

[185] This is true even if, as Maud Bracke has pointed out, the Prague Spring's revolutionary implications were not always immediately recognized by sectors of the New Left; Bracke, "French Responses to the Prague Spring."

[186] Katsiaficas, *The Imagination of the New Left.*

[187] Redaktion Partisan, "Solidarität mit den antiautoritären Kräften in der CSSR," in Lutz Schulenburg (ed.), *Das Leben ändern, die Welt verändern! 1968 – Dokumente und Berichte* (Hamburg: Edition Nautilus, 1998), 231–233, 231.

[188] Katsiaficas, *The Imagination of the New Left.*

[189] Kemp-Welch, "'To hell with sovereignty!'," 140.

[190] In a reference to violent protests against media monopoly in the Federal Republic, they wrote: "Your burning Soviet tanks are identical with the burning automobiles of the Springer press and the militaristic police. Your barricades stand together with those of France, Italy, and capitalist Germany." "Solidaritätsadresse der Roten Garde Berlin an die Tschechoslowakische revolutionäre Jugend," in Hartmut Sander and Ulrich Christians (eds.), *Subkultur Berlin: Kommunen Rocker subversiven Gruppen* (Darmstadt: März, 1969), 25.

[191] Another telegram, sent to the Politburo of the Communist Party of the USSR, read in part: "SHAKE IN YOUR SHOES BUREAUCRATS. THE INTERNATIONAL POWER OF THE WORKERS COUNCILS WILL SOON WIPE YOU OUT .... .

4.16 "Revolutionaries of East and West unite in the struggle against
capitalism and Stalinism." West Berlin solidarity demonstration with
Czechoslovakia, August 21, 1968 (photo: Klaus Lehnartz, courtesy of
Landesarchiv Berlin).

Far from being an attempt to ape Western democracy, indeed, the
Prague Spring was, again, precisely an attempt to come to grips with
a leading question of revolutionary history – the Bolshevik claim about
the leading role of the party and its relationship to the prospect of non-
party mass democracy from below. It was an attempt, to use Maude
Bracke's words, to answer the question, "which socialism?"[192] In this
respect, it resonated strongly with debates taking place both in Western
Europe and elsewhere in Eastern Europe. From this perspective, it is

LONG LIVE THE STRUGGLE OF THE KRONSTADT SAILORS AND OF THE
MAKHNOVSHCHINA AGAINST TROTSKY AND LENIN. LONG LIVE THE
1956 COUNCILIST INSURRECTION OF BUDAPEST ... . LONG LIVE
REVOLUTIONARY MARXISM" (all capital letters in the original). Two additional
telegrams were sent, one threatening the Chinese Communist Party, the other offering
support for the Zengakuren student militants in Japan; Occupation Committee of the
People's Free Sorbonne University, "Telegrams" (May 17, 1968), www.cddc.vt.edu/s
ionline/si/telegrams.html.
    The slogan was a *détournement* of an eighteenth-century saying: "Humanity won't be
happy till the last aristocrat is hung with the guts of the last priest."
[192] Maud Bracke, *Which Socialism, Whose Détente?*, 133.

important to avoid an overemphasis on the Warsaw Pact invasion of August 1968 and the corresponding tendency to take the project of "socialism with a human face" at face value. What was important about Prague in 1968 was not the Warsaw Pact invasion but the attempted socialist renewal on either side of it.

Down with the Red Bourgeoisie

In no small part because of the chilling effect of the post-1956 repression, Hungary was relatively quiescent in 1968, although there, too, currents of revolt, both global and local, coalesced in ways that challenged the authorities. Political repression after the Hungarian uprising of 1956 was intense through 1958. The regime of Janos Kádár executed hundreds of revolutionaries, including Kádár's predecessor Imre Nagy. The factory councils were suppressed, and the Hungarian Socialist Workers' Party (MSZMP) founded by the circle around Nagy was coopted into a strengthening of Stalinist rule.[193] The dissolution of the workers' councils was followed closely by the banning of the Hungarian Writers' Union and the National Association for Journalists.[194] At the beginning of the 1960s, with the most intense period of repression past, the regime attempted to let steam out of the situation by introducing market reforms and (relative) political liberalization. In 1962, the regime announced that the post-1956 "consolidation of socialism" was over and introduced an amnesty for those sentenced in connection with the 1956 uprising.

The New Economic Mechanism approved by the party in 1966 and inaugurated at the beginning of 1968 introduced limited market reforms and resulted in a higher standard of living and a relative openness to the "capitalist good life," symbolized by the Coca-Cola company beginning operations in Hungary in 1968.[195] Restrictions on movement between Hungary and other states were relaxed.[196] The attempt to smooth the surfaces of daily life within a context of continued state and party control – "Goulash Communism" as it was referred to in the West –

[193] The MSZMP was a reorganization of the previous ruling party, the Hungarian Working People's Party (MDP), which ruled Hungary from 1848 to 1956.

[194] "Kadar's terror," *Freedom. Anarchist Weekly*, 18(5) (February 2, 1957).

[195] The "New Economic Mechanism" was officially introduced at the beginning of 1968 and lasted until 1973. Máté Szabó, "Hungary," in Klimke and Scharloth, *1968 in Europe*, 209–218, 209–210. "In May 1968, the Communist daily Népszabadság reported indignantly how 'girls wearing Coca-Cola badges swayed to the blues tunes' in the Matthias Church"; Sándor Horváth, "The making of the Gang: Consumers of the Socialist *Youth Cultures, Music, and the State in Russia and Eastern Europe* (Lanham: Lexington, 2015), 100–115, 109.

[196] Csaba Békés, "Hungary 1968: Reform and the Challenge of the Prague Spring," in McDermott and Stibbe, *Eastern Europe in 1968*, 147–167, 149.

transformed Hungary into the "happiest barracks in the camp" of state socialism.[197] Stalinist hardliners resisted these concessions to public opinion, but market reforms were also opposed by members of the young intelligentsia, who, although they supported greater cultural and political freedom, were skeptical of a "Frigidaire socialism" that allowed greater access to consumer goods while ignoring the broader emancipatory content of Marxism.[198]

As part of its policy of cultural liberalization, the regime sought to coopt popular music, fostering "Pol-Beat," a genre that connected the rock 'n' roll impulse to a tradition of political song (also important in East and West Germany and elsewhere) with a regime-friendly version of left politics. The government sponsored festivals and prize competitions from 1966, in which bands such as Atlantis and Gerilla became prominent. The latter group was inspired politically by the Vietnam Solidarity Committee at ELTE, releasing a single featuring a track titled "Dissent." Yet the group also existed safely within the ideological energy field of the regime, winning official prizes and performing abroad in the German Democratic Republic on multiple occasions. Here, the regime succeeded in fostering "a commercial institutionalization of an apolitical new 'youth style,' which was co-opted through official recordings, competitions, and festivals to produce a 'Socialist' rock and youth culture."[199] Heavily infiltrated with informants, the Pol-Beat scene represented an ambiguous site of rebellion, serving the ideological goals of the regime and funneling youth rebellion in regime-friendly directions.

A key site for the attempt to renew Marxism in Hungary was the so-called Budapest School centered around the Marxist philosopher György Lukács. Lukács had been Minister of Culture in two revolutionary regimes in Hungary: the Hungarian Soviet Republic of 1919 and the government of Imre Nagy in 1956. In the aftermath of the latter, in which he sought to create an alliance of left-wing parties that would push for democratic change while remaining loyal to the Soviet Union, he narrowly escaped execution. In the 1960s, Lukács became a significant influence on the Western New Left, his work undergoing a major reassessment by those interested in Marxist alternatives to Stalinism. At home, a group of his students became an important locus of Marxist humanist thought in 1960s Hungary and in subsequent decades abroad. Strongly stamped by the

[197] Bill Lomax, "Twenty-five Years after 1956: The Heritage of the Hungarian Revolution," *Socialist Register*, 18 (March 18, 1982).
[198] Szilard Istvan Pap, "In the Hot Summer of '68, We Were the Tempest in the Hungarian Teapot," The Hungarian Maoist "Plotters," LeftEast (August 31, 2018), www.criticatac.ro/leftEast/hungarian-maoist-plotters.
[199] Szabó, "Hungary."

failed revolution of 1956, these students – notable among them Ágnes Heller, Ferenc Fehér, György Márkus, János Kis, and György Bence – were convinced of the need to create a socialism free from the smothering control of Moscow. They worked on an analysis in which Soviet Communism figured as "an abominable caricature of everything socialists have lived and fought for."[200]

Hungary's centrality on the continent made it a geographical conduit between East and West, and if its borders were not as open as those of Czechoslovakia or Yugoslavia, it was nevertheless fairly open.[201] As elsewhere in Eastern Europe, Hungarian youth were heavily influenced by the American and European New Left.[202] Their commitments were explicitly internationalist, concerned with events like the Vietnam War, the assassination of Martin Luther King, Jr., and the death of Che Guevara.[203] Their support for Castro and Guevara resonated with the commitments of the regime. Their interest in Marcuse did not, but since his works were translated into Hungarian only for high party leaders, it hardly mattered.[204]

Student unrest began to coalesce in 1963–1964 at ELTE University in Budapest, where a small politically interested circle of university students, disaffected from the official Hungarian Young Communist League (KISZ), began meeting to discuss new currents at the intersection of arts and politics, listening to music and considering alternative approaches to Marxism.[205] Members of this group participated in 1966 in the founding of a Solidarity Committee for Vietnam that, among other activities, demonstrated in front of the US embassy and passed out leaflets before the US pavilion at the 1966 International Fair in Budapest.[206] These protests were not just about Vietnam per se but were intimately linked to the issue of the extent to which the state held up its own socialist principles. As one activist put it, "we felt that our country's Socialism was not good enough."[207]

The Solidarity Committee was officially disbanded by the KISZ in December 1966 and its leading figures expelled from the organization

---

[200] Agnes Heller, Ferenc Fehér, and Gyorgy Markus, *Dictatorship over Needs: An Analysis of Soviet Societies* (London: Palgrave Macmillan, 1983), 235–236.
[201] Szabó, "Hungary."   [202] Borrero, "Spring Thaw, Summer Frost," 75.
[203] Szabó, "Hungary."   [204] Szabó, "Hungary."
[205] The Hungarian Young Communist League (KISZ) was founded on March 21, 1957 as a response to the failure of the Hungarian Revolution of the previous year, on the anniversary of the founding of the Hungarian Soviet Republic of 1919. George Ginsburgs, "Demise and revival of a Communist Party: An autopsy of the Hungarian Revolution," *The Western Political Quarterly*, 13(3) (September 1960), 780–802.
[206] Pap, "In the Hot Summer of '68."
[207] Writer Miklós Vámos to Mérce in Pap, "In the Hot Summer of '68."

altogether. A subsequent and smaller collection of activists – the "Hungarian Revolutionary Communists" – widened the remit of the first group's activities, undertaking continued actions around the Vietnam War, establishing relations with Greek Communist émigrés fleeing the 1967 right-wing coup in Greece, and creating a 36-point manifesto expressing the aim of "violently overthrow[ing] the revisionist, Bourgeois-bureaucratic system" in Hungary.[208] The participation of the Hungarian army in the Soviet-led invasion of Czechoslovakia in August 1968 only intensified disaffection with official socialism. Members of the "Budapest School" declared solidarity with the Prague Spring and condemned the invasion, a condemnation that, fittingly, was issued from the island of Korčula in Yugoslavia, where they were attending the summer school organized by the Yugoslav journal *Praxis*.[209]

Efforts to come to terms with the Prague Spring and with Hungary's own situation since 1956 entailed an attempt to come to grips with the content of socialism, to answer the question of what socialism *was*. As elsewhere, this involved historiographic work, in this case involving a key Hungarian revolutionary event – the Hungarian Soviet Republic of 1919. That uprising, under the de facto leadership of Béla Kun, lasted for 133 days. It saw a "Red Terror" against enemies of the regime, followed by a "White Terror" under Admiral Nicholas Horthy, who subsequently became head of the authoritarian interwar Nazi-collaborationist regime. This earlier revolutionary moment was not initially heralded by the post-war Communist regime, not least because of the uncomfortable fact that Béla Kun had been executed in the Soviet show trials of the 1930s.

The meaning of this event became central to the Communist regime's attempt to reestablish its legitimacy after the uprising of 1956, however. "[W]ithin the two and a half years that passed between October 1956 and March 1959," writes the leading scholar of these developments, "the Soviet Republic was transformed from a relatively insignificant event in the party's own history into the most important anniversary of the nation."[210] A main goal of this memory-political campaign was to draw a connection between the violence of the anti-Soviet uprising of 1956 and the White Terror of 1919, transforming "freedom fighters" against Communist tyranny into "murderers, fascists and counterrevolutionaries."[211]

---

[208] Pap, "In the Hot Summer of '68."

[209] On the response of the Praxis School, see Békés, "Hungary 1968," 162.

[210] Péter Apor, *Fabricating Authenticity in Soviet Hungary: The Afterlife of the First Hungarian Soviet Republic in the Age of State Socialism* (London: Anthem, 2014), 155.

[211] Adam Hudek, review of Péter Apor, *Fabricating Authenticity in Soviet Hungary*, *Hungarian Historical Review*, 4(1) (2015), 197–253, 234. The effort was backed by the

The New Left milieu in Hungary developed an alternative reading of 1919, one in which this previous revolutionary effort held an opposite meaning to the one intended by the authorities. This reading was expressed in Dezső Magyar's *Agitátorok* ("Agitators"), a 1969 film that recapitulated the past as an alternative version of the present. Here, the events of 1919 themselves were less important as historical events per se than as the model of a revolutionary moment with relevance for understanding other revolutionary moments such as 1956 and 1968. Based on the novel *Optimisták* ("Optimists") by Ervin Sinkó, the film also drew on interviews with actual participants in the Hungarian Soviet Republic, including György Lukács. In this act of historical recapitulation, activists of the present assumed the roles of those from the past. The author Gábor Révai, for example, played the role of his own father, József Révai, who had been a young Commissar in the events of 1919.[212] For the young protagonists involved with the film, as Péter Apor puts it, "the events of 1919 [were] actually the occurrences of 1968."[213]

In a way characteristic of 1968, the outstanding revolutionary issues of the past were dealt with using the radical source materials of the present, here in particular, as in a number of other national settings, Maoism. Maoism fulfilled multiple functions in the Hungarian setting. As part of a countercultural homology encompassing "Long hair, Eastern philosophy, the part guerilla, part peasant and part teacher Mao-jackets, and endless guitar music," it offered a means of attack "both against the Western bourgeois and the Eastern functionary."[214] It supplied ideological fuel for underground arts initiatives like Orfeo, the puppet-theater /band/theater troupe led by Péter Halász.[215] Most important of all, it offered both a metaphor for an attack on state socialism from the left and a template for action not sanctioned from above. It is no surprise in this regard that the "36-point program" elaborated by the "Hungarian Revolutionary Communists" called for the regime to be replaced by a "socialism with Chinese characteristics."[216] As the writer Miklós Haraszti put it in a recollection, Maoism expressed a truth that was "universal," in the sense that it bore directly on a Hungarian situation that he summarized in a slogan that could have been spoken by rebels on

---

proliferation in the international Communist press of atrocity images, alongside the production by the regime of so-called White Books establishing a link between the anti-Communist violence past and present.

[212] Gábor Révai in Pap, "In the Hot Summer of '68."

[213] Apor, *Fabricating Authenticity in Soviet Hungary*, 200. The film was banned until 1986.

[214] "Speech delivered at the Galeria Centralis of OSA Archivum, Budapest, 18 February, 2001. Transcript provided for Mérce by Miklós Haraszti," quoted in Pap, "In the Hot Summer of '68."

[215] Pap, "In the Hot Summer of '68."   [216] Pap, "In the Hot Summer of '68."

either side of the Cold War border around 1968: "they are abusing power and they are lying."[217]

The state made an example of the New Leftists, putting them on trial as members of an alleged "Maoist conspiracy." A number of activists were sentenced for "organizing to endanger the state order,"[218] forcing the Marxist philosopher György Lukács to weigh in (unsuccessfully) on their behalf.[219] In 1973, the preceding period of relative liberalization was brought to a close, the New Economic Mechanism abandoned.[220] As it had before 1968, New Left resistance in Hungary continued to take place mostly in the countercultural realm, organized around alternative theater and ballet, decorative arts and design, and underground music.[221] In this respect, the situation mirrored that in East Germany, where the impossibility of political resistance, proven in 1968 in connection with the Prague Spring, left only retreat into the psychic and literal spaces of the artistic and lifestyle-oriented subcultures.

The situation was very different in neighboring Yugoslavia, where the gains of the revolution were still in place. The real content of those gains, however, was subject to increasingly close questioning from the young dissident intelligentsia. Although Yugoslavia was one of the most liberal of the Eastern Bloc countries, 1968 tested the limitations of that permissiveness to and beyond its limits. As we have seen, the League of Yugoslav Communists (LCY) under Tito pursued its own path to socialism, breaking with the USSR's Cominform (Communist Information Bureau – successor to the Comintern) in 1948 and instituting a system of "workers' self-management" linked with concepts of "socialist democracy" according to which, in theory, society was directed from the bottom up in accordance with the direct will of the producers.[222] That system was meant not only as an antidote to Stalinist bureaucracy but held the implication of the "withering away of the state" predicted by Marx. In this respect, workers' self-management in Yugoslavia was a direct response to the central questions posed by Leninism and its subsequent degeneration into Stalinism – what was the role of the party? And what was the relationship between the "leading role" it claimed for itself under

---

[217] "Speech delivered at the Galeria Centralis of OSA Archivum, Budapest, 18 February, 2001."

[218] "Speech delivered at the Galeria Centralis of OSA Archivum, Budapest, 18 February, 2001." See also Anna von der Goltz and James Mark, "Encounters," in Robert Gildea, James Mark, and Anette Warring (eds.), *Europe's 1968: Voices of Revolt* (Oxford: Oxford University Press, 2013), 145, 188.

[219] Pap, "In the Hot Summer of '68."

[220] Rebecca Clifford, Juliane Fürst, Robert Gildea, James Mark, Piotr Osęka, and Chris Reynolds, "Spaces," in Gildea, Mark, and Warring, *Europe's 1968*, 190–192, 188.

[221] Szabó, "Hungary," 214.   [222] Borrero, "Spring Thaw, Summer Frost," 75.

Leninism and the will to direct workers' democracy that had underpinned the risings in Spain in 1936, Hungary and Poland in 1956, and France and Italy in 1968 and that was enshrined as the basis of the Yugoslav state?

On one level, the democratic content of workers' self-management in Yugoslavia was taken as a given, not least because of a level of cultural and political freedom unprecedented anywhere else in the Eastern Bloc. Citizens of Yugoslavia could easily obtain publications from, and travel to, both sides of the Iron Curtain.[223] Herbert Marcuse's works in particular, including his critique of "one-dimensional man," published in Serbo-Croatian in Yugoslavia, had a significant effect on the amplified political consciousness of Yugoslav youth in the mid-1960s. The Western musical *Hair* made its debut in Yugoslavia in the late 1960s. Simultaneously, new cultural expressions were created locally in dialogue with what was going on abroad. Given Yugoslavia's relative openness to the rest of the Europe and the world, as Boris Kanzleiter puts it, "citizens could feel that they related equally to the East, the West, and the South."[224]

The emancipatory patina of the Yugoslav experiment was further burnished by the status Tito enjoyed as the father of the nonaligned movement, which refused the artificial boundaries of the Cold War bloc system and gestured toward a less ossified, more open-ended set of sociopolitical possibilities. Yugoslavia's democratizing reputation was also strengthened by the influence of Yugoslav intellectuals on the international New Left. The journal *Praxis*, with its simultaneous critique of consumer capitalism and socialist bureaucracy, enjoyed a wide reputation, publishing an international edition with contributions in English, French, and German. In the annual Summer Schools on the Croatian island of Korčula, *Praxis* intellectuals sponsored leading theorists of the New Left such as Herbert Marcuse, Erich Fromm, Leszek Kołakowski, Ágnes Heller, and Ernest Mandel. The contribution of *Praxis* intellectuals to the rethinking of the Communist tradition, combined with the state's rhetorical support for the democratic potential of socialism, placed Yugoslavia in a unique position at the center of several "worlds."

---

[223] Boris Kanzleiter, "1968 in Yugoslavia: Student Revolt between East and West," in Klimke, Pekelder, and Scharloth, *Between Prague Spring and French May*, 84–100; Madigan Fichter, "East looks west: Belgrade's young people evaluate Western counterculture and student activism," in Chen Jian, Martin Klimke, Masha Kirasirova, Mary Nolan, Marilyn Young, and Joanna Waley-Cohen (eds.), *The Routledge Handbook of the Global Sixties: Between Protest and Nation-Building* (New York: Routledge, 2018), 193–204.

[224] Kanzleiter, "1968 in Yugoslavia."

Despite Yugoslavia's international reputation as an alternative to Stalinism, however, and notwithstanding the regime's emancipatory claims, there was a strong dissonance between the imaginary independence of "workers' self-management" and the reality of bureaucratic repression in Yugoslavia. The LCY still operated in a "vanguard" mode, still used its police power to control dissent, and still held political prisoners.[225] The "control" exercised by workers in the state-run enterprises, moreover, was more rhetorical than real, with the effect that official rhetoric regarding "workers' self-management" was widely understood to be mere propaganda.[226] The regime itself seemed to have understood the need to lend some form of reality to self-management. Economic reforms in the mid-1960s were accompanied by talk of political reform and democratization, which would entail greater involvement of workers in decision-making in the workplace.[227] Workers understood it too, launching strikes over working conditions that called attention to the disjuncture between official claims of self-management and the reality of bureaucratic party rule.

When reform came more strongly onto the agenda in the 1960s, it was not just the status of self-management that was at issue but the state's claim to a monopoly of legitimate speech and action. As in Czechoslovakia, the conversation expanded to previously taboo themes, such as inhumane conditions at the Goli Otok prison camp where the regime held its political prisoners.[228] The increasingly confident criticism voiced by the students and critical intellectuals was further encouraged by the removal of the feared chief of the Secret Service, Aleksandar Ranković, by those in the government attempting to create a reformed "socialist market economy." This, in turn, engendered a mass opening of political discussions of the imprisonment of "state enemies" in the 1940s and 1950s.

One result of those discussions was the release from prison of former partisan commander and leading Communist Milovan Ðilas. At one time considered a potential successor to Tito, Ðilas was imprisoned repeatedly for advocating democratic reform up to and including the abolition of one-party rule. His comments to the foreign press lamenting Yugoslavia's abstention from the vote condemning the 1956 invasion of Hungary brought him afoul of the regime, as did his book *The New Class*, published by the American press Praeger in 1957, which criticized the Communist

---

[225] For a cogent discussion of the fraudulent nature of "worker's control" in Yugoslavia, see Chris Harman, *The Fire Last Time: 1968 and After* (London: Bookmarks, 1995), 129.

[226] Kanzleiter, "1968 in Yugoslavia."   [227] Kanzleiter, "1968 in Yugoslavia."

[228] Kanzleiter, "1968 in Yugoslavia."

bureaucracy as a class in its own right whose very existence prevented the creation of the egalitarian society that communism promised.[229]

The critique of the ruling bureaucracy developed strongly in the universities, where a new generation of students sought to realize the democratic promises of Yugoslav society. As elsewhere in Europe, the 1960s in Yugoslavia saw a rapid influx of new students into universities, exposing the relatively backward state of higher education in terms of both facilities and instruction. Critical voices came forward in the magazine *Perspective*, founded in 1960 and banned in May 1964 for being too critical. Subsequently, *Susret* and *Student* (published by the Youth League of Serbia and the Student League of Belgrade University, respectively) became key sites of a new sensibility that was critical of developments at home while being explicitly internationalist in focus. This internationalism emphasized the importance of linking struggles on both sides of the Cold War divide.[230] Student journals closely followed events in West Germany, publishing a profile of Rudi Dutschke and printing his writings alongside those of figures such as Ernst Bloch, Daniel Guérin, and Herbert Marcuse.[231]

Attention to developments on both sides of the Cold War divide allowed Yugoslav students to develop a critique of what an article in *Student* called "the mythology of the 'welfare state' with its classical bourgeois democracy, and also the classical left parties – the social-democratic parties which have succeeded by all possible means in blunting revolutionary goals in developed Western societies, as well as the Communist parties which often discredited the original ideals for which they fought."[232] This line of analysis had an obvious relevance for state socialist societies, where the bureaucratization of Communist parties had reached its highest stage. *Student* reported approvingly on students' push for socialist democracy in Poland, criticizing both the Polish government's anti-Semitic campaign and the uncritical attitude of the Yugoslav press.[233]

The Yugoslav student movement also forged direct connections with European radical student networks. The Conference of the Student League of Yugoslavia (SSJ) hosted delegates from throughout Europe during a student conference in Belgrade in April 1968. The guests

[229] Milovan Ðilas, *The New Class: An Analysis of the Communist System* (New York: Mariner, 1982).

[230] Fichter, "East looks West."

[231] Kanzleiter, "1968 in Yugoslavia"; Perlman, *Birth of a Revolutionary Movement in Yugoslavia*.

[232] "The Topic is Action," *Student* (May 14, 1968), 4, quoted in Perlman, *Birth of a Revolutionary Movement in Yugoslavia*.

[233] Fichter, "East looks west."

included West German students who delivered a presentation on the International Vietnam Congress organized by the SDS in West Berlin two months earlier. Hundreds of Yugoslav students protested outside the embassy in Belgrade against the assassination attempt on Rudi Dutschke in April 1968 and against the passage of the Emergency Laws in West Germany.

Students initially saw their goals in terms of a convergence with the regime's declared goals of building a fair and equitable socialist modernity. As Kenneth Morrison writes, they "called for more, not less socialism."[234] They had reason to do so, for the Yugoslav government initially treated the global student rebellions as a confirmation of its ruling ideology. Indeed, as Boris Kanzleiter points out, the LCY was "probably the only ruling party worldwide to interpret the global student revolt as a confirmation of its own ideological and political groundwork."[235] Thus no less a figure than the Spanish Civil War veteran and LCY leader Veljko Vlahović could claim, in May 1968, that French demands for workers' self-management ("autogestion") showed the basic correctness of Yugoslavia's position, and Jean-Paul Sartre's interview with the young radical Daniel Cohn-Bendit could be published in the main party organ *Borba*.[236] Simultaneously, the party could support the right of socialist self-determination in Czechoslovakia, with Tito paying a visit of support to Dubček just a little over a week before the Warsaw Pact invasion of August 21, 1968.[237]

It was precisely in students' perception of a convergence of their goals with those of the regime that the potential for conflict lay. The developing oppositional consciousness was driven by a reaction against what a keen observer of the international student revolt, the Czech-born activist Fredy Perlman, called the "gap between theory and practice, between official proclamations and social relations."[238] Central to the revolt everywhere, as we have seen, in Yugoslavia this gap involved, in Madigan Fichter's words, a sense that "the state was not fully committed to the international, socialist cause."[239] This realization, wrote Perlman, was exposed precisely through the state's response to the developing critical consciousness of youth. When "students began to organize themselves in demonstrations and general assemblies," he observed, the critical moment of supreme dissonance came in which "the regime which

---

[234] Kenneth Morrison, "The 'June Events': The 1968 Student Protests in Yugoslavia," in McDermott and Stibbe, *Eastern Europe in 1968*, 215–229, 216.
[235] Kanzleiter, "1968 in Yugoslavia."   [236] Kanzleiter, "1968 in Yugoslavia."
[237] Kanzleiter, "1968 in Yugoslavia."
[238] Perlman, *Birth of a Revolutionary Movement in Yugoslavia*.
[239] Fichter, "East looks West," 194.

proclaims self-management reacted to this rare example of popular self-organization by putting an end to it through police and press repression."[240] As a statement of striking students and professors put it in June 1968, "Our program is the program of the most progressive forces of our society – the program of the LCY and the constitution. We demand that it should be put consequently into practice."[241]

The divergence between the goals of students and those of the regime developed in the course of the regime's own mobilizations. The fall 1966 series of anti–Vietnam War demonstrations in Zagreb, Belgrade, and Sarajevo were organized by the official student umbrella organization, the Student League. Despite their official nature, the protests created space for criticism of the government on the grounds that it was not doing enough to resist American imperialism. Students highlighted in particular what they saw as the hypocrisy of a Yugoslavian government that paid lip service to outrage against the Vietnam War but cooperated with the United States in other spheres.[242] In a demonstration on December 23, students who attempted to march on the US Embassy and American Cultural Center came into direct conflict with riot police.[243] This incident, in which the goals of students diverged visibly from those of the regime, was a watershed moment in Yugoslavia, spurring the creation of informal networks of activists who would prepare the ground for subsequent protest activity.[244] Expelled from the ruling League of Communists, key student protagonists of these protests began to forge connections with professors at Belgrade University, supporting their opposition to the rule of the party bureaucracy and the trend toward market socialism. By 1968, they were expressing strong support for the West German and Polish student movement while continuing their fierce opposition to the American war in Vietnam.[245]

As in Czechoslovakia, official rhetoric about "democratization" could prompt unexpected and unwelcome initiatives from below. This was the case in 1967, when students began to agitate for antibureaucratic reform in the official Student League. In March the following year, the Student League at the Faculty of Philosophy in Belgrade called for a "new activism," an impulse that increasingly came to be expressed in calls for "violent" action and the possibility of a student strike that was the subject of open discussion in student newspapers.[246] The growing radicalism was rooted in the conviction that all struggles were connected. "The

---

[240] Perlman, *Birth of a Revolutionary Movement in Yugoslavia.*
[241] Quoted in Kanzleiter, "1968 in Yugoslavia."
[242] Kanzleiter, "1968 in Yugoslavia," 91.   [243] Kanzleiter, "1968 in Yugoslavia," 91.
[244] Harman, *The Fire Last Time,* 130–131.   [245] Kanzleiter, "1968 in Yugoslavia."
[246] Kanzleiter, "1968 in Yugoslavia."

revolutionary role of Yugoslav students," read an editorial in *Susret*, the journal of the Belgrade Youth Federation,

lies in their engagement to deal with general social problems and contradictions (among which the problems and contradictions of the social and material situation of students are included). Special student problems, no matter how drastic, cannot be solved in isolation, separate from the general social problems: the material situation of students cannot be separated from the economic situation of the society; student self-government cannot be separated from the social problems of self-government; the situation of the University from the situation of society."[247]

A subsequent issue of *Susret* reinforced the point: "University reform is . . . not possible without . . . revolutionizing of the entire society, because the university cannot be separated from the wider spectrum of social institutions. From this it follows that freedom of thought and action . . . is only possible if the entire society is transformed, and if thus transformed it makes possible a general climate of freedom and self-government."[248]

Such views might be supported by the regime in theory, but not always at the level of practice. This was especially true when the objects of solidarity were citizens of other state socialist countries. In April 1968, when students at Belgrade University collected 1,500 signatures on a declaration of solidarity with Polish students, they were unequivocally condemned by the leadership of the Student League for interfering in the politics of another socialist country. The incident led to a debate in the pages of *Student* about the principle of democratic rights that could only have been unwelcome from the perspective of the authorities.[249]

In Yugoslavia, open revolt exploded out of one of the standard scenarios by which 1968 was characterized: a conflict with the police over entry to a music performance. In this case, on the night of June 2, 1968, the anger of students unable to squeeze into a room to see a music performance set off a chain reaction. As the crowd swelled into thousands of students and started to move in the direction of government buildings, it was set upon by the police with beatings and many arrests. As was so often the case in both East and West, the taste of police batons sharpened the political critique of those on the receiving end. The day after the riot, students held general assemblies on the campus of the University of Belgrade. An "Action Committee" was formed, and after being met with further violence, 10,000 students occupied the campus of the

---

[247] *Susret* (May 15, 1968), quoted in Perlman, *Birth of a Revolutionary Movement in Yugoslavia.*

[248] *Susret* (June 1, 1968), quoted in Perlman, *Birth of a Revolutionary Movement in Yugoslavia.*

[249] Kanzleiter, "1968 in Yugoslavia."

University of Belgrade.[250] In direct imitation of students at Frankfurt University, students renamed it the Red University Karl Marx.[251]

Now the frustration of the music performance revealed its true sources. "In their talks," reported an article the next day in a special issue of *Student*,

> students emphasized the gross social differentiation of Yugoslav society, the problem of unemployment, the increase of private property and the unearned wealth of one social layer, the unbearable condition of a large section of the working class and the need to carry out the principle of distribution according to labor consistently. The talks were interrupted by loud applause, by calls like "Students with Workers," "We're sons of working people," "Down with the Socialist Bourgeoisie," "Freedom of the press and freedom to demonstrate!"[252]

Demanding the "abolition of all privileges, democratization of all information media and freedom of gathering and demonstration," the students drew the widest possible conclusion from the humiliation of unjust authority delivered by police batons.[253] Once again, as in the dormitories at Nanterre or the Rolling Stones concerts in Zurich and West Berlin, it was on the terrain of daily life, in the wake of a seemingly trivial frustration, that the fuse of more substantial discontents was lit.[254]

The occupation of the university in Belgrade became the centerpiece of the outburst of protest. There developed a sort of political Happening in which "students, professors, and citizens discussed the country's problems" while crowds looked on and "[a]ctors, writers, artists, and delegations of workers showed solidarity."[255] It was out of this occupation, ringed in by police, that the students developed their "Political Action Program." That document announced its allegiance to the broader project of socialist democracy by mirroring the name of Prague's "Action Program," a document that had been published in *Rudé Právo* on April 10 and appeared the following day in the official Yugoslav party organ *Borba*.[256] As in France, "action committees" (*akcioni odbori*) were established as spontaneous forms of self-organization.[257] A popular slogan – "Down with the Red Bourgeoisie" – signaled the intent.[258]

[250] Borrero, "Spring Thaw, Summer Frost," 75.
[251] Kanzleiter, "1968 in Yugoslavia," 224.
[252] *Student* (June 4, 1968), 1, quoted in Perlman, *Birth of a Revolutionary Movement in Yugoslavia.*
[253] Quoted in Kanzleiter, "1968 in Yugoslavia."
[254] Perlman, *Birth of a Revolutionary Movement in Yugoslavia.*
[255] Kanzleiter, "1968 in Yugoslavia."   [256] Kanzleiter, "1968 in Yugoslavia."
[257] Kanzleiter, "1968 in Yugoslavia."
[258] Želimir Žilnik, "Yugoslavia: 'Down with the Red Bourgeoisie,'" in Gassert and Klimke, *1968*, 181–187; see also Harman, *The Fire Last Time*, 129.

The revolt quickly spread to universities in Ljubljana, Zagreb, and Sarajevo.[259] The party worried about the possibility of workers going into the streets, wondering about the possible deployment of troops.[260] The crisis became serious enough to compel Tito to appear on state television and promise to resign if he could not meet the demands of the striking students and professors, which was effective in convincing the majority to go back to class. However, the strikers at the Sociological and Philosophical Faculties at the University of Belgrade held out. For their resistance, the entire party organization at the Philosophical Faculty was expelled from the LCY, as the now-isolated resistance movement was steadily squashed.

Tito let the steam out of the student revolt by claiming, in a televised address on June 9, that he supported the students' demands. The "Guidelines" subsequently published by the party neglected to make any provision for the goals of increased democratization and self-management, however,[261] and the government quickly moved to repress critical intellectuals, starting with members of the Praxis group in Belgrade and Zagreb, who were blamed for stirring up student dissent. At the end of the summer, after the Soviet-led invasion of Czechoslovakia, measures were taken to stifle criticism in the student press as well. The action was well timed from Tito's perspective, since it now allowed the LCY to appeal to its independent role as protector of Yugoslav sovereignty. Using the fear of a Soviet intervention and mobilizing the reserves of the Yugoslav military, the government was able to master the crisis of authority that the student movement had helped to open. The early 1970s saw show trials, imprisonment, a superficial reform of the constitution of the Federal Republic, and the suppression of *Praxis*. Ultimately, attempts to link the nation's revolutionary image to its social reality were a failure.[262]

The Factory Is Our Vietnam

In Italy, student radicalism and working-class militancy converged in a way that Yugoslav activists could only dream of. Whereas in the latter, activists struggled to make the fiction of workers' control a reality, deploying official language that ultimately made their efforts easy to coopt, in the former, the combination of rapid industrialization and rising left-wing radicalism produced a social crisis with deep and long-lasting effects. This

---

[259] Kanzleiter, "1968 in Yugoslavia."   [260] Kanzleiter, "1968 in Yugoslavia."
[261] Quoted in Kanzleiter, "1968 in Yugoslavia."
[262] See the discussion of the repression in Morrison, "The 'June Events'," 228.

"Creeping May" saw widespread social unrest, countercultural resistance, and political violence converge with a force and duration not seen elsewhere. If it is true, as Jan Kurz and Marica Tolomelli claim, that "no other country can so clearly differentiate the before and after in historical time," it is in no small part because of the speed of the country's transformation and the violence of the response to it.[263]

That speed and violence was in part a consequence of Italy's late industrialization. At the end of the 1950s, Italy began to undergo one of the most dramatic demographic and structural shifts in its history. The "economic miracle" of the early 1960s saw the development of a skilled northern workforce with close ties to the Communist Party.[264] It also saw an influx of largely unskilled laborers from the agricultural regions of the south, a mass migration that radically transformed traditional conceptions of family and gender, religion, and the relationship between the generations.[265] Many of the new unskilled workers had previously belonged to agricultural communities with long experience of direct action and violent struggle including arson, occupations, and physical violence. With nothing to lose and everything to gain from workplace militancy, they were much less likely to be integrated into the political structures provided by the Socialist and Communist parties and difficult to coopt into traditional trade union channels.

The sense of culture shock was captured in the remarks of a young militant interviewed in the newspaper *Lotta Continua*: "I'd never seen anything like this in all my life," he recalled. "I come from Calabria and my town's a pretty small place. It's ruled by God, you might say: Three or four priests, who were all a bunch of shits, brought us up to be boy scouts and the like, and told us all about what they thought democracy was. Then there were the four or five Communists and the seven or eight fascists, and that's it."[266] Experiencing the high cost of living and poor working and living conditions, he simultaneously came into contact with radical students at the factory gate and became involved in radical labor

---

[263] Jan Kurz and Marica Tolomelli, "Italy," in Klimke and Scharloth, *1968 in Europe*, 83-96.

[264] Italy's "economic miracle" was particularly radical because it saw heavy urbanization alongside industrialization; see Stuart J. Hilwig, *Italy and 1968: Youthful Unrest and Democratic Culture* (Basingstoke: Palgrave Macmillan, 2009), 3.

[265] Kurz and Tolomelli, "Italy," 84. In the years 1950–1967, seventeen million people, more than a third of the Italian population, moved from one part of the country to another; Jim Kaplan, "Introduction to the revolutionary left in Italy," *Radical America*, 7 (2) (March/April 1973).

[266] "Anyway, down there, even if I only had 50 lire I could always buy myself a cheese roll or something. But I come up to Turin and fuck it: I find I'm paying out 200! It was all crazy to me"; "An interview with workers at Fiat, 1970," https://libcom.org/history/interview-workers-fiat-1970.

actions. His path into labor militancy was characteristic of the trajectory described by an activist in the Workers' Rank and File Committees: "They arrive in Turin, hunting the big wage packet they have heard so much about, but find instead that FIAT is a slave camp. Naturally they rebel."[267]

That rebellion took place against a historical backdrop that included the "Red Years" of factory occupations (1919–1920), Italian fascism (1922–1945) – the latter in part a direct response to the former – and the Communist-led partisan struggle during World War II. Antiunion labor codes of the fascist state remained well into the 1950s, and the Christian Democrats sought to maintain high unemployment and low wages, intentionally attempting to circumvent any collective workers' agency to significantly alter relations on the shop floor. Mass protests and strikes from 1960 to 1963 took an offensive character, successfully forcing Italian employers to raise wages, improve working conditions, and remove the most odious restrictions to collective bargaining contained within the labor code.

The transformation of workplace relations took place against a backdrop of rising student militancy. The Italian student revolt was one of Europe's most precocious, breaking out as early as 1964, around the time of the American student revolt in Berkeley. This new militancy arose in response to pressures similar to those in other European countries. As in France and elsewhere, the 1960s in Italy saw a massive expansion in higher education. Student enrollments increased by almost 200,000 from the beginning of the 1960s to the year 1968.[268] Students increasingly challenged the authoritarian relationships characteristic of higher education in Italy. The traditional headmaster-pupil relationship, the political nature of academic appointments, outdated curricula, and fixed quotas (*numero chiuso*) used to limit working-class students on campus were some of the first stimuli of discontent for Italian students, but the struggle against them would expand the articulation of social oppression into a far broader, radical perspective.[269]

The theoretical underpinning of the new militancy was provided by Operaismo ("workerism"), a doctrine that emerged at the beginning of the 1960s around the journal *Quaderni Rossi* ("Red Notebooks"). Rejecting the Leninist conception of the vanguard party, Operaismo

---

[267] *La Classe*, 13–14 (August 1969), reprinted in "Italy: New Tactics and Organization," *Radical America*, 5(5) (September/October 1971), 13.

[268] Sam Lowry, "Worker and Student Struggles in Italy, 1962–1973," http://libcom.org/history/1962-1973-worker-student-struggles-italy.

[269] Robert Lumley, *States of Emergency: Cultures of Revolt in Italy from 1968 to 1978* (London: Verso, 1990), 55–62.

emphasized the need for workers themselves to create the revolution. Rather than acting as a vanguard party imposing theory *on* the struggles of workers, the idea was to derive theory *from* workers' struggles. Targeting bureaucracy and hierarchy, especially as manifested in the Socialist and Communist parties and the trade unions, it rejected "reformism" – defined as that which happened outside the factory (unions and electoral politics) – in favor of "revolution," as that which happened inside it. Locating the revolution firmly at the point of production while emphasizing spontaneity and autonomy, Operaismo provided a fresh answer to the classical revolutionary dilemma about the relationship between intellectuals and the working classes that would prove uniquely suited to the Italian situation.

These theoretical developments took place against the backdrop of rising militancy in Italian universities, beginning in January 1966 with the occupation of the University of Trento.[270] Spreading to Turin and Pisa, and from there to universities around Italy, the wave of radicalization saw demands for the thoroughgoing democratization of the university that gradually extended their reach to the whole of society. Central to these demands was an operaist analysis in which the university was understood as an instrument of class domination and the student occupied a position analogous to a worker in the factory.[271] Such ideas were elaborated in the "Tesi della Sapienza" ("Theses of Wisdom") published at the University of Pisa in February 1967, which theorized student assemblies and occupations as instruments of grassroots democracy that could provide the basis for more thoroughgoing mobilizations.[272] The "Manifesto for a Negative University" published at Trento later the same year further developed these ideas with reference to the Frankfurt School and the Berkeley Free Speech Movement.[273]

Indeed, Italian student activism was formulated in explicitly internationalist terms, inspired by the American Civil Rights and Berkeley Free Speech Movements and figures such as C. Wright Mills and Herbert Marcuse.[274] It eagerly adopted tactics of civil disobedience like the sit-in

---

[270] See Gerd-Rainer Horn, *The Spirit of '68: Rebellion in Western Europe and North America, 1956–1976* (Oxford: Oxford University Press, 2006), 75–77.

[271] Lumley, *States of Emergency*, 63–65.

[272] "Occupiers of the Sapienza University: The Sapienza Theses (1967)," in Mohandesi, Risager, and Cox, *Voices of 1968*, 208–209. "Tesi della Sapienza" was a play on words employing *sapienza* ("wisdom") in the name of the university, "Sapienza University of Pisa."

[273] "Movement for a Negative University/Renato Curcio: Manifesto for a Negative University (1967)," in Mohandesi, Risager, and Cox, *Voices of 1968*, 210–212. See also Horn, *The Spirit of '68*.

[274] Horn, *The Spirit of '68*, 80.

and the teach-in, combining them with local labor traditions such as the "active strike."[275] This tactic had its antecedent in the Italian factory occupations of 1920, when rather than stay away from the workplace, workers had simply taken it over and run it themselves.[276] In the academic setting, similarly, students did not bother to disrupt official lectures but merely replaced them with their own "counter-seminars" (*controlezioni*) designed to expose the authoritarian nature of the university. In this way, moving beyond mere protest, they aimed to produce an alternative sphere of knowledge that would make possible emancipatory action, a goal it shared with student movements in West Germany, France, and elsewhere.

Student mobilization also saw a trajectory of increasing violence. This began with the April 1966 murder of the student Paolo Rossi in a conflict with fascist students at the University of Rome, an event that prompted mass protests, strikes, and occupations from Naples to Venice.[277] The events were notable for the strong presence of neo-fascists and for violence by the police and neo-fascists against student demonstrators. In February 1968, a neo-fascist group bombed the Faculty of Law at the University of Turin. Later the same month, neo-fascists violently confronted radical leftist students at the University of Rome following a police attack on the student occupation.[278] Violent conflict reached an initial culmination on March 1, 1968 with the so-called Battle of Valle Giulia and later became increasingly integrated into the movement's protest tactics.[279] In April 1968, a neo-fascist group attacked students occupying the university in Parma, backed by police, who drove students from campus, prompting a solidarity strike from local trade unions. In June, 300 right-wing students attacked leftist students occupying the University of Rome, backed by police, who took back the campus.[280] In this context, left-wing militants could come to understand themselves as insurgents against the forces of the bosses and the state, a conceit captured in the popular slogan: "The Factory Is Our Vietnam."[281]

---

[275] Horn, *The Spirit of '68*, 84.
[276] See Sidney Tarrow, *Democracy and Disorder: Protest and Politics in Italy, 1965–1975* (Oxford: Oxford University Press, 1989), 5–9. See also Tom Wetzel, "The Italian Factory Occupations of 1920," www.workerscontrol.net/theorists/italian-factory-occupations-1920.
[277] The murder took place on April 27, 1966. See Kurz and Tolomelli, "Italy," 88.
[278] Werenskjold, "A Chronology of the Global 1968 Protest," 285–287.
[279] Horn, *The Spirit of '68*, 84; Harman, *The Fire Last Time*, 137.
[280] Werenskjold, "A Chronology of the Global 1968 Protest," 291.
[281] George Katsiaficas, *The Global Imagination of 1968: Revolution and Counterrevolution* (Oakland: PM, 2018).

By the beginning of 1968, students had driven the Italian university system into crisis with occupations, strikes, and disruption of instruction.[282] As the limitations of activism within the space of the university became more and more apparent from the spring of 1968, students increasingly theorized their position within the broader society, with respect both to the university and to the working class. The strategies of the Italian movement from the end of the 1960s drew heavily on the example of France. There, as we have seen, student-worker militancy temporarily seemed ready to overturn the state, but quickly dissipated as workers in the factories were guided back into accommodation through the Grenelle Agreements. The issue in Italy, as it had been in France, was one of how to maintain revolutionary drive and produce long-term transformation. Italian militants explored new venues of activism, such as neighborhood organizing, and new vistas of radical subjectivity drawing on artistic and countercultural revolt. Above all, they set out in search of the revolutionary subject, which, especially given the nature of Italian society, could only be the working class.[283]

Operaist ideas manifested themselves organizationally from 1967 in the emergence of scattered local groups going under the name "Potere Operaio" ("Workers' Power").[284] The beginning of the following year saw major strikes in the northern factories, opening salvos in the *maggio striciante* (the "Drawn-Out May") of 1968–1969, a period of intense class conflict in Italy. Even before this, scattered workerist initiatives began to coalesce into political organizations. These included Potere Operaia ("Workers' Power"), founded in 1966–1967, associated with the reviews *Quaderni Rossi* and *Classe Operaia*; Avanguardia Operaia ("Workers' Vanguard"), a Trotskyist/Marxist-Leninist group founded in 1968–1969 and associated with *Avanguardia Operaia*; and Lotta Continua ("Continuous Struggle"), formalized in 1969 from elements of the student movement and ex-members of Potere Operaio and publishing a journal under its own name.

These groups drew on and fostered what Gerd-Ranier Horn has termed "the dynamic toward self-management," an impulse present in other great historical moments of social revolution such as Russia 1917–1921 and Spain 1936.[285] There was a direct Italian legacy, indeed, from the Turin movement of 1919–1920 and Gramsci's writings in *Ordine Nuovo*.[286] The revival of council Communist ideas in 1960s Italy was associated especially with the group around *Il Manifesto*, a council

[282] Kurz and Tolomelli, "Italy."   [283] Horn, *The Spirit of '68*, 85.
[284] Kaplan, "Introduction to the Revolutionary Left in Italy."
[285] Horn, "The Working Class Dimension of 1968," 108.
[286] Lumley, *States of Emergency*.

Communist tendency that split off from the PCI in 1969. In contrast to Leninists, who insisted on the leading role of the party, Il Manifesto advocated factory councils as means of establishing working-class democracy.[287] Drawing on historical leftist ideas, this impulse was also strongly shaped by left Catholicism, a key site in which impulses toward working-class democracy gathered strength in both France and Italy.[288] The impulse to self-management grew up in connection with new forms of political action rooted in the job site, from mass assemblies to smaller strike or factory committees as organs of working-class democracy.[289] These "new organs of factory democracy" were a hallmark of Italy's "Creeping May," just as they were of May 1968 in France.[290] The "process of democratization concerning factory and office life," writes Horn, was "the true hallmark of 1968 at the point of production."[291]

The new style of militancy associated with Potere Operaio and Lotta Continua played a major role in the industrial actions of the Hot Autumn of 1969, marked by working-class uprisings in Milan and Turin. The Hot Autumn saw the third-largest strike movement in history, second only to the British general strike of 1926 and the French general strike of May 1968.[292] Wildcat strikes proliferated, and industrial action spread to the south of the country, sucking trade unions into struggles they had not chosen but could no longer avoid. These actions were characterized by the emergence of joint student-worker militancy. As early as the summer of 1968, revolutionary student groups began to link up with workers on the picket lines, facilitated by "worker-students" who carried the militant ideas of the university onto the shop floor.[293] As mentioned earlier, the categories of "worker" and "student" interpenetrated each other in Italy in a way they elsewhere did not. Many rural and/or working class youth gained access to higher education for the first time in the 1960s, forming a living link between the university milieu and the shop floor.[294] This interpenetration of university and factory produced an unparalleled level of militancy.[295] Even middle-class students came to understand themselves to *be* workers, not only by dint of their "class role"

[287] Lumley, *States of Emergency.*
[288] Horn, "The Working Class Dimension of 1968," 108–109; see also Hilwig, *Italy and 1968,* 9.
[289] Horn, "The Working Class Dimension of 1968," 102.
[290] Horn, "The Working Class Dimension of 1968," 101.
[291] Horn, "The Working Class Dimension of 1968."   [292] Lumley, *States of Emergency.*
[293] Lowry, "Worker and Student Struggles in Italy, 1962–1973."
[294] Lowry, "Worker and Student Struggles in Italy, 1962–1973."
[295] Angelo Ventrone, "Revolution as a Quest for an Authentic Life: The 1960s and 1970s in Italy," in Joachim C. Häberlen, Mark Keck-Szajbel, and Kate Mahoney (eds.), *The Politics of Authenticity: Countercultures and Radical Movements across the Iron Curtain, 1968–1989* (New York: Berghahn, 2018), 25–44, 27.

within the university but in terms of their cultural practice, which saw the adoption of the historic symbols of working-class militancy and the rejection of bourgeois values, style, and comportment.[296]

Maoism was particularly popular among Italian militants for precisely this reason – it provided an idiom for expressing the idea of a revolution of daily life that was simultaneously a revolution in consciousness.[297] The association picked up steam in August 1966 when images of the Red Guards active in the Cultural Revolution were widely published in the Italian press.[298] There had already been some small Maoist groups founded, but after 1966, Maoism spread to become a more general radical template.[299] Maoism was received favorably in part because it tapped into young Italians' sense of unease about lost revolutionary momentum in the postwar period, the failure to live up to the legacy of the partisan struggle against fascism.[300] It was also easy to find Italian uses for Chinese practices and analyses, whether in the deployment of *dazibao* ("big character posters") in the factories or the use of the Red Guards' criticism of "bourgeois teaching practices" as a means of interpreting unhappiness with the nature of university instruction.[301]

This mass mobilization was accompanied by a "profound sea change of consciousness on the level of the rank and file."[302] Workers, observed an article in *Lotta Continua* during the mass strike actions of 1970, "are destroying constituted authority in the factory. They are taking apart the mechanisms that the bosses use to divide and control them, and are freeing themselves from the taboos that till now have kept them slaves." This process involved a change in workers' "ways of seeing themselves and seeing the world"; through the concrete experience of militant action they were "slowly beginning to free themselves."[303] The change of consciousness left a profound imprint on the struggles of the 1970s, above all in the building of alternative radical cultures of the left that manifested toward the end of that decade.

Ghosts of Revolution

In contrast to those in the state socialist countries and the Western liberal democracies, protest movements in Europe's capitalist authoritarian

---

[296] Lumley, *States of Emergency*.   [297] Lumley, *States of Emergency*.
[298] Dominique Kirchner Reill, "Partisan Legacies and Anti-Imperialist Ambitions: The Little Red Book in Italy and Yugoslavia," in Cook, *Mao's Little Red Book*, 185–205, 187.
[299] Reill, "Partisan Legacies and Anti-Imperialist Ambitions," 190.
[300] Reill, "Partisan Legacies and Anti-Imperialist Ambitions," 189.
[301] Reill, "Partisan Legacies and Anti-Imperialist Ambitions," 188–192.
[302] Horn, "The Working Class Dimension of 1968," 101.
[303] *Lotta Continua*, 18 (November 1970), www.prole.info/texts/culturalrevolution.html.

zone – Spain, Portugal, and Greece (from 1967 to 1974) – exhibited a strong tendency in the direction of Old Left organizational models and sensibilities.[304] This is not to say that New Left ideas and counter-cultural habitus did not penetrate those countries; far from it – but they did not become dominant against the backdrop of unresolved national-political issues.[305] The same may be said, indeed, of Northern Ireland – where citizens' initiatives influenced by the American Civil Rights Movement were quickly overwritten by religious-sectarian conflict – and Turkey, where identification with traditional Marxist-Leninist poli-tics far outweighed attraction to lifestyle revolution.[306] In general, where Old Left models predominated, as the case of Greece demonstrates in particular, debates about the relative merit of countercultural and hard political approaches were highly pronounced.[307]

After the defeat of the left-wing forces in the Civil War of 1946–1949, Greece suffered under a persistent anti-Communist ascendency. At the beginning of the 1950s, the country continued as a parliamentary democ-racy and joined NATO, but the roots of its democracy were shallow. Greek politics in the 1950s and 1960s were dominated by an anti-Communist "deep state" that continued to prosecute the Civil War by other means, including especially trying to place limitations on the activ-ities of the domestic left. As late as the mid-1960s, leftists imprisoned in the earlier conflict languished in internment camps, elements within the army and the police enjoyed close ties to the extreme right, and the Communist Party (KKE) remained banned. Thoroughly Stalinized, that party had repeatedly sabotaged its prospects by slavish adherence to the Moscow line, first in 1944 when it failed to take over from defeated Axis forces a Greece promised by Stalin to the British zone of influence, and again in 1948 when it backed Stalin against Tito at precisely the moment in the Civil War when it most needed aid and solidarity from neighboring Yugoslavia. In 1968, the KKE condemned the French upris-ing in May and endorsed the crushing of the Prague Spring by the Soviets

---

[304] This point comes out clearly in the recent collection edited by Jian, et al., *The Routledge Handbook of the Global Sixties.*

[305] See Kostis Kornetis, "Spain and Greece," in Klimke and Scharloth, *1968 in Europe,* 253–266; Nikolaos Papadogiannis, *Militant around the Clock? Youth Politics, Leisure and Sexuality in Post-dictatorship Greece, 1974–1981* (New York: Berghahn, 2015).

[306] On the former, see Simon Prince, "The Global Revolt of 1968 and Northern Ireland," *The Historical Journal,* 49(3) (September 2006), 851–875; on the latter, see Kenan Behzat Sharpe, "A Mediterranean Sixties: Cultural Politics in Turkey, Greece, and Beyond," in Jian, et al., *The Routledge Handbook of the Global Sixties,* 168–179.

[307] The same was true in Brazil; see Christopher Dunn, "Mapping Tropicália," in Timothy S. Brown and Andrew Lison (eds.), *The Global Sixties in Sound and Vision: Media, Counterculture, Revolt* (New York: Palgrave Macmillan, 2014), 29–42.

in August, continuing the unsuccessful line of analysis it had engaged in since the Civil War.[308]

At the beginning of the 1950s, the defeated forces of the left were gathered together in the United Democratic Left (EDA), which remained the only legal left-wing party in Greece through the establishment of the dictatorship in 1967. Initially intended as a front for the banned KKE whose activists filled its ranks, the EDA developed into a relatively autonomous left coalition party that prepared the ground for the emergence of a Greek New Left. The left gained strength in the late 1950s, with the EDA emerging as the second-strongest party in the 1958 elections, after the conservative National Radical Union.

The growing hegemony of the anti-Communist deep state was symbolized in 1963 by the murder of the charismatic EDA parliamentary deputy Grigoris Lambrakis. A former resistance fighter and champion athlete, Lambrakis was a picture-perfect representative of the new sixties style of grassroots democratic socialist politics. He had ties to the Aldermaston march in the UK and was a member of the Greek branch of Bertrand Russell's Peace Movement, the "Youth League for Nuclear Disarmament Bertrand Russell," a group that organized annual peace marches from Marathon to Athens starting in 1963. The inaugural march was banned by the authorities, but Lambrakis marched the route solo, protected by his parliamentary immunity. In May 1963, shortly after giving a speech at an antiwar rally, Lambrakis was assassinated by a club-wielding assailant in full view of security forces, who did nothing to intervene.[309]

The assassination of Lambrakis caused a political crisis that saw the resignation of Prime Minister Konstantinos Karamanlis and an investigation that uncovered links between the extreme right and the police and army. Signaling how far the deep state in Greece was willing to go to restrain popular movements, the brazenness of the murder lit a fire under a growing surge of left-wing sentiment among the young. Half a million people attended a demonstration on the day of Lambrakis's funeral. The same month saw the founding of the Democratic Youth Lambrakis (Dimokratiki Neolaia Lambraki or DNL), which rapidly developed a mass membership.[310] The Lambrakides, as they were known,

---

[308] The crushing of the Prague Spring caused a split in the KKE into Stalinist and Euro-Communist factions.

[309] Z, directed by Costa-Gavras (1969). Lambrakis's life and death inspired the Vassilis Vassilikos novel Z, made into a Costa-Gavras film of the same name staring Yves Montand as Lambrakis.

[310] The DNL had a membership of 37,000 in April 1965, spread over 150 regional groups, and could mobilize up to 100,000; Papadogiannis, *Militant around the Clock?*, 33.

4.17 CND funeral procession for Grigoris Lambrakis (Associated Press).

represented the first real youth movement in Greece, their sense of mission captured in the name of their newspaper: *Our Generation.*[311]

Skeptical of the memory-political hegemony of an Old Left that remained prominent in Greece in the specter of the banned KKE and the lost Civil War, the Lambrakides embraced pacifism, environmentalism, and nuclear disarmament.[312] They were also known for street activism, being key participants in the so-called July Events of 1965 that are sometimes referred to as Greece's "early 1968."[313] The Lambrakides were cautiously open to popular and youth culture as a site of emancipatory potential, although they were still relatively conservative in their

---

[311] Kostis Kornetis, *Children of the Dictatorship: Student Resistance, Cultural Politics, and the "Long 1960s" in Greece* (New York: Berghahn, 2013), 30. The DNL was predated by the larger Panhellenic Organization of Youth (EPON), the youth wing of the National Liberation Front (EAM) during the Axis occupation, but EPON had ceased to exist by 1958.

[312] Kornetis, *Children of the Dictatorship*, 26.

[313] Kostis Kornetis, "Spain and Greece," 256.

gender politics.[314] The mid-1960s saw the development of an indigenous youth culture aligned on Western models, although this took place against a backdrop of relative traditionalism in Greek society.[315] Early on, a Greek version of the British "Teddy Boy" subculture became prominent, its members treated brutally by the police, with arrests and forced haircuts reminiscent of how nonconformist youth were treated in East Germany and elsewhere behind the Iron Curtain.[316]

Nevertheless, Greece could not resist the cultural tide from the West, experiencing "Beatlemania" and a growing rock music–based subculture with its own style and mores.[317] Although its attitude changed over time, the Greek left in the 1960s tended to reject rock music as a debased artifact of an "American way of life," which it saw as a vehicle of undifferentiated mass culture of dubious artistic and political merit. Instead, the left emphasized the importance of "Greek popular tradition" as a more fitting source of cultural material for the popular struggle.[318] Intellectuals close to the EDA did, however, explore the political possibilities of popular culture. The emergence of a politically engaged "New Greek Cinema" in the 1960s suggested one possible outlet for such ideas, as did the DNL's attempts to foster so-called artistic popular music. Cultural initiatives were fostered through DNL clubs that existed in both big cities and smaller rural towns. Protest songs associated with the American Civil Rights movement, such as those of Joan Baez and Bob Dylan, were also deemed politically acceptable. Rock music continued to be criticized as a debased site of unpolitical mass cooptation, but in practice it was embraced in the DNL milieu as a means of harnessing youth enthusiasm for antiwar and other political themes.

This change in attitude was an inevitable response to the power, demonstrated across all three Europes in the 1960s, of popular culture and the arts as a site for developing youth identity. In Greece, as elsewhere, film and music could stir emotions in a way that a political rally could not, especially when the films were rich in subversive energy. Showings of films like *Woodstock* (1970) and *Easy Rider* (1970) became the occasion for mini demonstrations, and in the longer term, provided templates for the elaboration of radical identity, not least in their presentation of new models of personal appearance with a left-wing valence. In short, however much the Greek left might wish to restrain processes of Americanization and the spread of undifferentiated and politically

---

[314] Kornetis, *Children of the Dictatorship*, 25.
[315] Kornetis, *Children of the Dictatorship*, 16–17.
[316] On forced haircuts in East Germany, see Brown, "1968 East and West," 86.
[317] Kornetis, *Children of the Dictatorship*, 18.
[318] Papadogiannis, *Militant around the Clock?*, 34.

unreliable forms of mass entertainment, the cultural wind blowing from the West hinted at the possibility of freedom in a way that was irresistible to youth and activists alike.

Youth-countercultural and radical-political streams could not fully merge in Greece in the way that they did elsewhere in the West, however, not only because of the retarding effect of persistent "Old Left" value systems in Greece but because of the foreclosure of open political engagement. The unwillingness of elites to allow any leftward movement was symbolized by the unconstitutional removal of the centrist premier Georgios Papandreou by King Constantine in July 1965. This elite chicanery led to mass protests – the so-called July Events – which temporarily paralyzed the country.[319] Less than two years later, the deep state that had murdered Lambrakis stepped in to try and decisively destroy the left. The dictatorship of "the Colonels," established in April 1967, saw an intensification of the war against the left in which thousands were imprisoned, tortured, or killed. Political parties were banned, the press controlled, and the military and government purged of anyone suspected of left-wing or liberal sympathies.[320] Miniskirts and the music of the Beatles were banned, signaling the regime's intention of reinforcing patriarchal and conservative values.[321] Thousands of leftists fled the country, contributing to a wide Greek diaspora in both Eastern and Western Europe. By the following year, most student leaders had been expelled from university, jailed, or exiled. Some young radicals formed clandestine resistance cells practicing occasional violence, but in general, youth activism became chilled in a fog of resignation.

Starting in 1970, the regime began attempting to soften its international image, fostering consumerism and tourism and mitigating its most draconian domestic policies. Censorship was dialed down and martial law lifted in most of the country. This development opened the way for an explosion of publishing activity. Already as early as 1968, small left-wing publishing houses had been active, publishing classics of Marxism-Leninism, the Frankfurt School, and Third World liberation. The suspension of preventive censorship in 1970 saw an acceleration of this process leading to the founding of some 150 new houses publishing left-wing titles, including Greek translations of the latest in New Left thought from Guevara, Debray, and Debord. Meanwhile, left-wing bookshops became gathering-points where students of differing socialist persuasions could read and hold discussions.[322]

---

[319] Kornetis, "Spain and Greece."   [320] Kornetis, *Children of the Dictatorship*, 10.
[321] Bob Potter, "Greek Tragedy: The Failure of the Left," Solidarity Pamphlet No. 29 (1968), 37.
[322] Kornetis, "Spain and Greece."

This left-wing reading culture emerged at a time when student unrest was beginning to pick up steam, and young activists begin to engage in more open forms of struggle. This new militancy was exemplified in February 1973, when students occupied the law school of the University of Athens in response to a law aimed at drafting left-wing students into the military. It broke out in even more violent fashion in November, when students occupied the Polytechnic School of Athens. Crushed by a violent military intervention that famously saw a tank crash through the gates of the Polytechnic, this occupation involving thousands of students signaled the beginning of the end for the dictatorship of the Colonels. Less than a year later, in July 1974, the regime fell and Greece began its transition to democracy, the so-called *Metapolitefsi*. The occupation of the Polytechnic, sometimes referred to as a "late 1968," subsequently became central to the politics of memory around the Greek role in the uprisings of the global 1960s.[323]

The situation in Spain was similar to that in Greece in the sense that the regime in place in the 1960s was the product of a life-or-death struggle between left and right in which the latter had emerged victorious and which based the early period of its rule on executions and concentration camps while presiding over an ongoing repression of left alternatives and popular struggles. Under Franco, unlike in Greece prior to 1967, parliamentary democracy was suspended, but in other respects the situation of the left in the two countries was not dissimilar. In the 1960s, working-class and student struggle bubbled up underneath the surface of the Franco dictatorship in place since the end of the Civil War of 1936–1939. Despite the mass executions of leftists that accompanied Franco's victory in the war in 1939, the dictator faced an ongoing postwar insurgency that was not defeated until the early 1960s. The Asturian miners celebrated by the Situationists for their prowess with dynamite never ceased to go on strike even during the worst days of the repression, with the Asturian general strike of 1962 a notable instance in their continued militancy.[324]

New clandestine anarchist groups like the Spanish Libertarian Movement (MLE) and the Iberian Federation of Libertarian Youth (FIJL), with its armed wing, the "1st May Group," continued to defy Franco with a campaign of bombings.[325] Meanwhile, the outlawed Spanish Communist Party (PCE) strengthened its position through its

---

[323] Kornetis, "Spain and Greece," 263.
[324] Horn, "The Working Class Dimension of 1968," 96.
[325] There were also occasional guerrilla actions by student Maoist groups; Paul Harrison and Ian H. Birchall, "Spain: The Prospects," *International Socialism* (1st series), 88 (May 1976), 25–29.

clandestine networks. Marginal in support during the time of the Civil War, when it had backed the worst abuses of Stalinism, the party remained active as a clandestine force under Franco and gained support that had previously belonged to the Socialist Party and the anarcho-syndicalist CNT. The PCE broke with Moscow over the crushing of the Prague Spring, moreover, becoming an advocate of broad front reform, and emerged as an important force both in student mobilization and in labor militancy.[326]

As elsewhere in Europe during the 1960s, Spain saw a dramatic increase in the numbers of university students. Dissent increased accordingly, as students too young to remember the chilling effect of the Civil War chafed against the conservatism of the official student union SEU (Sindicato Español Universitario) and became increasingly militant in pressing for their rights of free expression and political participation. Unrest at the University of Madrid broke out as early as February 1956.[327] By the mid-1960s, the Spanish universities faced "an explosive situation," in part because of rising knowledge of youth unrest elsewhere in Europe and the world.[328] The second half of the 1960s saw an increasing radicalization of Spanish students, involving strikes, occupations, and invasions of public space.[329] Opposition to the Vietnam War was a staple issue, as was opposition to America's support for the Franco regime. Particularly violent clashes took place in the spring of 1968. As in Greece, a relaxation of censorship laws precipitated an explosion of left-wing publishing in Spain that introduced students to the Marxist classics alongside the output of the international student rebellion.[330] From the end of 1968, in parallel with the development of this left-wing reading public, the movement in Spain began to self-consciously radicalize and internationalize itself, "boycotting exams, proclaiming communes, paying homage to Che Guevara, occupying the dean's office, and smashing Franco's portraits on university premises."[331]

In contrast to Greece, and unsurprisingly given Spain's strong tradition of anarcho-syndicalism, trade unionism remained lively. In the postwar period, the vestigial fascism of the Falange Party had increasingly been sidelined in favor of the Catholic sect Opus Dei, which sought to enact economic reforms that would strengthen the position of the regime. One of these was the Collective Bargaining Law of 1958, which was meant displace responsibility for labor disputes from the government onto

---

[326] Jean Monds, "Syndicalism and Revolution in Spain: The Workers' Commissions," *Radical America*, 9(2) (March/April 1975), 52.
[327] Kornetis, "Spain and Greece," 254.   [328] Kornetis, "Spain and Greece."
[329] Kornetis, "Spain and Greece."   [330] Kornetis, "Spain and Greece."
[331] Kornetis, "Spain and Greece."

business owners. In theory, this would tie workers more closely to their employers, but in practice, it rejuvenated trade unionism in Spain in the form of the so-called Workers' Commissions (Comisiones Obreras).[332] Strong in Barcelona, Madrid, and the Basque country, the commissions became a key vehicle of industrial militancy through the early 1970s.[333]

The economic crisis of the late 1960s saw an intensification of struggles involving the Workers' Commissions. These came to an initial head in October 1967 with a day of mass protest against economic hardship and in favor of greater political freedom that saw workers battle the police in the streets.[334] This activity prompted a crackdown on the Workers' Commissions, and the period from November 1968 to February 1969 saw the arrests of thousands of working-class militants.[335] But from the end of 1967 onward, the struggles of workers took on a more and more explicitly political character, which continued through the process of democratic transition following Franco's death in 1975.[336]

The previous year saw an even more explosive rebellion in neighboring Portugal, which, like both Spain and Greece, had suffered under a prolonged right-wing ascendency that circumscribed the possibilities of left-wing politics. For over half a century, Portugal was ruled under the corporatist-authoritarian "New State" (Estado Novo), first under António de Oliveira Salazar (1932–1968) and then under Marcelo Caetano (1968–1974). Like the KKE in Greece, the Portuguese Communist Party was Stalinist in orientation, rejecting the "Eurocommunism" of the Italian and Spanish Communist parties.[337] Portugal was Europe's last major colonial power, and the anticolonial uprisings in Africa played a major role in growing student discontent, not least because of the threat of conscription to fight in brutal anticolonial wars in Angola, Mozambique, and Guinea-Bissau.[338] The colonial war drained the treasury, while the threat of conscription, in Guya Accornero's words, "hung like a sword of Damocles over young Portuguese men of all social classes."[339] Begun in 1961, the war was absorbing almost 50 percent of the state budget by 1970. "By the early

---

[332] Harrison and Birchall, "Spain: The Prospects." On the Workers' Commissions, see also Horn, "The Working Class Dimension of 1968," 95.

[333] Harman, *The Fire Last Time*, 330.

[334] Gerd-Rainer Horn, "The Changing Nature of the European Working Class: The Rise and Fall of the 'New Working Class' (France, Italy, Spain, Czechoslovakia)," in Fink, Gassert, and Junker, *1968*, 351–371, 356.

[335] Monds, "Syndicalism and Revolution in Spain."

[336] Horn, "The Working Class Dimension of 1968," 98.

[337] Harman, *The Fire Last Time*, 280–281.   [338] Harman, *The Fire Last Time*.

[339] Guya Accornero, "The Revolution before the Revolution: Student Protest and Political Process at the End of the Portuguese dictatorship," in Jian, et al., *The Routledge Handbook of the Global Sixties*, 305–323.

1970s," Nancy Bermeo observes, "it was rare to find a Portuguese family who did not have someone fighting in Africa."[340] From 1969, the draft was used as a weapon against left-wing students, who were threatened with conscription on the basis of "conduct." For the left, the draft became a vehicle for the subversion of the military from the inside.[341]

Resistance to the draft was one cause of a broader youth insurgency that saw students demand university reforms and clash with the police. Student unrest had existed in Portugal from the mid-1950s, and it began to be regarded as a serious threat by the regime by the mid-1960s. An early crisis occurred in May 1962 when protesting students carried out a hunger strike. The failure of the Communist Party to foreground the issue of the colonial war was one reason for its eclipse in the affections of student activists, especially Maoists, who increasingly came to foreground the role of the African liberation movements as the vanguard of the revolution.[342] In this context, the Vietnam War took on a dual valence as an imperial war that should be resisted on its own terms and as a symbol of the wars that Portugal was involved in but should not be. A major protest against the Vietnam War in Lisbon in February 1968 became a key moment in the politicization of Portuguese students. It led to the founding of Maoist-oriented New Left groups – above all, the Movement for the Reorganization of the Party of the Proletariat (MRPP) – that represented the desire of students to break once and for all with the Portuguese Communist Party (PCP). Alongside a number of other newly founded Maoist groups, the MRPP subsequently became a major force in campus mobilizations in Portugal.

The New State was overthrown in April 1974 by an opposition movement within the army, the Armed Forces Movement. This "carnation revolution" – so named because of scenes of citizens giving flowers to soldiers – represented less an end than a radical new beginning.[343] Even though it was enacted by the army, the coup drew on very significant popular support and was accompanied by a wave of strikes which saw 100,000 workers out on May Day 1975.[344] The coup initiated the so-called Ongoing Revolutionary Process (PREC), a period of intense mobilization that saw young leftists expand the boundaries of the political, linking up with the poor in the city and the countryside, engaging in house

---

[340] Nancy Bermeo, "War and Democratization: Lessons from the Portuguese Experience," *Democratization*, 14(3) (2007), 388–406, 391.

[341] Accornero, "The Revolution before the Revolution."

[342] Accornero, "The Revolution before the Revolution."

[343] See this invaluable oral history: Raquel Varela, *A People's History of the Portuguese Revolution* (London: Pluto, 2018).

[344] Harman, *The Fire Last Time*, 278.

occupations, and other social-revolutionary actions outside the university campus.

From April 1974 to November 1975, Portugal saw an antiauthoritarian explosion that far outstripped its initial character as a revolt of the armed forces against the dictatorship.[345] The task of clearing away the vestiges of the dictatorship gave the impulse toward participatory democracy a special charge in Portugal, a country where "the anti-hierarchical radiance of strike committees and similar organs of popular power was even more profound and all-pervasive than in Italy or France."[346] Rank-and-file democracy extended from the factory to the neighborhood, creating networks of popular self-management "evoking faint echoes of the institutions of dual power in the Russian and Catalan Revolutions [of 1917 and 1936, respectively]."[347] The force of revolution was blunted at the end of 1975 with the ascendency of the conservative faction in the Armed Forces Movement. But during the revolution's high point in 1974–1975, the left in Portugal may be rightly seen as the most powerful in Europe in the postwar period.[348]

The Politics of Truth

We have seen that 1968 in all three Europes was characterized by impulses toward workers' self-management and participatory democracy, inflected by the attempt to come to grips with the classical dilemmas of revolutionary organization and identity. In every case, an emphasis on *truth* grew directly out the experiences of cognitive dissonance that helped generate the various movements in the first place. That cognitive dissonance was intensified by the blatantly false way in which protest movements were portrayed in the media. On both sides of the Iron Curtain, activists saw their motives questioned and their actions misrepresented. In West Germany, relatively clean-cut students were "Gammler" (Beatniks), "Polit-Gammler," "academic Gammler," or "Red Guards."[349] It Italy, they were the "filochinesi," ("China-lovers"), a term that "conjured up the red menace and the yellow peril all in one."[350] In Poland, they were "spoiled brats;" in Yugoslavia, privileged self-seekers. Such labeling was always closely linked with attempts to place the offending students into the camp of the Cold War enemy. In this way, support for local status quos doubled as Cold War

---

[345] Horn, "The Working Class Dimension of 1968," 112.
[346] Horn, "The Working Class Dimension of 1968."
[347] Horn, "The Working Class Dimension of 1968."
[348] Horn, "The Working Class Dimension of 1968."
[349] Brown, *West Germany and the Global Sixties*, 68.
[350] Lumley, *States of Emergency*, 73.

border-policing. Whatever the system, the smear tactics were similar. "What surprised me," recalls the Polish dissident Adam Michnik in a conversation with Daniel Cohn-Bendit, "was the tone that the Polish press used to write about May '68 in France. It was the tone that they used to write about us."[351]

To be sure, mainstream reporting in the West could sometimes be more nuanced, as Stuart Hilwig and others have shown.[352] But it is not for nothing that protests against false press reports became a staple of the revolt in Poland and West Germany, France and Czechoslovakia, Italy and Greece, Yugoslavia and the UK. In every country, dictatorial media power, either of the state or privately owned variety, was understood by activists as an impediment to rational debate about solutions to society's problems.[353] Coming to grips with the power of mass media to deform consciousness and prevent informed debate was a necessity in societies where the channels of social meaning were monopolized by elites hostile to change. And this coming to grips meant not only movements criticizing official lies but those presenting their own truths through independent channels of dissemination.

In Eastern Europe, police-state censorship made the battle lines especially clear. It is no accident that in the Prague Spring, it was the elimination of censorship that allowed the revolt to develop so swiftly and the failure to control the media that was one of the biggest mistakes of the old regime.[354] As the Situationists noted, counterinformation was the most important, and from the perspective of the authorities most dangerous, weapon at the disposal of the insurgents. "The first reflex of the people of Prague," they wrote, " . . . was to defend not the Palace of the Republic, but the radio station, which was considered the symbol of their main conquest: truth of information against organized falsehood." In this way the rebels yielded "what had been the nightmare of all the Warsaw Pact bureaucracies – the press and the radio."[355]

Official media strategies went far beyond mere censorship but aimed at smearing the reputation of dissenters in the eyes of their fellow citizens. In Poland, as noted earlier, student protestors were depicted as "spoiled brats" cut off from the interests of workers and peasants. In Yugoslavia, similarly, state media depicted students' demands as ones of narrow self-interest. Reform was not to be for the greater good but for greater privileges. This

---

[351] Adam Michnik, *Letters from Freedom: Post–Cold War Realities and Perspectives* (Berkeley: University of California Press, 1998), 46.
[352] Hilwig, *Italy and 1968.*   [353] Garsztecki, "Poland," 183.
[354] Jan Pauer, "Czechoslovakia," in Klimke and Scharloth, *1968 in Europe*, 163–177, 174.
[355] "Reform and Counterreform in the Bureaucratic Bloc," *Internationale Situationniste*, 12 (1969).

problem was expressed openly in the banned June 4 issue of *Student*, which claimed: "The press has once again succeeded in distorting the events at the University, [claiming that] students are fighting to improve their own material conditions. Yet everyone who took part in the meetings and demonstrations knows very well that the students were already turned in another direction – toward a struggle which encompasses the general interests of our society, above all a struggle for the interests of the working class."[356] The press failed to "quote a single speaker who talked about unjustified social differences," complained the article, and "omitted the main slogans called out during the meetings and demonstrations: For the Unity of Workers and Students, Students with Workers, and similar slogans which expressed a single idea and a single feeling: that the roads and interests of students are inseparable from those of the working class."[357]

As in Poland, authorities in Yugoslavia succeeded in driving a wedge between students and workers, portraying the former to the latter as spoiled brats, and spread brazen lies accusing the students of practicing violence against the state militia instead of the other way around. As an article in *Student* put it: "According to what is written and said, it turns out that it was the students who used force on the National Militia, that they blocked militia stations and surrounded them. Everything which has characterized the student movement from the beginning, in the city and in the university buildings, the order and self-control, is described with the old word: violence."[358]

A similar claim was made against student protestors in the Western democracies, where mainstream media served to police Cold War boundaries in both political conviction and cultural behavior. In Italy and West Germany, press coverage of the revolts was mostly negative and one-sided; student protestors were branded not only spoiled brats but "left wing fascists."[359] Newspapers like the Fiat-owned *La Stampa* and the right-wing *Corriere della Sera* in Italy and the papers of the Springer Press in West Germany were fiercely anti-Communist, uncritically supported the American war in Vietnam, and placed critical voices automatically in the camp of the Cold War enemy.[360] In Italy,

---

[356] *Student* (June 4, 1968), 1, quoted in Perlman, *Birth of a Revolutionary Movement in Yugoslavia.*

[357] *Student* (June 4, 1968), 1, quoted in Perlman, *Birth of a Revolutionary Movement in Yugoslavia.*

[358] *Student* (June 4, 1968), 1, quoted in Perlman, *Birth of a Revolutionary Movement in Yugoslavia.*

[359] Hilwig, "Constructing a Media Image of the Sessantotto: The Framing of the Italian Protest Movement in 1968," in Fahlenbrach, et al., *Media and Revolt*, 114–115.

[360] The Springer Press owned 67 percent of West Berlin's daily newspapers; see Nick Thomas, *Protest Movements in 1960s West Germany: A Social History of Dissent and Democracy* (Oxford: Berg, 2003), 165.

mass media framed student protest in ways designed to limit damage to the existing order.[361] These strategies – trivialization, polarization, marginalization, disparagement, delegitimization – sought to portray protesters "as either figures of ridicule or dangerous threats to public order and morality."[362] The Springer Press in West Germany behaved similarly, falsifying the viewpoints of the New Left and caricaturing student protestors as club-wielding biker-barbarians threatening the life and limb of ordinary citizens.[363]

One of the biggest goals of the movements in the two countries, correspondingly, became to combat the lies of the mainstream media. This was done in part through protest actions and alliance-building. In West Germany, an "expropriate Springer" campaign was launched by the student organization SDS, with significant participation from trade unions, critical intellectuals, and others worried about the state of West German democracy. The term "expropriate" in the title of the campaign signaled the Marxist inclinations of student activists, but more broadly, it suggested the idea that control of information should not be a private affair but a public good. The Springer Press, the campaign argued, turned "the fundamental right of freedom of information and opinion" into a matter of private profit, manipulating opinion and thereby diminishing citizens' abilities to make informed political judgment.[364] The dangers of press disinformation were crystalized for activists by the assassination attempt against Rudi Dutschke in April 1968, which followed months of demonization in the press. Activists hurled Molotov cocktails against newspaper delivery vans, and Italian militants acting in solidarity conducted a "picket against *disinformazione*" of the *Corriere della Sera* and a bomb attack against the offices of the Springer Press.[365]

A second important goal involved attempts to develop a sphere of counter-knowledge rooted in various forms of underground media. The "expropriate Springer" campaign was explicitly conceived in terms of establishing a "counter–public sphere" (*Gegenöffentlichkeit*) that would make it possible to distinguish *authentic* communication from communication corrupted by official lies, providing a space for alternatives to Establishment untruth. In France, as we have seen, the work of the Atelier Populaire was explicitly grounded in the same needs. In Italy, activists

---

[361] See the discussion in Hilwig, *Italy and 1968*.

[362] Hilwig, "Constructing a Media Image of the Sessantotto," 109.

[363] Brown, *West Germany and the Global Sixties*, 218.

[364] Elmar Altvater, Bernhard Blanke, Rudi Dutschke, Hans-Jürgen Krahl, and Helmut Schauer, "Die demokratische Öffentlichkeit ist zerstört," in Bernd Kramer (ed.), *Gefundene Fragmente, 1967–1980* (Berlin: Karin Kramer, 2004), vol. 1, 63–66.

[365] Lumley, *States of Emergency*.

developed the idea of "counterinformation" (*controinformazione*) to contend with the bourgeois media's *disinformazione*.[366] In all three countries, as elsewhere in Europe, this goal was pursued through means ranging from leaflets and graffiti to underground newspapers and alternative books and journals disseminated through newly founded left-wing publishing houses, bookstores, and distribution networks.[367] Developing alternative sources of information became central in both countries to the development of long-lasting left-alternative cultures in the 1970s.

The UK was a particularly important site for the new politics of truth. Relatively quiescent in 1968 when compared to continental hotspot countries like France, West Germany, and Italy, the UK nevertheless saw its own significant variant of the international New Left. There was substantial cross-fertilization with student movements in the United States and continental Europe, with Americans in London founding the anti–Vietnam War "Stop It Committee" (originally called "Americans against American Aggression"). Strikes and sit-ins took place at the universities of Essex, Hull, Leicester, Warwick, and Birmingham, as well as at the Hornsey Art College in London.[368] The Socialist Society at the London School of Economics made the LSE a major site of radicalism, exemplified by the occupation in March 1967. An anti–Vietnam War demonstration of March 17, 1968 saw 10,000–20,000 participants march on the American Embassy in Grosvenor Square, with many arrests and injuries.[369]

The International Marxist Group (IMG) and the International Socialists (IS), in connection with the Vietnam Solidarity Campaign, were active in trying to strengthen and ideologically codify the rebellion. A Revolutionary Socialist Student Federation, organized by editors of the *New Left Review*, was explicitly modeled on the West German SDS.[370] Black immigrants were organized in the Campaign Against Racial Discrimination (CARD), and Stokely Carmichael's visit to the UK in 1967 inspired the Universal Coloured People's Association (UCPA).[371] Meanwhile, the "London underground," a loose scene of persons, publications, shops, clubs, bands, and independent initiatives of all sorts, became a site of psychedelic ferment at once personal and political,

---

[366] Lumley, *States of Emergency*, 120–123, 139, note 3.
[367] On alternative media and the arts, see the essays in Brown and Lison, *The Global Sixties in Sound and Vision*.
[368] Madeleine Davis, "The Origins of the British New Left," in Klimke and Scharloth, *1968 in Europe*, 44–56, 53–54.
[369] Holger Nehring, "Great Britain," in Klimke and Scharloth, *1968 in Europe*, 130.
[370] Celia Hughes, *Young Lives on the Left: Sixties Activism and the Liberation of the Self* (Manchester: Manchester University Press, 2015), 133.
[371] Nehring, "Great Britain," 127–128.

a cultural revolution in which new ways of understanding and being were elevated to the forefront of radical praxis.

Percolating with themes that would characterize the radical afterlives of the 1970s, the underground was notable in particular for its role in propagating the politics of truth central to 1968. A striking early example of this politics, one in which diverse elements of the sixties cultural-political revolution converged and coalesced, was the July 1967 "Dialectics of Liberation" congress in London. Organized by the American "antipsychiatrist" Joseph Berke, the congress billed itself as "a unique gathering to demystify human violence in all its forms, the social systems from which it emanates, and to explore new forms of action."[372] The congress brought together a who's who of the international counterculture and New Left. "The Provos were there from Amsterdam," remembered Berke's friend Susan Sherman. "There were students from West Berlin, political activists from Norway and Sweden as well as a large contingent from the New Experimental College, Thy, Denmark. There were representatives from the West Indies, Africa, France, Canada, America, Holland, India, Nigeria and Cuba."[373] The congress featured speakers ranging from Herbert Marcuse to Allen Ginsberg, from the antipsychiatrist R. D. Laing to the Living Theater's Julian Beck, from the American anarchist philosopher Paul Goodman to the African American firebrand Stokely Carmichael. The congress even had its own Happening, led by the American artist Carolee Schneemann. LSD, still legal in the UK at the time, flowed freely.[374]

Deploying wide-ranging expertise in search of a "clarification" of the current condition of society, the Dialectics of Liberation congress drew on a longstanding left-wing commitment to critical inquiry and self-education.[375] It is no surprise, indeed, that leading figures in the British New Left such as E. P. Thompson and Raymond Williams were heavily involved in adult education, and this impulse toward self-education dovetailed with a characteristic feature of 1960s radicalism: the will not only to challenge official expertise but to posit counter-expertise.

---

[372] Dialectics of Liberation, *Dialectics Introduction*, www.dialecticsofliberation.com/1967-dialectics/dialectics-introduction. Berke's London Institute of Phenomenological Studies was actually little more than a working group including Berke, R. D. Laing, David Cooper, and Leon Radler. Joseph Berke, interview with the author, March 26, 2017. For the best account of the conference, see Joseph Berke, *Counterculture* (London: Peter Own, 1969). See also the account in Jonathon Green, *Days in the Life: Voices from the English Underground 1961–1971* (London: Minerva, 1988), 238–239.

[373] Dialectics of Liberation, *Dialectics Introduction*.

[374] Dialectics of Liberation, *Dialectics Introduction*.

[375] "Antiuniversity of London Manifesto," in Peter Stansill and David Zane Mairowitz, *By Any Means Necessary (BAMN: Outlaw Manifestos and Ephemera, 1965–1970* (New York: Autonomedia, 1999), 83.

Marshaling the latest scientific knowledge and mobilizing the most progressive thinkers, the New Left sought to build upon and extend Enlightenment values of free inquiry and intellectual antiauthoritarianism. This impulse both reflected and helped to produce the popularity in the 1960s of psychoanalysis and sociology, alongside the creation of "critical" or "anti"-initiatives – antipsychiatry, antiuniversities, critical universities, and so on – that sprouted like mushrooms in the antiauthoritarian soil of the 1960s.

Joseph Berke had been active in the free universities movement in the United States and was also strongly attracted to the Scotsman Alexander Trocchi's concept of a "spontaneous university."[376] A direct outcome of the Dialectics congress was the founding the following year of the Antiuniversity of London. This project unfolded in parallel with various alternative-educational experiments in the United States and the so-called Critical Universities in the Netherlands and West Germany, as well as with initiatives connected to Trocchi's Project Sigma. Offering "Music, Art, Poetry, Black Power, Madness, Revolution,"[377] the Antiuniversity was to be a home to global radicalism, bringing together "original and radical artists, activists, and intellectuals of London as well as Europe, America and the Third World."[378] If in practice the Antiuniversity suffered from all the problems inherent to the project of psychedelic self-liberation, its founding nevertheless perfectly represented the antiauthoritarian pedagogical impulse central to 1968.[379]

An underlying tension in the Dialectics congress derived from its position at the intersection of differing conceptions of what "revolution" entailed. The most basic division was between what Berke called the "culture wizards" and the "politicos" – that is, between those who believed in the power of free underground culture to change human consciousness and thereby society, and those who held that explicit political struggle, perhaps even including violence, was required. Writing a couple of years after the Dialectics congress, Berke defended his conception against critics on the left who insisted on the primacy of the working class in the political struggle.

[376] Berke was involved in the Free University of New York (FUNY), which, as early as 1965, was offering courses on topics such as "Theory and Practice of Radical Social Movements," "Marxist Approaches to the Avant Garde Arts," "The Search for Authentic Sexual Experience," and Anarchistic and Synergetic Politics"; *Peace News* (October 1965), 6.

[377] "Antiuniversity of London," document collection published by Mayday Rooms archive.

[378] "Antiuniversity of London Manifesto," 87.

[379] "[T]he anti-university got off to an anti-start," wrote a sympathetic contemporary. "Within an hour the room, jammed with poets, painters, sculptors, publishers, novelists, psychoanalysts, sociologists, and just people, was a howling underground cell of clashing ideologies and aims"; Harold Norse, "Free University of Love" (February 16–29, 1968), 6, in "Antiuniversity of London."

"For the middle class," he wrote, "political confrontation and struggle is primarily CULTURAL, because political power over the middle class is exercised through cultural channels. To rip aside the façade of bourgeois institutions is to expose them for what they have become, what they are now – mechanisms for social control and manipulation."[380] Berke insisted that culture – understood as the realm of the production and dissemination of consciousness – was to be the "battleground" on which the war for the future of society would be waged.[381]

There was strong disagreement about this assertion, as we will see in Chapter 5. But it is also true that the boundaries between the hard political and the countercultural were more fluid than Berke's scheme suggested.[382] Celia Hughes has emphasized this point in connection the Socialist Society at the LSE, which, in her words, became "a haven of activist sociability" in which IS militants mingled freely with students engaged in lifestyle experimentation. The convergence was expressed especially in knowledge-political initiatives that included "radical theater, art and information groups: CAST, Agitprop Information, Agitprop Street Players and Poster Workshop ... drawing upon political and cultural traditions from Russian agitprop, the San Francisco Mime Troup theater and rock n' roll to the Parisian Atelier Populaire and surrealist ideas circulating in the art schools."[383] The cultural theorist and memoirist Phil Cohen has made a similar point, noting that differences between political activists and counterculturalists, although expressed strongly on paper, were less pronounced in person, where protagonists occupied the same spaces and habitus.[384]

Nevertheless, Berke was not wrong to assert the existence of fundamental disagreements about the nature of the revolutionary project. The easy assumptions that fueled the high moment of 1960s optimism in which the Dialectics congress took place – about the community of interests between Marxist revolutionaries and psychedelic gurus, between black people and white people, between men and women – would be difficult to sustain once the synergizing spell of the "year of the barricades" was broken.[385] Then, as we will see in Chapter 5, the path forward would become at once more clear and more unclear than ever before. Herbert Marcuse warned of the danger in his speech at the Dialectics

---

[380] Joseph Berke, "The creation of an Alternative Society," in Joseph Berke (ed.), *Counterculture* (London: Peter Own, 1969).
[381] Berke, "The Creation of an Alternative Society."
[382] Hughes, *Young Lives on the Left*, 133.   [383] Hughes, *Young Lives on the Left*.
[384] Interview with the author, January 23, 2019.
[385] David Caute, *The Year of the Barricades: A Journey Through 1968* (New York: Harper & Row, 1988).

congress. "I am very happy to see so many flowers here," he said, "and that is why I want to remind you that flowers, by themselves, have no power whatsoever, other than the power of men and women who protect them and take care of them against aggression and destruction."[386] It might be true, as Marcuse asserted, that the counterculture's "refusal to play the rules of a rigid game," along with its rejection of aggression-producing "puritan morality," were inherently political, but Marcuse recognized, as did many others on the left, that alternative lifestyles and the impulse toward sharpened analysis and truth-telling in which they were enfolded had a limited power to produce change in the world.[387] After 1968, militants who sought to bring about a classical Marxist revolution involving the industrial working class would come up hard against the ideological divisions that made common action so difficult, and activists who rejected hard political militancy in favor of a liberation of consciousness won through grassroots cultural production would learn that evolution could be almost as difficult as revolution.

---

[386] Herbert Marcuse, "Liberation from the Affluent Society" (1967 lecture in London), in David Cooper (ed.), *The Dialectics of Liberation* (Harmondsworth: Penguin, 1968), 175–192, www.marcuse.org/herbert/pubs/60spubs/67dialecticlib/67LibFromAfflSocie ty.htm.

[387] Marcuse, "Liberation from the Affluent Society."

"All self-respecting publishers are falling over themselves to cash in on the events of May," wrote Daniel Cohn-Bendit and his brother Gabriel in the introduction to *Obsolete Communism*; "all they want is something they can sell – a revolutionary gadget with marketable qualities."[1] As we have seen, the publication of the book was a striking example of the self-analysis and self-historicization that characterized the 1968 revolt. With its fierce criticism of historical Bolshevism and its modern defenders like the French Communist Party, it was at the same time a high-profile salvo in the war between differing conceptions of the revolutionary project that characterized 1968. But it was also, as the Cohn-Bendits observed, part of the process by which mainstream culture got its hands on the revolt and marketed it back to the rebels. As such, it was already part of a post-1968 moment in which radicals faced the task not only of how to keep the rebellion alive but of how to fight the battle over what it meant.

If the twin poles of Paris and Prague had inspired the radical imagination, the aftermath of the events in France and Czechoslovakia exposed the limitations of radical activism. For left-wing radicals across Europe, the year 1968 served as a wakeup call. In the spring of 1968, radicals across Europe and beyond could dream of creating "French conditions" in their respective countries, en route to creating a bloc-spanning socialism with a face that was truly human.[2] The failure of these turning points to turn, the dashed hopes and the repression that followed in their wakes, prompted radicals to make hard-eyed reassessments of the utopian optimism and revolutionary expectations that had swelled throughout the 1960s. The decline of the French May events was heavily debated in Turin, for example, where activists diagnosed the shortcomings of spontaneous activism and sought ways to strengthen the structural integrity of

---

[1] Daniel Cohn-Bendit and Gabriel Cohn-Bendit, *Obsolete Communism: The Left-Wing Alternative* (London: AK, 2000), 13.

[2] Hans Magnus Enzensberger, in Bernhard Pollmann (ed.), *Lesebuch zur deutschen Geschichte*, vol. 3, *Vom deutschen Reich bis zur Gegenwart* (Dortmund: Chronik, 1984), 253–254.

the radical left in order to increase the staying power of its actions.[3] This impulse was mirrored in the so-called "organization debate" in West Germany, where the twin failures of the campaigns against the Emergency Laws and the Springer Press produced a sense of stagnation and decline that could only be overcome by rethinking approaches to radical politics.

It was by no means merely the outcome of Prague and Paris that prompted these reassessments, however, but the inherent difficulties of radical action more generally. Uncertainty about the proper goals of such action – and the all-too-frequent failure to achieve such goals as were agreed upon – was exacerbated by a more fundamental problem: that alongside the failure to achieve the revolution lay a worrisome inability to reach agreement about what the revolution in fact *was*. Even before 1968, and especially afterward, radicals had to grapple with the hard truth that what appeared to be an unstoppable revolutionary convergence was in fact a loosely cobbled-together set of shifting alliances lacking any easily agreed-upon programs or goals. The task thus became one of deciding how to go forward in a situation in which there were no rules and few certainties. Increasingly, this task involved attempts to distinguish between different approaches to radical activism, one of the key themes of the Cohn-Bendits' book.

Here, activists did not invent problems and dilemmas out of whole cloth or face entirely new ones, as we have seen; rather, they strove to come to grips with the classical problems of the modern revolutionary era: who was to make the revolution? Who was it to benefit? What were the means to be, and to what ends? Was the revolution to be the work of artists and avant-garde cultural troublemakers? Or of serious-minded students allied with trade unions and an older generation of intellectuals? Or of pop-culture-oriented youth consumers? Would society be transformed by revitalized Marxist-Leninist vanguard parties? For activists in the West, would the revolution be allied with or opposed to Eastern Communist orthodoxies? And was it to be fundamentally a revolution of the people or a revolution of the self, or of both simultaneously?

R/Evolutionary Subjects

The uniformity of the different national responses to this impasse is striking. On both sides of the Cold War divide, activists chose between a set of options seemingly inherent in the radical project: (a) a will to organization

---

[3] Jan Kurz and Marica Tolomelli, "Italy," in Martin Klimke and Joachim Scharloth (eds.), *1968 in Europe: A History of Protest and Activism, 1956–1977* (London: Palgrave Macmillan, 2008), 92.

in the Marxist-Leninist sense, linked to attempts to connect with the working class; (b) a rejection of rigid cadre-party models in favor of radical grassroots democracy and anarchist direct action; (c) a focus on local activism aimed at contesting the conditions of daily life, sometimes involving attempts to connect with working-class immigrant populations; (d) a dropping out of both society and left-wing activism into a politics of countercultural lifestyle in either urban or rural environments; (e) a move away from "revolution" as a rigid model in favor of an increased attention to personal subjectivity, as in both subcultures generally and in the nascent women's movement, which, in highlighting issues such as childcare and abortion rights, sought to reorient the radical conversation in the direction of the concerns of daily life; and (f) an embrace of armed struggle against the state as the only remaining option for those opposed to the system.[4]

These "radical options" represent trends or tendencies only; in practice, the different options often cut across each other, even if, in some instances, they were diametrically opposed. It was a natural, if not always fortunate, response to this perceived impasse to attempt to impose order on the chaos, either through greater organization, through increased ideological rigidity, or by becoming more firmly rooted in constituencies perceived to be more authentically revolutionary. Across Western and Central Europe, the post-1968 moment saw a turn away from utopian optimism in the direction of stock-taking, reassessment, and the founding of new organizational initiatives.

A major feature of this reorientation was a "back to basics" return to Leninist cadre politics, heavily leavened with Maoism. The embrace of Marxism-Leninism enabled activists to sidestep the dubious record of Soviet Communism – irrevocably tarnished for all but the most diehard Communists by the Soviet crushing of the Prague Spring – by reference to the earliest configuration of Bolshevism and its particular interpretation of Marxism. Maoism, meanwhile, presented an "antiauthoritarian" alternative to bureaucratic communism of the Soviet variety, providing an ideological and psychological framework for all sorts of radical grassroots initiatives. Marxist-Leninist and/or Trotskyist and/or Maoist cadre groups included the Communist League (Ligue Communiste) in France, the Student Movement (Movimento Studentesco or MS) in Italy, the Movement for the Reorganization of the Party of the Proletariat (Movimento Reorganizativo do Partido do Proletariado or MRPP) in Portugal, Rigas in Greece, the Communist Party of Germany-Marxist-Leninist (KPD-ML) in

---

[4] For France, see the detailed discussion in Julian Bourg, *From Revolution to Ethics: May 1968 and Contemporary French Thought* (Montreal: McGill-Queen's University Press, 2007), 179–186.

West Germany, and the International Socialists in the UK. If these foundings represented one prominent solution to the question of how to "make
the revolution" after the high-water mark of 1968, it is important to recognize that Communist cadre politics were not just a post-1968 phenomenon;
rather, the potential for different types of left politics – Communist, anarchist, lifestyle – were present from the beginning in every situation, even if
existing tensions were exacerbated in the post-1968 moment.

The question of vanguardism was intimately bound up with the question
of the revolutionary subject. After the high-water mark of 1968, radicals once
again came face to face with another of the classical revolutionary problems –
the need for largely middle-class radicals to connect with the broader
working-class population. If, for the Russian Narodniks of late-Tsarist
Russia who "went to the people," this meant largely the peasantry, for
twentieth-century leftists it meant connecting with the working class, defined
primarily as the industrial proletariat, but also including the poor, the marginal, and in some cases immigrant worker communities. This was in turn
connected to a shift in emphasis away from university campuses as the key
site of struggle to the street and the factory. Notable in West Germany and
the UK, this shift was especially prominent in Italy and Portugal.[5]

The influence of Italian groups like Lotta Continua and Avanguardia
Operaia was strongly felt in West Germany, particularly in the Sponti
("spontaneous") scene in Frankfurt. Even though West Germany generally lacked the favorable conditions for the combined militancy of workers
and activists that characterized Italy, the early 1970s saw the founding of
so-called Factory Project Groups with names such as Workers' Cause,
Workers' Struggle, and Revolutionary Struggle, which had some notable
success in organizing and supporting the struggles of immigrant workers
in the early 1970s.[6] Many of these immigrants were Italian and had been
members of Lotta Continua or otherwise involved in labor militancy.[7] As
in Italy, industrial actions bled over into attempts to seize control of the
urban environment through rent strikes and building seizures, notably in
the early 1970s *Häuserkampf* ("war for the buildings").

This work focused on working-class immigrants was part of a broader
project of mobilizing social out-groups with little stake in the system in West
Germany. This effort included work with runaways and children in group
homes, some of it conducted by militants of what would become the Red

---

[5] See Vladimir Tismaneanu (ed.), *Promises of 1968: Crisis, Illusion and Utopia* (New York:
Central European University Press, 2011), 93–94).

[6] See Timothy Scott Brown, *West Germany and the Global Sixties: The Anti-Authoritarian
Revolt, 1962–1978* (New York: Cambridge University Press, 2013; 2015), 302.

[7] Geronimo, *Fire and Flames: A History of the German Autonomist Movement* (Oakland: PM,
2012), 54.

Army Faction. Mobilizing delinquent youth, as we have seen, was an early goal of avant-garde groups like the Provos. From late 1968 and 1969, with broad swathes of youth increasingly unmoored from moderating institutions and increasingly steeped in antiauthoritarian and countercultural values, attempts to mobilize society's outcasts came to the front and center of radical practice. The emergence of a fully fledged drug scene, in particular, provided the opportunity for antiauthoritarian praxis cum marginal group mobilization. An early example was English drug self-help group Release, founded in London in 1967, which advised young people on drug safety and represented defendants in drug cases. Release quickly caught on the continent, with chapters established in the Scandinavian countries, the Netherlands, and West Germany. In the Federal Republic, Release quickly became the site of a variety of self-organized cultural-political initiatives, ranging from a macrobiotic restaurant to a multimedia lab, a publishing house, and the initiative "Rock Liberation Front." The Release mission was not just to get people off drugs, in other words, but to create an alternative to capitalist society rooted in the self-organization of daily life.[8]

This mission was part of a broader strategy of mobilizing marginalized groups such as institutionalized children, mental patients, and criminals – in short, the various members of Marx's "Lumpenproletariat" – whose revolutionary potential was foregrounded in the "Marginal Group Theory" of Marcuse.[9] Groups like Socialist Self-Help Cologne (SSK) and Action Southern Front in Munich dedicated themselves to fighting gentrification, securing the rights of tenants, and working with juveniles from youth homes and patients from psychiatric clinics.[10] In the UK, the London Street Commune sought to place street youth and squatters at the center of the struggle. "Our project," they wrote, "is that the Underground should dissolve itself into a street level mobilization/unification of all the sub-cultural groups – greasers, skinheads, beats, heads, student drop-outs."[11] Lamenting the effect of a two-pronged recuperative assault led on the one hand by "well-meaning liberals – often ex-CND pacifists, who, as social workers, probation officers, teachers, etc., are quite unconscious of how repressive their role actually is" and on the other by "the so-called Flower Children and their ideology of love," the London Street Commune concluded: "The only

---

[8] Brown, *West Germany and the Global Sixties*, 288.
[9] Attitudes differed about the relative worth of marginalized groups in the revolutionary struggle; see Sven Steinacker, "Die radikale Linke und soziale Randgruppen: Facetten eines ambivalenten Verhältnisses," in Rotaprint 25 (ed.), *Agit 883: Bewegung Revolte Underground in Westberlin 1969–1972* (Berlin: Assoziation A, 2006), 201–214, 204–205.
[10] Brown, *West Germany and the Global Sixties*.
[11] "An Open Letter to the Underground from the London Street Commune," in Peter Stansill and David Zane Mairowitz (eds.), *BAMN (By Any Means Necessary): Outlaw Manifestos and Ephemera, 1965–1970* (New York: Autonomedia, 1999), 214.

force at present capable of hitting back are the kids who are trying to fight their way out of their parents' culture."[12]

Attempts to politicize youth delinquency were fraught with danger for activists. West Berlin's Kommune I drew to itself all the vaguely political bohemians in its immediate area, not least political desperadoes like the Hash Rebels and Red Army faction cofounder Andreas Baader. The commune's dealings with working-class youth gangs were difficult, however. Young toughs drove the Kommune I out of its second location, the so-called KI Factory, leading to the disbanding of the commune.[13] The Provos experienced a similar unintended consequence when working-class Nozem burned down the "Provo houseboat" that Hans Tuynman had purchased using money earned from the sale of his book, *Full-Time Provo*.[14] The efforts of King Mob and other groups to establish ties with working-class skinheads in Ladbroke Grove met with mixed results. It was one thing to turn the power of delinquency against middle-class values and the power of the state, represented by the police; it was another to have that power – fundamentally anti-ideological and therefore unpredictable – turned against oneself.

In the UK, the drive to revolutionize daily life in the street and at the point of production was embodied in the group East London Big Flame. A self-described "Revolutionary Socialist Feminist organization with a working class orientation," Big Flame was founded in Liverpool in 1970 before branching out to other cities, including London, where the group was known as "East London Big Flame." Originally oriented toward Trotskyism, Big Flame moved in the direction of "libertarian Marxism" and had ties to the Solidarity group. The group was strongly influenced by Italian Autonomism and possessed tactical links with Lotta Continua. It acknowledged the need to found a party but resisted the impulse to found one itself. Instead, it focused on the struggles of daily life across a number of different spheres. The group was involved in initiatives ranging from a food co-op, strike organizing at the Ford Motors plants at Halewood and Dagenham, involvement in the Building Workers campaign, squatting and rank-and-file housing redevelopment, the Claimant's Union and unemployment, and also work with so-called Red Therapy.[15]

---

[12] "An Open Letter to the Underground from the London Street Commune," 212–213. On the London Street Commune, see also the account of one of its founders in Phil Cohen, *Archive That, Comrade! Left Legacies and the Counter Culture of Remembrance* (Oakland: PM, 2018).

[13] See the account in Rolf Ulrich Kaiser, *Protokolle einer Kommune und 23 Trips* (Düsseldorf: Droste, 1970), 26.

[14] Richard Kempton, *Provo: Amsterdam's Anarchist Revolt* (Southport: New Autonomy, 2007), 77.

[15] ELBF/A4/1–11, Mayday Rooms, London.

5.1 The Portuguese Revolution depicted on the cover of the British publication *Big Flame* (Big Flame Archive).

Big Flame's answer to the classical revolutionary dilemma of top down/ bottom up was to focus on "autonomous" or decentralized organization. Here they parted ways from what an unofficial historian of the group called a "traditional Marxist-Leninist Left ... blinkered by a hierarchy of white, male, middle-class elitist central committee leaderships."[16] Instead, they embraced a new feminist politics emphasizing local decision-making in accordance with local needs. "We understood," the former activist continued, "how exploitation is carried out in all areas of our lives, and hence understood the importance of housing, child care, health, sexuality, food and all the extra labour of reproducing capital that is carried out in the home."[17] Ideologically, the group drew on an eclectic mix of nonconformist (Luxemburg and Gramsci) and psychoanalytic (Wilhelm Reich) Marxism, anticolonialism (Franz Fanon), autonomist feminism (Mariarosa Dalla Costa), and Situationism (Raoul Vaneigem), all with a focus on self-organization at the level of daily life.[18] Rejecting top-down models of organization associated with traditional Communist parties, along with the narrow definitions of struggle with which that model was often associated, the group instead embraced perspectives from feminism and gay rights to New Age psychotherapy of the California variety and the sex-drugs-and-rock-'n'-roll culture of "swinging London."[19] Even as it focused on local struggles, Big Flame was explicitly internationalist. The American influence was strong, and there was a good deal of interchange with the European continent, not only with Lotta Continua in Italy but with activists in Spain, Portugal, and West Germany.[20]

Going Underground

Big Flame represented one salient post-1968 attempt to answer the question: what now? Alongside the post-1968 tendency to connect with ongoing social struggles, Big Flame and other groups developed a countervailing urge to escape – or, more usually, redefine – the arena of political struggle altogether by establishing countercultural enclaves. These could exist within the city, in squats and other alternative living arrangements, or in the countryside, where the rural environment seemed to offer the possibility of a fresh start. This tendency was lent force by the repression that followed 1968 on both sides of the Iron Curtain. Dropping out had a different meaning in the West and East. On both sides of the Iron Curtain, it could spring from a desire to find rest from the

---

[16] "East London in the 70s – one woman's view," Mayday Rooms, London.
[17] "East London in the 70s."   [18] "East London in the 70s."
[19] "East London in the 70s."   [20] "East London in the 70s."

rigors of activism and heal the wounds of political struggle, but in the East, it was frequently a response to the lack of space that had existed for that activism in the first place.

Ideas of the "underground" in West and East were similar in the sense that both posited an escape from direct political engagement (or at least from certain kinds of political engagement) but different in terms of their relationship to the broader society. Whereas in the West the underground could serve simultaneously as a conceptual location for scenes, a discursive category, and a marketing slogan, in the East it tended to connote a "defensive" space, a literal escape from the dangers of political engagement.[21] The "artistic movement which neither supports nor attacks the establishment, but remains outside of it" (Béla Hap) was a far cry from Western models, which saw the "underground" as a site of political engagement that could range from simple communal living to armed guerrilla struggle.[22]

A key feature of the post-1968 moment, as we have seen, was a widening gulf between countercultural and hard political tendencies. The inability of the two to get along was less like the sudden shattering of a blissful union than a case of a divorce in a marriage that was not particularly happy to begin with. Mutual suspicion verging on hostility was present in relations between "revolutionaries" and "flower children" even prior to the post-1968 parting of ways, even if they frequently adopted aspects of each other's appearance and political ethos. It could be possible thus for Barry Miles of *International Times* to cite "The League of Spiritual Discovery, The Diggers, N.Y. Provos, Amsterdam Provos, Drop City, L.S.E., Psychedelic Community, U.S.C.O., Haight Ashberry [sic], Free People of the World, The Tribe of the Sacred Mushroom" as "giving a pointer to the direction of the next epoch"[23] while ignoring how little in practice student militancy at the London School of Economics (e.g.) had to do with the spiritual seeking of the counterculture. Meanwhile, others could forcefully suggest that the battle against US imperialism in Vietnam was the signature struggle of the moment and that hippie was a divergence from it, an abdication of real responsibility in an age of conflict.

---

[21] See the essays in Cathleen M. Giustino, Catherine J. Plum, and Alexander Vari (eds.), *Socialist Escapes: Breaking Away from Ideology and Everyday Routine in Eastern Europe, 1945–1989* (New York: Berghahn, 2013).

[22] Rebecca Clifford, Juliane Fürst, Robert Gildea, James Mark, Piotr Osęka, and Chris Reynolds, "Spaces," in Robert Gildea, James Mark, and Anette Warring (eds.), *Europe's 1968: Voices of Revolt* (Oxford: Oxford University Press, 2013), 190–192, 188.

[23] Barry Miles, "Design for Positive Effectiveness," *International Times*, 27 (March 8, 1968), 3.

To be sure, as noted above, even when actors embraced them at the level of rhetoric, hard distinctions between countercultural and militant wings of different movements were sometimes less important at the level of lived reality. In the UK, as Celia Hughes shows, multisided connections existed between the student movement and counterculture, labor movement and neighborhood and other local struggles, connections that were forged by avant-gardes that moved among the different milieux.[24] The situation was similar in the continental democracies, where the lines between countercultural and hard political scenes were extremely blurry around 1968. In Eastern Europe, the confined space for nonconformist activity of any type, along with the greater explosive power of artistic interventions in general, made the distinction between culture and politics even less important.

Nevertheless, from the end of the 1960s, revolutionary disappointments accelerated tendencies toward fracture and division. The demand for greater political discipline and personal sacrifice was on many lips. A West German radical expressed what many thought when he complained, "[i]t is clear beyond a doubt that where pot is smoked, where flower power is practiced, that there Marx's *Kapital* and Guevara's *Guerilla – Theory and Method* are probably seldom read."[25] Others strongly rejected such views. As the West German filmmaker Gerd Conradt put it retrospectively: "The SDS, the APO [Extra-Parliamentary Opposition] had little appreciation for culture. Only a few cared about fantasy and beauty. The cadres held fast to buzzwords: fascism, working class, bourgeoisie – enemy, struggle, freedom, victory, revolution. But I remember other words: drugs, music, dance, love – sexuality, commune."[26]

The split between cultural and political revolutionaries was one that reproduced itself in locations as diverse as Hungary and France, Denmark and Russia, West Germany and Poland.[27] In West Berlin, as early as 1967, student officials whom the Kommune I had mocked as "lame-asses [and] careerists" expelled the communards, charging that their emphasis on the liberation of the self represented "the means of an impotent rebellion."[28] The K1-Ost in East Berlin experienced similar

---

[24] Celia Hughes, *Young Lives on the Left: Sixties Activism and the Liberation of the Self* (Manchester: Manchester University Press, 2015), 1.

[25] Werner Olles, "Kiff und Revolution," *Agit 883*, 28 (August 21, 1969), 5. Olles was a member of the Frankfurt branch of the SDS Frankfurt and later became close to the K-Group KPD-ML.

[26] Gerd Conradt, *Starbuck: Holger Meins – Ein Porträt als Zeitbild* (Berlin: Espresso, 2001), 9.

[27] See Agnes Heller, "The Year 1968 and its Results: An East European Perspective," in Tismaneanu, *Promises of 1968*, 157–166, 160.

[28] Quoted in Brown, *West Germany and the Global Sixties*, 72.

debates over the relative value of lifestyle as a revolutionary tool.[29] In and around the East London Big Flame commune, a split developed between factions that one participant dubbed the "primal screamers" and the "politicos."[30] In France, Maoists rejected the lifestyle focus of hippies, and the Vive la Révolution commune split over the issue of sexual liberation.[31] In Denmark, Maoists broke with the Redstockings.[32] In Leningrad's Yellow Submarine commune, fissures between "politicals" and "counterculturalists" became a defining feature of communal life.[33]

Dealing with such divisions became part of the self-theorization of the left scene. The basic antinomies were sketched out in the Danish countercultural journal *Superlove*, which distinguished between types like "Warriors and Freaks" and "Activists and Dropouts."[34] To be sure, revolutionary action was increasingly understood to rely on both inner and outer transformation. "Certainly we are going to destroy capitalism," read a characteristic quote in *Superlove*, "but it is not only an attack on those in power; it is also an attack on the deepest structures within ourselves."[35] Denmark represents a particularly striking example of the interpenetration of the political and cultural around 1968, but in this respect it was not unique.[36] As Laura Skardhamar has shown, questions about what kind of politics a commune represented – a preparation for socialism or a cultural revolution in its own right? A revolutionizing of society by other means versus revolution of the self as sufficient in its own right? – ran through the commune movement itself.[37]

This fundamental disagreement could take on an element of East-West competition as well. One former Russian activist recalls being simultaneously intrigued and repelled by the French May, applauding the "joyous" nature of the rebellion while criticizing activists for being

---

[29] Anna von der Goltz and James Mark, 161.

[30] John Davis and Juliane Fürst, "Drop-outs," in Gildea, Mark, and Warring, *Europe's 1968*, 193–210, 207.

[31] This occurred in connection with issue 12 of the group's newspaper *Tout!*, edited by a group of male homosexual and female feminist activists, the publication of which saw, instead of the delineation of a clear line of struggle, a multiplication of divergent perspectives on the nature of the "sexual revolution"; see Bourg, *From Revolution to Ethics*, 182–183.

[32] Clifford, et al., "Spaces," 245.

[33] Juliane Fürst, "'We all live in a yellow submarine': Dropping out in a Leningrad Commune," in Juliane Fürst and Josie McLellan, *Dropping out of Socialism: The Creation of Alternative Spheres in the Soviet Union* (Lanham: Lexington, 2017), 179–206.

[34] Marie Černá, John Davis, Robert Gildea, and Piotr Osęka, "Revolutions," in Gildea, Mark, and Warring, *Europe's 1968*, 107–130, 108.

[35] Quoted in Černá, et al., "Revolutions."

[36] Laura P. Skardhamar, "'Real Revolution' in Kana Commune," *Scandinavian Journal of History*, 33(4) (2008), 441–463, 448.

[37] Skardhamar, "'Real Revolution' in Kana Commune," 447–448.

"spoiled."[38] In a similar spirit, the Polish Commandos saw what they regarded as Western hedonism as a waste of time, a distraction from the tasks of the revolution.[39] In Greece, as we have seen, Communist organizations tended to look upon Western-oriented rock music with suspicion, seeking instead to foster reliance on folk-musical traditions from Greece itself.[40] In Yugoslavia, similarly, the value of currents from the West was the subject of fierce dispute. There, activists discussed rock 'n' roll in a way that would have been familiar in West Germany, England, and other Western countries, where, as we saw earlier, the political merit of pop- and subcultural forms was a source of burning concern.[41]

Turning Rebellion into Money

Perhaps the greatest danger perceived by radicals struggling to launch or sustain underground initiatives was *recuperation*, that process through which capitalism disarmed rebellion by packaging it and selling it back to its originators. This process was a major source of concern in the underground nearly from the beginning. As early as October 1967, San Francisco's Diggers staged the "death of hippie," demonstrators bearing a symbolic coffin in a procession through the Haight Ashbury epicenter of media hype about the new youth culture. Part of a transatlantic wave of symbolic "death" Happenings that included the "Death of IT" staged by London's *International Times* in March 1967 and the "Death of Provo" staged in Amsterdam in May of the same year, the event signaled its intention in the legend inscribed on the Diggers' coffin: "Hippie – Son of Media."[42] Hippie was dead, the Diggers argued, because it was a media creation that had never existed to begin with.[43]

These worries were in part about the deforming power of mass media, but this concern was intimately related to a broader fear that only became more acute as the decade wore on: that authentic rebellion was being replaced by rebellion-as-commodity. As the Italian Worker-Student Committee at the Sorbonne said of one of its "combat flyers" distributed

---

[38] Victor Yerofeyev in Philipp Gassert and Martin Klimke (eds.), *1968: Memories and Legacies of a Global Revolt* (Washington, DC: Bulletin of the German Historical Institute, 2009), 171.

[39] Von der Goltz and Mark, "Encounters," 143.

[40] Nikolaos Papadogiannis, "Greek Communist Youth Identities and Rock Music in the late 1970s," in Timothy S. Brown and Lorena Anton (eds.), *Between the Avant-Garde and the Everyday: Subversive Politics in Europe, 1957 to the Present* (New York: Berghahn, 2011), 77–91.

[41] See Madigan Fichter, "East looks," 204.

[42] Stansill and Mairowitz, *BAMN*, 69; Kempton, *Provo*, 82.

[43] See the discussion of Provo's self-dissolution in response to the danger of assimilation by mass media in Stansill and Mairowitz, *BAMN*, 69.

in the factories in 1968, "[i]t appeared as a way of preventing the government from digesting the barricades by transforming them into repetitive phenomena and turning the cobblestone into a consumer product."[44] The protagonists of the Atelier Populaire were similarly attuned to the danger of recuperation. "The posters produced by the Atelier Populaire," they wrote, "are weapons in the service of the struggle and are an inseparable part of it. Their rightful place is in the centers of conflict, that is to say in the streets and on the walls of the factories. To use them for decorative purposes, to display them in bourgeois places of culture or to consider them as objects of aesthetic interest is to impair both their function and their effect."[45]

Worries about the commodification of underground culture came to expression especially with regard to popular music, a cultural arena in which great stock was put as a means of rebellion. The West German underground newspaper *Fizz* condemned, for example, the American group Grand Funk Railroad as "the prototype of a capitalist pop group," praising other more "authentic" performers such as Jimi Hendrix and the American radical rock band MC-5.[46] Similarly, a Dutch alternative magazine sympathetic to the Provos, *Hitweek*, pronounced anathema on The Golden Earrings (aka Golden Earring), whom it deemed "filthily commercial" for having recorded a hit song for Coca-Cola.[47] Such critiques took place in a broader context of skepticism about mass media. Journals like *Song* in West Germany shared the skeptical outlook of the Frankfurt School, which regarded popular culture as a key site in establishing capitalism's cultural hegemony and identified precisely rock and "hip" culture as key sites of that recuperation.

By the end of the decade, the issue of recuperation had reached a crisis point, exacerbated by an influx of younger adherents who learned what they knew about the underground not initially from firsthand experience but from media depictions and advertising. For English Diggers writing in the magazine *Hapt*, the danger was embodied in the figure of the "subhippie," a debased species acted upon by, rather than acting against, the forces of capitalist recuperation. "Subhippie is dead," they wrote, "and we are handing back the corpse to the promoters who sold him his image and his music, and the manipulators and ego-trippers who ripped off his

---

[44] Andrew Feenberg and Jim Freedman, *When Poetry Ruled the Streets: The French May Events of 1968* (Albany: State University of New York Press, 2001), 157.

[45] Johan Kugelberg and Philippe Vermès (eds.), *Beauty Is in the Street: A Visual Record of the May '68 Paris Uprising* (London: Four Corners, 2011).

[46] *Fizz*, 1, reprinted in *Fizz Re-Print 1–10* (Berlin: Anti-Quariat Reprint, 1989).

[47] Robert Adlington, "Expressive revolutions: '1968' and Music in the Netherlands," in Beate Kutschke and Barley Norton (eds.), *Music and Protest in 1968* (Cambridge: Cambridge University Press, 2013), 12–28, 18.

passive gatherings – and killed him."[48] Across the English Channel, West German activists working with elementary school students expressed the fear that "many of us are beginning to fit ourselves to the image that the old culture has cobbled together out of our revolutionary positions and symbols and with them rejuvenated itself. Today in many classes and subcultural groups the very pupils are honored who have best imitated us, without however having really been touched by us, the very pupils who are able to put on the revolutionary façade most slickly."[49]

These worries reflected tensions at the heart of the relationship between the counterculture and radical politics, as well as unease about American influence. The London Street Commune worried openly about the influence of "a succession of psychedelic merchants, media, media-freaks and guru hustlers [who] confused the ideological issues .... in a stifling haze of hashsmoke and Amerikan hipkulchur [sic]."[50] A West German militant similarly questioned the adoption of American terms like "cool" and "dig it," asking: "is it in and of itself logical when the scene as a symbol of [Marcuse's] great refusal is adopted on the basis of expressions adapted from the language of the occupier?"[51] Concerns over the theft of subcultural authenticity reached a high point of sorts when anarchists attacked the West Berlin premier of the musical *Hair*, claiming that it represented little more than an attempt to "gratify capitalist demands" at the expense of the "real subculture."[52]

Worries about recuperation were bound up with the hardening of attitudes that characterized the post-1968 moment. The Beatles song "Revolution" is a case in point. "Musically, Revolution was superb," remembers John Hoyland, a founding editor of the New Left journal *Black Dwarf*,

but the lyrics were a bitter disappointment. Instead of identifying with the rebellious ferment among the young, [John Lennon] was hostile to it. He complained about "minds that hate." He said "When you talk about destruction, don't you know that you can count me out." Above all, he said: "You tell me it's the institution/You better free your mind instead." Those sentiments might have fitted the previous year and the dreamy mind expansions of the "summer of love," but things had moved on and they now seemed entirely off the mark.[53]

---

[48] "Tribal drum," editorial in English Digger magazine *Hapt* (1970), in Stansill and Mairowitz, *BAMN*, 88.
[49] "Sexualität nach der Sexwelle," *konkret*, 17 (August 11, 1969), 20.
[50] "An Open Letter to the Underground from the London Street Commune," 212.
[51] "Underground," *Ulcus Molle INFO*, 9/10 (1973), 424.
[52] "Ist 'Hair' Subkultur?," in Bernd Kramer (ed.), *Gefundene Fragmente, 1967–1980* (Berlin: Karin Kramer, 2004), 24.
[53] John Hoyland, "Power to the People," *The Guardian* (March 14, 2008).

In "An Open Letter to John Lennon" published in *Black Dwarf*, Hoyland wrote: "Perhaps now you'll see what it is you're (we're) up against. Not nasty people. Not even neurosis, or spiritual under-nourishment. What we're confronted with is a repressive, vicious, authoritarian system."[54]

It is no surprise in this context that *Oz* editor Richard Neville could refer to the bitter dustup between Hoyland and Lennon as "a classic New Left/psychedelic left dialogue."[55] Such conflicts were encoded into the very DNA of the 1968 revolt. Characterized by the attempt to fill the vessel of the revolt with appropriate content, lacking in most cases institutional forms and fixed political organizations, 1968 had of necessity to involve a struggle about which sort of content was best and about whether different sorts of content could or could not fit together.

Activists in the East struggled with the danger of recuperation as well, albeit not because of the mechanisms of capitalism. Rather, it was official attempts to coopt youth fashion that represented the problem. In Poland, the Communist regime turned from criminalizing youth's embrace of Western fashions in the 1950s to fostering it in the 1960s, prompting the author Stefan Kisielewski to confide to his diary in the summer of 1968: "How odd that one fought, true to ideals, for these things [music, fashion, cinema, music festivals, and so on] during the Stalinist period, because they represented Western culture. And now the Communists have understood that the whole show works in their favor." This "political stylization of a generation," he complained, had the effect of "turning people completely stupid and making them completely harmless for the authorities."[56] The same complaint could be made in other Eastern Bloc countries, where official sponsorship of popular music blurred the boundaries between rebellion and conformism.

Recuperation was in any case not the opposite of the repressive power of the state but its complement, and not just in the East. For the Surrealist authors of the Platform of Prague, "police intimidation and the allure of consumption" were two pillars of a "technocratic order" against which youth struggled. Citing Marcuse, they noted that the concept of class struggle alone was no longer enough to deal with a social landscape overlain by the production of desires and their fulfillment.[57] The dominance of recuperation made it indispensable to support new revolutionary actors capable of escaping it. "One will certainly not find the

---

[54] Hoyland, "Power to the people."   [55] Hoyland, "Power to the People."
[56] Anna Pelka, "Youth Fashion in Poland in the 1950s and 1960s: Ideology, Resistance, and Manipulation," in Kathrin Fahlenbrach, Martin Klimke, Joachim Scharloth, and Laura Wong (eds.), *The Establishment Responds: Power, Politics, and Protest since 1945* (New York: Palgrave, 2012), 197–210, 197.
[57] The "Platform of Prague."

expression of a genuine political renewal among the apparatchiks of the Communist Parties," they wrote, "(especially those of France and Czechoslovakia), whose essential work consists in paralyzing or congealing all revolutionary thought. It is rather among student minorities that one must expect the decisive impetus."[58]

Recuperation, thus, had to do with much more than commodification. It was also bound up with the question of the New Left's attempts to remain independent of existing political organizations seen to be too closely tied to old ways of thinking. "What is completely new and extremely important in the new revolutionary movement of the Paris students – but also of German, Italian and US students – is that the movement was possible only because it was independent of all existing political organizations," wrote a contributor to the Yugoslavian journal *Student*. "All of these organizations, including the Communist Party, have become part of the system; they have become integrated into the rules of the daily parliamentary game; they have hardly been willing to risk the positions they've already reached to throw themselves into this insanely courageous and at first glance hopeless operation."[59]

Strategies of Tension

Students, workers, and others engaged in a whole range of activism aimed at protecting the integrity of revolutionary struggle. At its most militant, this activism adopted the logics of struggles being waged in the Third World, where a hot war against imperialism was being fought alongside the Cold War between the competing superpowers. Increasingly, solutions to the revolutionary conundrum were drawn from the iron logic of political struggle generated not just from fantasies about Third World hero figures like Che but from realities of conflict with state power. In West Germany, one of the two European countries to experience the rise of significant armed left-wing groups from the end of the 1960s, the question of violence was a focus of debate early on. The editorial accompanying an interview with Rudi Dutschke reprinted in the *International Times* wrote: "Understanding violent vs. non-violent action is not only a pragmatic problem of tactics and strategy but a phenomenological problem, because most of us ... have learned the Establishment's lesson too well: that state violence is legitimate while popular opposition, especially reactive violence is unlawful.'"[60]

[58] The "Platform of Prague."
[59] *Student* (May 21, 1968), quoted in Fredy Perlman, *Birth of a Revolutionary Movement in Yugoslavia* (Kalamazoo: Black & Red, 1969).
[60] "Dutschke Intervue," *International Times*, 29 (May 2, 1968), 6.

In Italy, the other country to produce significant armed left-wing groups, violence was understood as an admissible and necessary concomitant to revolutionary struggle. Coming into contact with the violence of police and fascists fostered a hardening of attitudes and the development of theory and tactics of self-defense against the forces of the state.[61] As an article in a radical organ of the student revolt, *La Sinistra*, put it in 1968: "The fight against 'academic' and 'societal' authoritarianism is now visibly unified; the whole state apparatus is behind the academic structure not only culturally but physically. The truncheon reinforces professorial concepts, the water-cannon speaks for parliamentary majorities, and the old-style exam stands behind the blanket of tear-gas."[62] This analysis was connected to the emergence of a "politics of violence" that saw violence come to be regarded as a revolutionary act in its own right and Molotov cocktails become a key item of insurrectionary technology. "Pacifism," writes Robert Lumley, "was pronounced dead by common consent," as expressed in a popular graffito: "A revolutionary pacifist is like a vegetarian lion."[63]

The turn to violence in Italy and West Germany must be understood against the backdrop of the two countries' histories, which were marked by exterminationist violence of the right against the organizations and personnel of the left. In the rise of Italian fascism between 1919 and 1922 and of German National Socialism between 1930 and 1933, physical destruction of left-wing opponents was seen not only as a winning political strategy but as a vehicle for spiritual regeneration. Everywhere, however, violence was a possibility, because everywhere activists faced police violence, and everywhere they were influenced by the backdrop of anticolonial wars and the dilemmas and rhetoric they produced. Everywhere, moreover, violence, or at least the readiness for it, could be seen to offer the possibility of a liberation of consciousness that allowed activists to break with the conditioning that had taught them to exist peacefully within structures of oppression.

As student movements increasingly became involved in contests of power with the forces of the state, in the UK, in the protests organized by the Vietnam Solidarity Committee, and in confrontations between student demonstrators and riot police from West Germany to Poland, from France to Yugoslavia, the question of what "liberation" meant – and what were the necessary means to achieve it – came strongly to the fore. In both West Germany and Italy, key moments of open, "offensive" struggle

[61] Robert Lumley, *States of Emergency: Cultures of Revolt in Italy from 1968 to 1978* (London: Verso, 1990), 68–70.
[62] Quoted in Lumley, *States of Emergency*, 67.   [63] Lumley, *States of Emergency*.

against the police became central to the escalating militancy of the movements. In Italy, this was the "Battle of the Valle Giulia" of March 1968, which saw students successfully fight back against the police for the first time.[64] In West Germany, the decisive event was the "Battle of the Tegeler Weg" in November of the same year, which saw armed militants wearing motorcycle helmets attack and drive back the police.[65] A radicalization on the terrain of violence was also encoded in the avant-garde tradition. In West Germany there was a process through which Situationist-inspired pranks – the burning of a Christmas tree, or a flyer likening the fatal fire in a Belgian department store to the US use of napalm in Vietnam – prefigured and perhaps inspired actual acts of arson and physical violence.[66]

If these events lay outside the realm of bourgeois normality inasmuch as they disputed the state's monopoly on arms, they did not depart from the traditions of working-class militancy stretching back to the French Revolution. Nor were they out of place in an information sphere in which Third World guerrilla struggle was seen to represent the apex of ethical action in the face of murderous imperial aggressions like the one carried out by the USA in Vietnam and a publishing environment making easy-to-obtain books justifying the need for, or explaining how to enact, violent anti-imperialism.[67]

The spring of 1968 saw a wave of bombings of targets such as the US embassy in Madrid, the Spanish embassy and a US officers' club in London, the US consulate in Turin, and the Spanish, Greek, and Portuguese embassies in The Hague.[68] The Spanish "1st May Group" claimed responsibility for a range of actions, including the kidnapping of Monsignor Marcos Ussia, ecclesiastical attaché to the Spanish embassy to the Vatican, an attack on the US embassy in London, and attacks on the Greek and Bolivian embassies in Bonn, Germany. The group explained these actions as part of a strategy of "counter-escalation" against a US-led campaign of terror encompassing the war in Vietnam, various Latin American interventions, and support for right-wing dictatorships in Spain, Portugal, and Greece.[69]

---

[64] Stuart Hilwig, "Constructing a Media Image of the Sessantotto: The framing of the Italian protest movement in 1968," in Kathrin Fahlenbrach, Erling Sivertsen, and Rolf Werenskjold (eds.), *Media and Revolt: Strategies and Performances from the 1960s to the Present* (New York: Berghahn, 2014), 112.

[65] Brown, *West Germany and the Global Sixties*, 336.

[66] Brown, *West Germany and the Global Sixties*.

[67] For example, the works of Che and Castro, or Carlos Marighella's *Minimanual of the Urban Guerilla*.

[68] Rolf Werenskjold, "A Chronology of the Global 1968 Protest,"

[69] Federacion Internacional Juventudes Libertaria/Grupo I. Mayo, "Erklärung an die Presseagenturen und revolutionären Gruppen," in Lutz Schulenburg (ed.), *Das Leben*

At least one attack, the bombing of the Faculty of Law at the University of Turin in February 1968, was carried out by an Italian neo-fascist group as part of the "strategy of tension," according to which the state could be empowered to act forcefully against the left.[70] The Piazza Fontana bombing of December 1969 served just such a function. Carried out by the far right, the bombing supplied the excuse for an all-out campaign against the left which saw the arrests of militants of Lotta Continua and other organizations as well as thousands of trade unionists.[71] The death of the anarchist militant Giuseppe "Pino" Pinelli in police custody provided the inspiration for Dario Fo's play *Accidental Death of an Anarchist*.

In West Germany, the so-called Red Army Faction and other groups like the Movement 2nd June undertook an escalating campaign of violence, as did the Red Brigades in Italy. These groups represented a small minority of activists, but the logic of their actions was encoded within the long sweep of working-class resistance to capitalism, imperialism, and fascism. After all, state violence did not just range itself against Molotov cocktail–wielding demonstrators. It targeted equally the pacific elements of the counterculture. It is easy to forget, to take the example of a country where the violence question was hotly debated, that underneath the marketing category "Swinging London" – the term itself created by *Time* magazine in April 1966 – lay a political-cultural project that challenged dominant values, including not only those around gender and sexuality but those around money and private property. It is thus unsurprising that the counterculture had to contend with constant police harassment, including violence and arrests.

The campaign of the Angry Brigade, the UK's own contribution to the politics of violent struggle, intervened at precisely this point. A loosely knit collection of antiauthoritarian socialists, the Angry Brigade unleashed a campaign of bombings in London beginning in October 1967. Unlike the Red Army Faction and the Red Brigades, the Angry Brigade was less a clandestine urban guerrilla group than a multifaceted ad hoc initiative of the increasingly militant London counterculture.[72] Members of the Brigade were heavily involved in community organizing and in the

---

ändern, die Welt verändern! 1968 – Dokumente und Berichte (Hamburg: Edition Nautilus, 1998), 133–135, 133–134.

[70] Werenskjold, "Chronology of Events of Protest in Europe 1968," 285.

[71] Gerd-Rainer Horn, "The Working Class Dimension of 1968," in Gerd-Rainer Horn and Padraic Kenney (eds.), *Transnational Moments of Change: Europe 1945, 1968, 1989* (Rowman & Littlefield, 2004), 99.

[72] On this point, see Samantha Christiansen "'We are all Angry': Violence and Spectacle in the British Counterculture," in Brown and Anton, *Between the Avant-Garde and the Everyday*, 47–57.

London squatting scene.[73] The campaign of bombings they unleashed in London, beginning in October 1967, targeted both "political" and "cultural" targets. Alongside symbolic bombs aimed at official installations (only property was attacked), the Angry Brigade targeted a BBC news van outside the Miss World pageant[74] and the fashionable Biba boutique in Kensington, an epicenter of "swinging London" countercultural cooptation.[75]

The question of violence was hotly debated. "Violence has become such a channel for emotional release," argued a voice in the *International Times*, "a religion, complete with bishops and holy martyrs. A lot of people rave on as if it was the direction in which we all have to go. The fact of the matter is that violence is part of the screwed up business that we are trying to cool out."[76] When an anti–Vietnam War march in March 1967 saw students in the streets confront police, underground guru John Hopkins published "An open letter to Mr. Tariq Ali" in which he advised the student leader that, if he was going to flirt with violence in confrontations with the police, he should "[f]ind out how German, Italian, Japanese students organize their demonstrations. Read what literature exists on street fighting & urban guerila warfare. Read Guevara, Fanon, Debray, Canetti, Engels. Or else cop out & start thinking."[77] Hopkins's semi-facetious point was not that the anti–Vietnam War left should adopt the increasingly violent stance of other student movements or the tactics of Third World guerrilla movements, but that it should think more carefully about the consequences of escalation in the contest with authority.

For student radicals, however, a failure to come to grips with the possibility of violence was an abdication of the responsibility imposed on the radical subject by the reality of state violence. Rudi Dutschke, a key participant in the "violence debate"[78] in West Germany, forcefully

---

[73] Some members of the Brigade lived in a commune at 29 Grosvenor Avenue in Islington. The anarchist newspaper *Black Flag* was printed in the basement; Stuart Christie, *Granny Made Me an Anarchist: General Franco, the Angry Brigade, and Me* (Oakland: AK, 2007), 328.

[74] On November 20, 1970. The bombing was followed the next day by a radical feminist assault on the proceedings themselves in which three women from the Grosvenor Street commune took part; Christie, *Granny Made Me an Anarchist*, 329.

[75] On May 1, 1971. Two warning phone calls were made to clear people from the shop. "Biba had a long tradition of exploitation of their young shop assistants," writes Stuart Christie, "who were paid miserable wages, as were their cutters, but the Angry Brigade intended it as an attack on trendy consumer capitalism"; Christie, *Granny Made Me an Anarchist*, 335.

[76] *International Times*, 32 (May/June 1968).

[77] *International Times*, 29 (April/May 1968).

[78] See Berliner Redaktionskollektiv, "Gewalt," *konkret*, 6 (June 1968), 24–28.

expressed the latter perspective in an interview with the *International Times*:

IT: A large part of the people are in sympathy with student demands, but terrorist methods like breaking windows, street battles over tram fare increases and bloodshed are to be deplored. Don't you dissociate yourself from violence?

Dutschke: No! The pitch of our counter-violence is set by the violently repressive methods of our rulers. We accept the activities of the underground groups because they are a continuous learning process for those who take part. Only by practice, gone over again and again, can clear and effective forms of opposition be evolved. In the long term, this means nothing less than a revolutionary struggle for a free society, a free world in which no one has to labour too much and will really have a great deal of time for creative development of personal capacities.[79]

The fact that by the time of the interview's publication in May 1968 Dutschke was in hospital recovering from an assassin's attempt on his life reinforces the point that in the face of violence perpetrated by the state and by the extreme right – Dutschke's would-be assassin was connected to German far-right circles – the question of what Dutschke called "counter-violence" was unavoidable.

It is this fact, rather than the fascist past,[80] anti-Semitism,[81] or left-wing bloodlust,[82] that accounts for the proliferation of armed left-wing groups across Europe in the late 1960s and 1970s. Nor was violence necessarily separate from projects of personal liberation, including feminism.[83] To make these points is not to deny that, as Jeremy Varon and others have shown, violence in left-wing scenes produced and reinforced its own internal, frequently pathological, logics, nor is it to make an argument about whether revolutionary violence was or is "justified" or not; rather, it is to state the simple fact that the turn to violence was one logically derived path to which the contest with authority might lead.[84]

---

[79] *International Times*, 29 (April/May 1968).

[80] Hans Kundnani, *Utopia or Auschwitz: Germany's 1968 Generation and the Holocaust* (London: Hurst, 2010).

[81] Jeffrey Herf, *Undeclared Wars with Israel: East Germany and the West German Far Left, 1967–1989* (Cambridge: Cambridge University Press, 2015).

[82] Jillian Becker, *Hitler's Children: Story of the Baader-Meinhof Terrorist Gang* (London: Michael Joseph, 1977).

[83] See Katharina Karcher, "Women in Armed Leftist Struggles," in Nancy Naples, Renee C. Hoogland, Maithree Wickramasinghe, and Angela Wong (eds.), *The Wiley-Blackwell Encyclopedia of Gender and Sexuality Studies* (Chichester: Wiley-Blackwell, 2016), 1–6; Katharina Karcher, *"Sisters in Arms"? Militant Feminisms in the Federal Republic of Germany since 1968* (New York: Berghahn, 2017); Patricia Melzer, *Death in the Shape of a Young Girl: Women's Political Violence in the Red Army Faction* (New York: New York University Press, 2015).

[84] See Jeremy Varon, *Bringing the War Home: The Weather Underground, the Red Army Faction, and Revolutionary Violence in the Sixties and Seventies* (Berkeley: University of California Press, 2004); see also Holger Nehring, "The Era of Non-Violence: 'Terrorism'

Year of the Militant Woman

The processes of divergence mirrored in conflicts between sectarian-Communist and countercultural streams of activism emerged in particularly potent form on the terrain of gender. Across Europe, autonomous women's groups evolved out of New Left organizations, typically through the discovery by women of the fact that the general oppression of women in society was also present – indeed, sometimes in concentrated form – in left-wing organizations otherwise devoted to emancipation. The rise of women's groups and a transnational women's movement exacerbated previously existing disagreements about the legitimate focus of revolutionary activity. Who had the right to act, for what reason, and with what goals? A key discovery for women around 1968 was that the vulgar Marxist dismissal of the gendered dimension of daily life as a "secondary contradiction" was often indistinguishable from a persistent male chauvinism that differed little from that in society at large.[85]

The growth of women's activism took place in connection with a wide-ranging assault from student and countercultural circles on the basis of bourgeois society at its roots in the family, and specifically on the terrain of sexuality. This intervention was underpinned by broad-based cultural changes in sexual matters, driven not least by the introduction of the birth control pill, which were reflected both in fashion and in the proliferation of media images depicting a more open sexuality in both mainstream and (especially) countercultural publications. Attempts to refine the subversive potential from this proliferation of sexual imagery drew on theoretical approaches rooted in psychoanalysis, and they were concretized in the rise of left-wing reading cultures dedicated to the in-depth exploration of the works of theorists like Wilhelm Reich and, in West Germany, the formation of Reichian "Sex-Pol" groups.

It also saw the formation of communes such as the Kana commune in Copenhagen, the Kommune I and II in West Berlin, the K1 Ost in East Berlin, and many others across Europe.[86] Communal living situations such as these were intended to serve as sites for sexual-political experimentation aimed at breaking out of traditional and restrictive gender roles

---

in West German, Italian and French Political Culture, 1968–1982," in *European Review of History/Revue Europeenne d'Histoire*, 14(3), 343–371.

[85] See Sarah Colvin and Katharina Karcher (eds.), *Gender, Emancipation, and Political Violence: Rethinking the Legacy of 1968* (London: Routledge, 2018); Sarah Colvin and Katharina Karcher (eds.), *Women, Global Protest Movements and Political Agency: Rethinking the Legacy of 1968* (New York: Routledge, 2018); Kristina Schulz (ed.), *The Women's Liberation Movement: Impacts and Outcomes* (New York: Berghahn, 2017); Hughes, *Young Lives on the Left*.

[86] See Skardhamar, "'Real Revolution' in Kana Commune."

that, it was argued, contributed not only to individual oppression but to authoritarian social relationships. These goals were easier to articulate than to realize, however, and one typical feature of attempts to "smash the bourgeois family" was the proliferation of tensions and jealousies, the very sort of "hang-ups" that activists were striving to eliminate. Communes also sometimes saw the exacerbation of the conditions of male dominance that continued to exist in the left-wing scene more broadly.

Radical feminism developed in part as a reaction against the failings of these difficult experiments. Although the feminist movement really only took off in Europe in the late 1960s and 1970s, women's realization of their subordinate status within left-wing movements was present early on. A French activist recalls an action as early as 1962, during the World Youth Festival in Helsinki, where she and a friend gave a presentation on birth control only to be roughed up by Communist Party militants. They were "furious with us," she remembers. "They wanted to know where we came up with foolishness like that, that it was necessary to have children ... . That was the party line, but it wasn't ours; we had our own."[87] The same activist faced an even more violent reaction as a "pied rouge" in Algeria, when she accompanied Algerian women on an International Women's Day demonstration in 1965 only to see them ostracized and completely cut off from the community immediately afterward.[88] This particular episode was rooted in local mores, but it was not foreign to the broader experience of female activists in the metropole. As one put it: "There's no denying though that in '68 it was a period of sexual liberation, of living your life, but it was also one of a strong machismo."[89]

The female rage that fueled the birth of second wave feminism in Europe was placed on brief but impressive display at the July 1967 Dialectics of Liberation Congress, which exhibited a near-complete lack of attention to women and women's issues.[90] "Having ... eloquently if implicitly ... established that the future, rather like the past, was male," remembers the R. D. Liang patient and playwright David Gale, "the Congress stage was invaded by a group of six incensed women. Without prefatory cries or rumblings from the floor, they jumped onto the platform ... seized some hand mics and began to denounce the entire structure and organization of the Congress. The women were not beautiful – something that, in the Summer of Love, men had come to expect of

---

[87] Mitchell Abidor, *More May Made Me: Additional Elements of an Oral History of the 1968 Uprising in France* (Oakland: AK, 2018), 34.
[88] Abidor, *More May Made Me*, 36.   [89] Abidor, *More May Made Me*, 106.
[90] Dialectics of Liberation, *Memories of the Congress*, www.dialecticsofliberation.com/1967-dialectics/memories.

expressive females." The women, who, Gale notes tellingly, "had working class accents,"

shouted, raged and swore at the audience, giving ground to no-one and, in fact, receiving very little audible reaction from a stunned crowd. The lack of local friction did not deter them in the least for they were, it quickly became apparent, not merely vexed by the maleness of this revolutionary occasion, they took it as absolutely typical of the whole, burgeoning late 60s revolutionary enterprise. The Dialectics of Liberation Congress was just one more kick in the teeth . . . .

It was only a few years later, he continued, with second wave feminism more firmly established, that "the men who shuffled out of the Roundhouse, muttering defensively and making jokes about mad, ugly chicks, were probably becoming more ruminative."[91]

If they did so, it was in no small part due to a growing militant self-confidence on the part of women, who were beginning to draw broader conclusions from their previous activism. The first women's workshops in the UK were founded in 1969, and the first national women's liberation conference took place in 1970.[92] As early as 1966, the British feminist Juliet Mitchell decried the status of women within the movement in the pages of *New Left Review*. In an essay subsequently reprinted in her book *Women's Estate* (1971), she recalled a bitter experience in Paris, the home of the French May:

As we walked around we handed out leaflets, particularly to women. A crowd of about a hundred people followed us around; most of them were hostile. We had been prepared for significant opposition from men, even afraid of it; but even so were not prepared for such depth and breadth of outrage. Here were "movement" men shouting insults at us: "Lesbians," "Strip," "What you need is a good fuck."[93]

Against this experience, she wrote, "[n]ot one single left-wing movement: working-class, Black or student can offer anything to contradict."[94] It was precisely "from the ashes of this type of socialism," she continued, that radical feminism was born. "If socialism is to regain its status as *the* revolutionary politics (in addition to the scientific analysis it offers of capitalist society)," she wrote, "it has to make good its practical sins of commission against women and its huge sin of omission – the absence of an adequate place for them in its theory."[95]

---

[91] Dialectics of Liberation, *Memories of the Congress*.
[92] Chris Harman, *The Fire Last Time: 1968 and After* (London: Bookmarks, 1995), 351.
[93] Juliet Mitchell, "Women: The Longest Revolution," *New Left Review*, 40 (December 1966); subsequently published in Juliet Mitchell, *Women's Estate* (London: Penguin, 1971), 75–122.
[94] Mitchell, "Women."   [95] Mitchell, "Women."

Militant women on the continent found themselves in a similar situation. In Italy, an attack by male members of Lotta Continua on a women's abortion rights march in December 1975 led to a major crisis in the organization. The resulting conversation about the meaning of feminism saw "sexist comrades" denounced amidst a mass exodus of women from the organization.[96] "It is a little difficult," a woman at a mass meeting sarcastically observed, "to support the Men's Revolutionary Party."[97] Much earlier, in West Germany, women feeling silenced by the dominance within the movement of high-profile male theoreticians (literally) launched an attack against male dominance by pelting a male speaker of the SDS with tomatoes.[98] Around the same time, women in West Germany were helping to initiate the founding of radical kindergartens meant to socialize the task of childcare and thus free women's time for political agitation.[99] Around Europe, meanwhile, women responded to exploding tensions with left-wing men by founding autonomous institutions such as the women's commune, intended to allow women to pursue issues of interest to them free of male interference.

If the most important impetus for the creation of autonomous women's organizations was women's sense of lacking a voice in the left-wing organizations to which they belonged, it was combined with a growing realization of the Janus-faced nature of a "sexual revolution" in which the freedom gained often seemed to redound more to the benefit of men. Here, the infamous West German slogan – "Who sleeps more than once with the same person already belongs to the establishment" – expressed a generalized assumption.[100] "I hated the term 'sexual revolution,'" recalls one activist, for "we knew that it was only a revolution for men and that women were supposed to be available without hesitation, as often as possible, and if possible, on a rotating basis."[101] The demeaning content of the "sexual revolution" was captured visually in the West German milieu in the covers of important left-wing magazines like *Pardon* and *konkret*, the latter in particular featuring covers depicting "radical women" that were often indistinguishable from soft-core pornography.[102] The British activist

---

[96] "Italy 1977–8: Living with an Earthquake" (London: Red Notes Pamphlets, no date). The decision of many women to leave Lotta Continua to go into the women's movement was aided by a feeling of disenchantment with the course of the revolution in China; Harman, *The Fire Last Time*, 353.
[97] "Italy 1977–8."   [98] See Brown, *West Germany and the Global Sixties*, 286–287.
[99] For a contemporaneous German treatment of the project in English translation, see Helke Sander, "Project: Company kindergartens," *Radical America*, 4(2) (1970), 68–79, https://libcom.org/library/radical-america-0402-women.
[100] "Wer zweimal mit derselben pennt, gehört schon zum Establishment."
[101] Frigga Haug of the Socialist Women's League West Berlin, quoted in Ute Kätzel (ed.), *Die 68erinnen: Porträt einer rebellischen Frauengeneration* (Berlin: Rohwolt, 2002), 197.
[102] See Brown, *West Germany and the Global Sixties*, 315–317.

5.2 Publication of the women's group in Revolutionary Struggle, West German allies of Lotta Continua (Archiv des Hamburger Instituts für Sozialforschung).

Sheila Rowbotham remembers how, when she submitted a piece for a special issue of *Black Dwarf* on the "1969 Year of the Militant Woman," her text returned from the designer overlaid with images of female nudity that rendered it almost impossible to read.[103] "The designer ... had heard 'women,'" she remembers," and thought 'ridicule.'"[104] The growing female response at the end of the 1960s was captured in a piece in *Tout!*, the magazine of the French group Vive la Révolution: "Your sexual liberation is not the same as ours."[105]

The militant end of American second wave feminism quickly exerted its influence in Europe, where it resonated precisely because left-wing women were responding to similar dilemmas on both sides of the Atlantic. Key feminist texts from America circulated widely in Europe, from Betty Friedan's *The Feminist Mystique* (1963) to Germaine Greer's *The Female Eunuch* (1970) and Shulamith Firestone's *The Dialectic of Sex* (1970). The years 1968–1969 in the United States saw the proliferation of groups such as New York Radical Women, Cell 16, and Redstockings, producing influential periodicals like *Feminist Revolution*, *Lilith*, and *No More Fun and Games*. These groups pioneered concepts ("the personal is political"), practices (consciousness-raising), and actions (public protests, like those against the Miss America Pageant, beginning in 1968) that exerted a strong influence in Europe.

Redstockings, which sought to overcome earlier "bourgeois" versions of feminism in favor of a socialist ("red") feminism, inspired the founding of a "Redstocking Movement" in Denmark that attempted a similar combination of socialist and feminist politics under one roof.[106] The American group Bread and Roses, similarly, inspired a West German model, which was an outgrowth in turn of disagreements within groups such as the Action Council for the Liberation of Women and the "Old Wives Soviets" (Weiberräte) about the proper relationship between the personal and the political. As in America, the attempt to shove the square peg of women's issues into the round hole of student Marxism produced

---

[103] Sheila Rowbotham, *Promise of a Dream: Remembering the Sixties* (London: Penguin, 2001) 210.

[104] Rowbotham, *Promise of a Dream*.

[105] Clifford, et al., "Spaces," 247; on the founding of *Tout!*, see Antoine Idier, "A Genealogy of a Politics of Subjectivity: Guy Hocquenghem, Homosexuality, and the Radical Left in post-1968 France," in Joachim C. Häberlen, Mark Keck-Szajbel, and Kate Mahoney (eds.), *The Politics of Authenticity: Countercultures and Radical Movements across the Iron Curtain, 1968–1989* (New York: Berghahn, 2018), 89–109, 98.

[106] Rebecca Clifford, Robert Gildea, and Anette Warring, "Gender and sexuality," in Gildea, Mark, and Warring, *Europe's 1968*, 239–257, 245.

5.3 Biological direct action. Women of the "Ad Hoc Group Prisma" perform taking the birth control pill. West Berlin, January 1, 1969 (photo: Klaus Lehnartz, courtesy of Landesarchiv Berlin).

irreconcilable friction as groups split into "feminist" and "socialist" factions. These splits were part of a rebellion within second wave feminism not only against Marxism as the dominant ideological lens but against "the cult of the genuine revolutionary who subordinated the personal to the political, and the emotional to the reasoned, in the quest for the proletarian revolution."[107]

Women's growing awareness of specifically female issues paved the way for the development in the 1970s of a full-fledged second wave feminist movement with concerns stretching beyond the remit of Marxist politics as commonly constituted. Many radical women resisted the danger of abandoning the socialist content of women's activism, but the new focus on issues of daily life like sexuality and childcare, combined with an awareness of the psychological costs of sustained political militancy in general and the dominating personality of male militants in particular, saw new concerns rise to prominence over issues of class and revolution.

[107] Clifford, Gildea, and Warring, "Gender and sexuality," 246.

The struggle for abortion rights, in particular, became the focus of national and transnational legalization campaigns.[108]

The development of the gay rights movement that grew out of 1968 proceeded from a position similar to that of the women's movement inasmuch as it privileged daily life as the new terrain of struggle, fought against longstanding prejudices, and discussed themes that had previously figured little in left politics. Like the women's movement, the gay liberation movement exhibited a Janus face, one represented by Marxist ideas of class struggle transposed onto the terrain of the personal – in this case, sexual orientation – the other by the birth of a sensibility oriented more closely toward the concerns of personal and group sexual identity free of its Marxist overlay. Starting in 1970–1971, gay rights groups were founded in the UK, France, Italy, and West Germany. In the latter, where activists fought to overturn statutes criminalizing male homosexuality still on the books from the nineteenth century, the main gay rights group, Homosexual Action West Berlin, sought to fuse gay rights with larger issues of social justice on the model of the Gay Liberation Front in New York City. In 1973, in East Germany, Homosexual Initiative Berlin was founded as the first gay liberation group in the state socialist bloc.[109]

The new politics of identity required a delicate balancing act that was not always successful. There was the question, first, of whether socialism provided a suitable analytical lens through which to envision a liberation based on gender identity and sexual orientation. There was strong resistance within the sectarian far left to the idea that an issue like abortion rights, for example, could reasonably exist outside socialist politics. Too great a concession to "bourgeois feminism," according to this line of analysis, risked throwing the socialist baby out with the patriarchal bathwater. A similar conflict emerged within the gay rights movement. In West Germany, Homosexual Action West Berlin required its members to belong to other New Left organizations so as to avoid lapsing into a pure sexual-identitarian movement. This organizational requirement, however, failed to solve deeper problems. In a 1973 Berlin meeting of homosexual action groups from around West Germany, French and Italian drag queens disrupted a demonstration, prompting a discussion about "revolutionary respectability" within the left-wing student movement.[110]

Alongside conflicts within the gay rights movement about the proper content of gay politics, there were conflicts between gay and straight

---

[108] From mid-decade, the legalization of abortion became a major issue in West Germany, Italy, Spain, and the UK; Harman, *The Fire Last Time*, 352.

[109] See Idier, "A Genealogy of a Politics of Subjectivity."

[110] See the discussion in Brown, *West Germany and the Global Sixties*, 320–328.

people. As with the development of sexual identity politics in Europe more generally, these evolved in part out of origins in the United States.[111] In this respect, they were rooted fundamentally in the same sorts of conflicts over goals and methods that characterized the New Left more generally. Groups like the French Psych et Po (Psychologie et Politique) advocated a strict separatism, part of a broader conflict around the balance between the private and the political, separatism and inclusion.[112] "Feminism and gay liberation were never unified phenomena," writes Julian Bourg. "Although feminists and some male activists often found common cause with one another in attacking the sexual and gender 'old order,' such solidarity did not always materialize."[113] Indicative was the fate of the feminist collective Movimento Feminista Romano in Rome, which, after a decade-long period of relative success, dissolved due to tensions between gay and straight women.[114] Similar tensions existed in the UK.[115] It was another irony of the multifaceted phenomenon of 1968 that, in Bourg's words, sometimes "sexual politics . . . fought other sexual politics all in the name of liberation."[116]

The Search for Social Power

In this respect, sexual politics around 1968 reproduced disputes common to the broader radical project. One of the biggest unresolved tensions of 1968 was the one between individualism and collectivism; that is, between the claims of personal and group identity and rebellion. If it came out clearly in the battle between men and women, between differing sexual identities, between Marxists and counterculturalists, and between different tendencies within the hard left itself, this tension underpinned the entirety of 1968. In the early period of radical convergence, before utopian optimism ran hard up against the unwillingness of elites to countenance change, different impulses were mutually supporting, or at least seemed to be so. Amidst euphoria and optimism, it was easy to believe that personal liberation necessarily fed into the project of social transformation. In the period of divergence that followed the

---

[111] Clifford, et al., "Gender and sexuality," 254.
[112] Clifford, et al., "Gender and sexuality," 255–256.
[113] Bourg, *From Revolution to Ethics*, 180.
[114] Clifford, et al., "Gender and Sexuality," 254.
[115] See the discussion in Big Flame Education Program, "Women's liberation" (May 1974), 1–6. Mayday Rooms.
[116] Bourg, *From Revolution to Ethics*, 180.

defeat of left insurgencies, inherent contradictions came to the fore as different tendencies reproduced themselves in increasingly exaggerated iterations.[117]

A significant minority of activists sought to reestablish the forms and practices of the "old" left as a necessary continuation of the "new" (the groupuscules in France, the K-Gruppen in West Germany, Maoist and Trotskyist sects in various Eastern Bloc countries). Others followed the logic of self-management and independent cultural practice to extend the gains that had been made, even if these failed to resemble previously conceived notions of "revolution." To be sure, no political movement is ever a purely fresh creation of the present moment, but for all its newness and orientation to the future, the revolt of 1968 in Europe was, with all the ideological-archeological work before it, a more-than-usually hybrid phenomenon.

From this perspective, we can conclude that there was in fact no unitary phenomenon known as 1968; rather, what we refer to as "1968" or the "long 1960s" must be seen as the proliferation of a generalized rebellion that acquired different ideological and organizational shapes in different locations, even while driven by universalizing urges. Because political ideologies and action forms were secondary to these urges, 1968 was characterized above all by a search for the answer to the question of *how* to be political within prevailing local and global contexts. This search was linked in turn to the question of *social power* – that is, the question of how to take political action that would not represent a mere "refusal" or merely achieve emotional catharsis through symbolic revolutionary gestures but instead create actual change, if not in the external world, then at least in the realm of personal subjectivity.

As we have seen, this search necessitated coming to grips with the classical revolutionary problems about the role of authority and the relationship of the individual to the collective, the cultural to the political, and the personal to the political. We have also seen that the possibility of *enacting* the politics uncovered – actively discovered by the restless grappling with the local revolutionary past and the global revolutionary present – was decisively shaped by the political space available. The degree of available space did not negate the basic impulses at work, but it did shape them, even as they were shaped by the broader historical and power-political contexts. The principles that

---

[117] On "convergence" and "divergence" as ways of thinking about 1968, see Timothy Scott Brown, "1968 in West Germany: The anti-authoritarian revolt," *The Sixties: A Journal of History, Politics and Culture. What Was Politics in 68? A Special Issue on the West German Sixties*, 7(2) (2014), 99–116.

underpinned the activism of 1968 thus did not provide a unified concept and approach; on the contrary, they were by their very nature inconsistent and sometimes contradictory.

A key problem was that the revolutionary traditions and sources that activists inherited or sought to draw on, whether from the Old Left legacy or from contemporary postcolonial struggles, were themselves ambiguous precisely regarding central questions of the relative merits of organization versus spontaneity, about the relationship between discipline and antiauthoritarianism, and about the proper ratio between personal and social liberation. Even as they challenged power relations at every level, for example, a significant portion of activists worked with source materials – Marxism-Leninism or Maoism – in which authoritarianism and antiauthoritarianism were heavily intertwined. In the West, and to a smaller degree in the East, a reinvented anarchist tradition represented an important counterweight to the authoritarian tendencies present in aspects of the Marxist tradition. Still, the failure to come to terms with the dichotomy at the heart of this mixed legacy may be seen to represent the blind spot in the antiauthoritarian gaze.

The realm of cultural production was characterized by its own ambiguities. If the interpenetration of culture and politics was a key feature of 1968, the terms of the relationship between them was open to interpretation. There was wide agreement that culture *should* be political, but the question of exactly of *how* it should be political was open. In the West, debates about the politics of culture were connected to worries about capitalist recuperation – that is, about the question of whether it was possible to seek revolutionary ends through nonrevolutionary means. Was radical literature, for example, really "radical" if it was produced and distributed, as it so often was, by a mainstream publishing house? Such conflicts became increasingly bitter when the battles over capitalist recuperation took place not between the underground and the mainstream but within the underground itself, as they often did.

As such examples make clear, the question of what politics actually *were* in 1968, and the linked question of what activists understood to be social power, is not one that scholars have to superimpose back over the political terrain of the 1960s; it was *the* question that activists posed themselves. This is one reason why, as the scholarship is continually revealing, the 1960s were "long," or, put differently, the reason why the end of "1968" is indistinguishable from 1968's afterlives. Key aspects of the politics pioneered in the 1960s did not unfold until the 1970s (and sometimes even the 1980s), in some societies because their development was retarded by police state Marxism, in others only in the natural course of activists understanding what they actually wanted and what was possible to accomplish. Thus, in the final analysis, for the question "what *kind* of politics?" there can be no easily agreed-upon answer.

Afterword

To think about sixties Europe is to do more than consider Europe as a geographic space and the 1960s as a time period. It is to reflect on fundamental unresolved problems of modernity. In a moment when the processes of cultural and economic globalization are more advanced than at any time in human history, a particular vision of free market capitalism appearing under the sign of "neoliberalism" seems so solid as to represent a form of common sense. "Yet, since the financial collapse of 2008, and especially with the economic disruption caused by the global pandemic of 2020, the capitalist order looks a lot less certain than it used to. The political consequences of that uncertainty have thrown politics open in a way they have not been for decades."

A particularly disquieting feature of the present moment is the way in which radical right-wing movements in Europe and America have made themselves beneficiaries of the widespread anger about neoliberal globalization. The liberal establishment, in both in Europe and America, has been shocked by widespread resistance to the political-economic consensus it has done so much to put in place. On the right, paradoxically, the reaction to the crisis of capitalism focuses its anger on various perceived challenges to white identity (e.g. immigration), positioning itself as a defensive bulwark against a radical left whose threat is more symbolic than real. If this development should come as no surprise to the student of interwar European fascism, it has nevertheless shattered easy assumptions about the triumph of capitalism in place since 1989. With the success of authoritarian capitalisms in China and Russia and the rise of right-wing populisms in Europe and North America, meanwhile, easy assumptions about the natural link between capitalism and democracy are increasingly called into question.

Against this backdrop, a new generation of the left increasingly rejects mainstream liberalism, so voluble about identity yet silent about class, in favor of a renewed approach to the classical Marxist and anarchist traditions. It does not do so by rendering invisible the struggles of the LGBTQ community, women, and people of color, however; rather, it recognizes the essential indivisibility of issues of identity and class. In this sense, contemporary activists are inheritors of a key 1960s assumption, updated for the twenty-first century, that all struggles are connected. With rising inequality, the challenges posed to capitalism around 1968 appear less chimerical than they did in the immediate period of triumphalism after 1989. Indeed, in a moment in which socialism and Marxism are slowly being shed of their negative Cold War associations, the upheavals of the 1960s are taking on a new meaning and importance.

To be sure, conditions are very different now than in the 1960s. The politics of Third World liberation no longer serve as a critical backdrop in the way they once did, the "heroic guerrilla" having been supplanted by the "bloodthirsty jihadi" in the pantheon of Third World militancy. In the metropole, a toothless establishment liberalism struggles to understand why members of the working class it long ago abandoned go off in search of darker models of political self-assertion. Much of what was culturally new in the 1960s, meanwhile, is no longer so, having long since been commodified – "recuperated," in 1960s parlance – and turned into just more product in a world in which literally everything is for sale. Where popular culture does retain a subversive edge, it is as likely to be a site of reactionary as of progressive politics. The same goes for the youth sub-cultures that once offered hope to the Amsterdam Provos or the theorists of the Birmingham School.

And what of 1968's politics of truth? Fifty years ago, activists insisted that media must accurately reflect social reality, demanding honest reporting "from above" in the mainstream media and creating left-wing counter-media to expose the lies of power "from below." Today, if the distinction between "above" and "below" is less clear, the result is far from politically salutary. Corporate and extreme right-wing news empires are more capable than ever of trafficking in untruth, denying actually existing problems such as global climate change while drumming up hysteria about made-up ones such as immigration. The explosion of raw information through the Internet, meanwhile, has produced ambivalent results. Far from alleviating the problems of truth that sixties radicals saw as impediments to effective political action, the proliferation of insurgent voices has only amplified them. The democratization of media alone does not lead to emancipation, but sixties radicals never argued that it would; for that, as they would be the first to insist, politics is required.

This is one reason why, despite the changed terrain, the classical revolutionary problems adduced by 1960s radicals are still with us. The core question of 1968 – what *is*, after all, the correct means of organizing society? – is open again in a way it has not been for decades. The fall of communism in 1989 was supposed to have ushered in a new millennium of liberal-democratic ascendency. Instead, it opened the way for a neoliberal hollowing out of society that crushed the economic hopes of all but an elite few and opened up a Pandora's Box out of which has stepped a rogues' gallery of right-wing populist demagogues. But the crisis has also awakened a resurgence of interest in socialism among the young. In that resurgence, like the one of the 1960s, radicals have had to rediscover or reinvent the left-wing tradition in accordance with the changed circumstances in which they find themselves.

Sixties radicals fought against the attempts, so successful today, to make a market out of everything, to insist that young people place all their energies into the creation of the entrepreneurial self as the price of entry into adulthood and citizenship. As many commentators have argued, the "neoliberal subject" is itself a product of the 1960s cult of individual liberation, but the flipside of that equation is the will to collective empowerment that is also a legacy of 1968, and, critically, one that connects it to the century-and-a-half of revolutionary moments that preceded it.

To reject neoliberalism's insistence that all loss, like all profit, is an individual affair, to replace private desperation with collective empowerment, will require an act of the imagination perhaps even greater than that required by 1960s activists trying to develop a path forward in the frozen landscape of the Cold War. Today, 1968 still matters because, in a world marked by the persistence of war, poverty, racism, and the threat of environmental collapse – not to mention insurgent right-wing extremism – the questions it posed about the proper organization of human society refuse to go away. Fifty years on, the questions posed around 1968 remain more open than ever.

Bibliography

Abidor, Mitchell, ed. *May Made Me: An Oral History of the 1968 Uprising in France* (London: Pluto, 2018).

Abidor, Mitchell. *More May Made Me: Additional Elements of an Oral History of the 1968 Uprising in France* (Oakland: AK, 2018).

Alekseeva, Ludmilla, and Paul Goldberg. *The Thaw Generation: Coming of Age in the Post-Stalin Era* (Boston: Little, Brown, 1990).

Ali, Tariq. *Street-Fighting Years: An Autobiography of the Sixties* (London: Verso, 2005).

Álvarez, Alberto Martín, and Eduardo Rey Tristán. *Revolutionary Violence and the New Left: Transnational Perspectives* (New York: Routledge, 2017).

Anderson, Terry H. *The Movement and the Sixties* (New York: Oxford University Press, 1995).

Apor, Péter. *Fabricating Authenticity in Soviet Hungary: The Afterlife of the First Hungarian Soviet Republic in the Age of State Socialism* (London: Anthem, 2014).

Arrighi, Giovanni, Terence K. Hopkins, and Immanuel Wallerstein. *Anti-Systemic Movements* (London: Verso, 1989).

Avrich, Paul. *Kronstadt 1921* (Princeton: Princeton University Press, 1970).

Avrich, Paul. *The Russian Anarchists* (Princeton: Princeton University Press, 1967).

Baas, Jacquelynn, ed. *Fluxus and the Essential Questions of Life* (Chicago: University of Chicago Press, 2011).

Babiracki, Patryk, and Austin Jersild, eds. *Socialist Internationalism in the Cold War: Exploring the Second World* (New York: Palgrave Macmillan, 2016).

Barker, Colin, ed. *Revolutionary Rehearsals* (London: Bookmarks, 1987).

Baumann, Michael. *How It All Began* (Vancouver: Arsenal Pulp, 1977).

Bazin, Jérôme, Pascal Dubourg Glatigny, and Piotr Piotrowski, eds. *Art beyond Borders: Artistic Exchange in Communist Europe (1945–1989)* (Budapest: Central European University Press, 2016).

Becker, Jillian. *Hitler's Children: Story of the Baader-Meinhof Terrorist Gang* (London: Michael Joseph, 1977).

Berger, Stefan, and Holger Nehring, eds. *The History of Social Movements in Global Perspective: A Survey* (New York: Palgrave Macmillan, 2017).

Bergmann, Uwe, Rudi Dutschke, Wolfgang Lefèvre, and Bernd Rabehl. *Rebellion der Studenten oder die neue Opposition* (Hamburg: Rororo Aktuell, 1968).

Berke, Joseph. *Counterculture* (London: Peter Own, 1969).

Bhambra, Gurminder K., and Ipek Demir, eds. *1968 in Retrospect: History, Theory, Alterity* (London: Palgrave Macmillan, 2009).

Bieling, Rainer. *Die Tränen der Revolution: Die 68er zwanzig Jahre danach* (Berlin: Siedler, 1988).

Birchall, Ian H. *Workers against the Monolith: The Communist Parties since 1943* (London: Pluto, 1974).

Böckelmann, Frank, and Herbert Nagel, eds. *Subversive Aktion: Der Sinn der Organisation ist ihr Scheitern* (Frankfurt: Neue Kritik, 1976).

Bokina, John, ed. *Marcuse: From the New Left to the Next Left* (Lawrence: University Press of Kansas, 1994).

Bolton, Jonathan. *Worlds of Dissent: Charter 77, The Plastic People of the Universe, and Czech Culture under Communism* (Cambridge, MA: Harvard University Press, 2012).

Borkenau, Franz. *The Spanish Cockpit: An Eye-Witness Account of the Political and Social Conflicts of the Spanish Civil War* (London: Faber & Faber, 1937).

Bourg, Julian. *From Revolution to Ethics: May 1968 and Contemporary French Thought* (Montreal: McGill-Queen's University Press, 2007).

Bracke, Maud. *Which Socialism, Whose Détente? West European Communism and the Czechoslovak Crisis of 1968* (Budapest: Central European University Press, 2007).

Bracke, Maud. *Women and the Reinvention of the Political: Feminism in Italy, 1968–1983* (London: Routledge, 2014).

Bragança, Manuel, and Peter Tame. *The Long Aftermath: Cultural Legacies of Europe at War, 1936–2016* (New York: Berghahn, 2015).

Breines, Paul, ed. *Critical Interruptions: New Left Perspectives on Herbert Marcuse* (New York: Herder, 1970).

Bren, Paulina. *The Green Grocer and His TV: The Culture of Communism after the 1968 Prague Spring* (Ithaca: Cornell University Press, 2010).

Brinton, Maurice. *The Bolsheviks and Workers' Control: The State and Counter-Revolution* (London: Solidarity, 1970).

Brinton, Maurice. *Paris: May 1968* (London: Solidarity, 1968).

Broué, Pierre. *The German Revolution: 1917–1923* (Berlin: Historical Materialism, 2006).

Brown, Timothy Scott. *West Germany and the Global Sixties: The Anti-Authoritarian Revolt, 1962–1978* (New York: Cambridge University Press, 2013).

Brown, Timothy Scott, and Lorena Anton, eds. *Between the Avant-Garde and the Everyday: Subversive Politics in Europe, 1957 to the Present* (New York: Berghahn, 2011).

Brown, Timothy Scott, and Andrew Lison, eds. *The Global Sixties in Sound and Vision: Media, Counterculture, Revolt* (New York: Palgrave Macmillan, 2014).

Byrne, Jeffrey James. *The Mecca of Revolution: Algeria, Decolonization, and the Third World Order* (Oxford: Oxford University Press, 2016).

Callaghan, John. *The Far Left in British Politics* (Oxford: Basil Blackwell, 1987).

Carey, Elaine, and Alfred J. Andrea, eds. *Protests in the Streets: 1968 across the Globe* (Indianapolis: Hackett, 2016).

Carr, Gordon. *The Angry Brigade: A History of Britain's First Urban Guerilla Group* (Oakland: PM, 2010).

Carr, Raymond, and Juan Pable Fusi Aizpurua. *Spain: Dictatorship to Democracy* (London: Allen & Unwin, 1982).

Castoriadis, Cornelius. *Political and Social Writings: Volume 1, 1946–1955* (Minneapolis: University of Minnesota, 1988).

Catanzaro, Raimondo, ed. *The Red Brigades and Left-Wing Terrorism in Italy* (London: Pinter, 1991).

Caute, David. *The Year of the Barricades: A Journey through 1968* (New York: Harper & Row, 1988).

Cerny, Petr. *Czechoslovakia 1968: What "Socialism"? What "Human Face"?* (London: Solidarity, 1985), pamphlet no. 55.

Chamberlin, Paul Thomas. *The Cold War's Killing Fields: Rethinking the Long Peace* (New York: HarperCollins, 2018).

Chaussy, Ulrich. *Die drei Leben des Rudi Dutschke* (Berlin: Fischer, 1993).

Christiansen, Samantha, and Zachary A. Scarlett, eds. *The Third World in the Global 1960s* (New York: Berghahn, 2013).

Christie, Stuart. *Granny Made Me an Anarchist: General Franco, the Angry Brigade, and Me* (Oakland: AK, 2007).

Cohen, Phil. *Archive That, Comrade! Left Legacies and the Counter Culture of Remembrance* (Oakland: PM, 2018).

Cohen, Phil. *Reading Room Only: Memoir of a Radical Bibliophile* (Nottingham: Five Leaves, 2013).

Cohn-Bendit, Daniel. *Wir haben sie so geliebt, die Revolution* (Frankfurt: Athenäum, 1987).

Cohn-Bendit, Daniel, and Gabriel Cohn-Bendit. *Linksradikalismus: Gewaltkur gegen die Alterskrankheit des Kommunismus* (Hamburg: Rowohlt, 1968).

Cohn-Bendit, Daniel, and Gabriel Cohn-Bendit. *Obsolete Communism: The Left-Wing Alternative* (London: AK, 2000).

Cohn-Bendit, Daniel, and Reinhard Mohr. *1968: Die letzte Revolution, die noch nichts vom Ozonloch wußte* (Berlin: Wagenbach, 1988).

Colvin, Sarah, and Katharina Karcher, eds. *Gender, Emancipation, and Political Violence: Rethinking the Legacy of 1968* (London: Routledge, 2018).

Colvin, Sarah, and Katharina Karcher, eds. *Women, Global Protest Movements and Political Agency: Rethinking the Legacy of 1968* (New York: Routledge, 2018).

Conradt, Gerd. *Starbuck: Holger Meins – Ein Porträt als Zeitbild* (Berlin: Espresso, 2001).

Cook, Alexander, ed. *Mao's Little Red Book: A Global History* (New York: Cambridge University Press, 2014).

Cooper, David, ed. *The Dialectics of Liberation* (Harmondsworth: Penguin, 1968).

Cooper, Sam. *The Situationist International in Britain: Modernism, Surrealism, and the Avant-Garde* (New York: Routledge, 2017).

Cornils, Ingo. *Writing the Revolution: The Construction of "1968"* (Rochester: Camden House, 2016).

Daniels, Robert V. *The Year of the Heroic Guerrilla: World Revolution and Counterrevolution in 1968* (Cambridge, MA: Harvard University Press, 1996).

Davey, Eleanor. *Idealism beyond Borders: The French Revolutionary Left and the Rise of Humanitarianism, 1954–1988* (New York: Cambridge University Press, 2015).

Davies, Meredid. *Writing and the West German Protest Movements: The Textual Revolution* (London: Institute for Modern Language Research, 2015).

Davis, Belinda, Wilfried Mausbach, Martin Klimke, and Carla MacDougall, eds. *Changing the World, Changing Oneself: Political Protest and Collective Identities in West Germany and the US in the 1960s and 1970s* (New York: Berghahn, 2010).

DeGroot, Gerard J., ed. *Student Protest: The Sixties and After* (London: Longman, 1998).

Della Porta, Donatella, Hanspeter Kriesi, and Dieter Rucht, eds. *Social Movements in a Globalizing World* (New York: Palgrave Macmillan, 1999).

Dhoest, Alexander, Steven Malliet, Jacques Haers, and Barbara Segaert, eds. *The Borders of Subculture: Resistance and the Mainstream* (London: Routledge, 2015).

Đilas, Milovan. *The New Class: An Analysis of the Communist System* (New York: Mariner, 1982).

Dirke, Sabine Von. *"All Power to the Imagination!": The West German Counterculture from the Student Movement to the Greens* (Lincoln: University of Nebraska Press, 1997).

Dubček, Alexander, with Jiří Hochman, ed. and trans. *Hope Dies Last: The Autobiography of Alexander Dubček* (New York: Kodansha International, 1993).

Dubinsky, Karen, Catherine Krull, Susan Lord, Sean Mills, and Scott Rutherford, eds. *New World Coming: The Sixties and the Shaping of Global Consciousness* (Toronto, ON: Between the Lines, 2009).

Duchen, Claire. *Feminism in France: From May '68 to Mitterand* (London: Routledge, 1986).

Duteuil, Jean-Pierre. *Nanterre 1965–66–67–68: Vers le mouvement du 22 mars* (Mauléon: Acratie, 1988).

Duteuil, Jean-Pierre. *Nanterre 1968: Notes on the Background to the 22 March Group* (ChristieBooks, electronic edition, 2014).

Dutschke, Rudi. *Ausgewählte und kommentierte Bibliographie des revolutionären Sozialismus von K. Marx bis in die Gegenwart* (Heidelberg: Druck- und Verlagskooperative HFHB, 1969).

Edwards, Phil. *More Work! Less Pay!: Rebellion and Repression in Italy, 1972–77* (Manchester: Manchester University Press, 2017).

Eley, Geoff. *Forging Democracy: The History of the Left in Europe, 1850–2000* (Oxford: Oxford University Press, 2002).

Engler, Wolfgang, ed. *Die Ost-deutschen: Kunde von einem verlorenen Land* (Berlin: atb, 2005).

Enzensberger, Ulrich. *Die Jahre der Kommune I: Berlin 1967–1969* (Cologne: Kiepenheuer & Witsch, 2004).

Fahlenbrach, Kathrin, Erling Sivertsen, and Rolf Werenskjold, eds., *Media and Revolt: Strategies and Performances from the 1960s to the Present* (New York: Berghahn, 2014).

Fahlenbrach, Kathrin, Martin Klimke, Joachim Scharloth, and Laura Wong, eds. *The Establishment Responds: Power, Politics, and Protest since 1945* (New York: Palgrave, 2012).

Fainberg, Dina, and Artemy M. Kalinovsky, eds. *Reconsidering Stagnation in the Brezhnev Era* (Lanham: Rowman & Littlefield, 2016).

Falk, Barbara. *Dilemmas of Dissidence in East-Central Europe: Citizen Intellectuals and Philosopher Kings* (Budapest: Central European University Press, 2003).

Feenberg, Andrew, and Jim Freedman. *When Poetry Ruled the Streets: The French May Events of 1968* (Albany: State University of New York Press, 2001).

Fenemore, Mark. *Sex, Thugs and Rock 'n' Roll: Teenage Rebels in Cold-War East Germany* (New York: Berghahn, 2007).

Fink, Carole, Philipp Gassert, and Detlef Junker, eds. *1968: The World Transformed* (Cambridge: Cambridge University Press, 1998).

Fišera, Vladimir, ed. *Workers' Councils in Czechoslovakia, 1968–69: Documents and Essays* (New York: St. Martin's, 1978).

François, Etienne, ed. *1968: Ein europäisches Jahr?* (Leipzig: Leipziger Universitätsverlag, 1997).

Fraser, Ronald, ed. *1968: A Student Generation in Revolt* (New York: Pantheon, 1988).

Frei, Norbert. *1968: Jugendrevolte und globaler Protest* (Munich: Deutscher Taschenbuch, 2008).

Fürmetz, Gerhard, and Thomas Kleinknecht, eds. *Schwabinger Krawalle: Protest, Polizei und Öffentlichkeit zu Beginn der 60er Jahre* (Essen: Klartext, 2006).

Fürst, Juliane. *Flowers through Concrete: Explorations in the Soviet Hippieland* (Oxford: Oxford University Press, 2018).

Fürst, Juliane, and Josie McLellan. *Dropping out of Socialism: The Creation of Alternative Spheres in the Soviet Union* (Lanham: Lexington, 2017).

Ganser, Daniele. *NATO's Secret Armies: Operation Gladio and Terrorism in Western Europe* (London: Routledge, 2005).

Gassert, Philipp, and Martin Klimke, eds. *1968: Memories and Legacies of a Global Revolt* (Washington, DC: Bulletin of the German Historical Institute, 2009).

Gassert, Philipp, and Martin Klimke. *1968: On the Edge of World Revolution* (Chicago: University of Chicago Press, 2018).

Gehret, Jens. *Gegenkultur: von Woodstock bis Tunix 1969–1981* (Asslar: MarGis, 1985).

Gerhardt, Christina, and Marco Abel, eds. *Celluloid Revolt: German Screen Cultures and the Long Sixties* (Rochester: Camden House, 2019).

Geronimo. *Fire and Flames: A History of the German Autonomist Movement* (Oakland: PM, 2012).

Geserick, Rolf, ed. *Unsere Medien, Unsere Republik 2: 1965: Warten auf den Frühling*, vol. 4 (Marl: Adolf Grimme Institut, 1993).

Getzler, Israel. *Kronstadt 1917–1921: The Fate of a Soviet Democracy* (Cambridge: Cambridge University Press, 1983).

Gilcher-Holtey, Ingrid, ed. *1968: Vom Ereignis zum Gegenstand der Geschichtswissenschaft* (Göttingen: Vandenhoeck & Ruprecht, 1998).

Gilcher-Holtey, Ingrid. *"Die Phantasie an die Macht": Mai 68 in Frankreich* (Frankfurt: Suhrkamp, 1995).

Gildea, Robert, James Mark, and Anette Warring, eds. *Europe's 1968: Voices of Revolt* (Oxford: Oxford University Press, 2013).

Giustino, Cathleen M., Catherine J. Plum, and Alexander Vari, eds. *Socialist Escapes: Breaking Away from Ideology and Everyday Routine in Eastern Europe, 1945–1989* (New York: Berghahn, 2013).

Golan, Galia. *The Czechoslovak Reform Movement: Communism in Crisis 1962–1968* (Cambridge: Cambridge University Press, 1971).

Golan, Galia. *Reform Rule in Czechoslovakia: The Dubček Era 1968–1969* (Cambridge: Cambridge University Press, 1973).

Goldman, Emma. *My Disillusionment in Russia* (New York: Doubleday, Page & Company, 1923).

Goldman, Emma. *Trotsky Protests Too Much* (Glasgow: The Anarchist Communist Federation, 1938).

Goldstücker, Eduard, František Kautman, and Paul Reimann, eds. *Franz Kafka aus Prager Sicht* (Berlin: Voltaire, 1966).

von der Goltz, Anna, ed. *"Talkin' 'bout My Generation": Conflicts of Generation Building and Europe's 1968* (Göttingen: Wallstein, 2011).

Gordon, Daniel. *Immigrants & Intellectuals: May '68 & and the Rise of Anti-Racism in France* (Pontypool: Merlin, 2012).

Gorsuch, Anne E., and Diane P. Koenker, eds. *The Socialist Sixties: Crossing Borders in the Second World* (Bloomington: Indiana University Press, 2013).

Grace, Nancy M., and Jennie Skerl, eds. *The Transnational Beat Generation* (New York: Palgrave Macmillan, 2012).

Green, Jonathon. *All Dressed Up: The Sixties and Counterculture* (London: Pimlico, 1999).

Green, Jonathon. *Days in the Life: Voices from the English Underground 1961–1971* (London: Minerva, 1988).

Gregoire, Roger, and Fredy Perlman. *Worker-Student Action Committees: France May '68* (Kalamazoo: Black & Red, 1969).

Gross, Alex. *The Untold Sixties: When Hope Was Born – An Insider's Sixties on an International Scale* (New York: Cross-Cultural Research Projects, 2009).

Gruenwald, Oskar. *The Yugoslav Search for Man: Marxist Humanism in Contemporary Yugoslavia* (South Hadley: Bergin & Garvey, 1983).

Häberlen, Joachim. *The Emotional Politics of the New Left: West Germany, 1968–1984* (New York: Cambridge University Press, 2018.

Häberlen, Joachim, Mark Keck-Szajbel, and Kate Mahoney, eds. *The Politics of Authenticity: Countercultures and Radical Movements across the Iron Curtain, 1968–1989* (New York: Berghahn, 2018).

Hamsik, Dusan. *Writers against Rulers* (New York: Vintage, 1971).

Hanshew, Karrin. *Terror and Democracy in West Germany* (New York: Berghahn, 2012).

Harman, Chris. *Bureaucracy and Revolution in Eastern Europe* (London: Pluto, 1974).

Harman, Chris. *The Fire Last Time: 1968 and After* (London: Bookmarks, 1995).

Havel, Vaclav, and John Keane. *The Power of the Powerless: Citizens against the State in Central Eastern Europe* (New York: Routledge, 1985).

Hecken, Thomas. *Gegenkultur und Avantgarde 1950–1970: Situationisten, Beatniks, 68er* (Tübingen: Francke, 2006).

Hejzlar, Zdenek, and Vladimir V. Kusin. *Czechoslovakia, 1968–1969: Chronology, Bibliography, Annotation* (New York, Garland, 1975).

Heller, Agnes, Ferenc Fehér, and Gyorgy Markus. *Dictatorship over Needs: An Analysis of Soviet Societies* (London: Palgrave Macmillan, 1983).

Herf, Jeffrey. *Undeclared Wars with Israel: East Germany and the West German Far Left, 1967–1989* (Cambridge: Cambridge University Press, 2015).

Hilwig, Stuart J. *Italy and 1968: Youthful Unrest and Democratic Culture* (Basingstoke: Palgrave Macmillan, 2009).

Hjartarson, Benedikt, Andrea Kollnitz, Per Stounbjerg, and Tania Ørum, eds. *A Cultural History of the Avant-Garde in the Nordic Countries 1950–1975* (Leiden: Brill, 2016).

von Hodenberg, Christina. *Das andere Achtundsechzig: Gesellschaftsgeschichte einer Revolte* (Munich: C. H. Beck, 2018).

von Hodenberg, Christina. *Konsens und Krise: eine Geschichte der Westdeutschen Medienöffentlichkeit, 1945–1973* (Göttingen: Wallstein, 2006).

Horn, Gerd-Rainer. *1968 und die Arbeiter: Studien zum "proletarischen Mai" in Europa* (Hamburg: VSA, 2007).

Horn, Gerd-Rainer. *The Spirit of '68: Rebellion in Western Europe and North America, 1956–1976* (Oxford: Oxford University Press, 2006).

Horn, Gerd-Rainer. *The Spirit of Vatican II: Western European Progressive Catholicism in the Long Sixties* (Oxford: Oxford University Press, 2015).

Horn, Gerd-Rainer, and Padraic Kenney, eds. *Transnational Moments of Change: Europe 1945, 1968, 1989* (Lanham: Rowman & Littlefield, 2004).

House, Jim, and Neil MacMaster. *Paris 1961: Algerians, State Terror, and Memory* (Oxford: Oxford University Press, 2006).

Hughes, Celia. *Young Lives on the Left: Sixties Activism and the Liberation of the Self* (Manchester: Manchester University Press, 2015).

Internationale Situationiste. *On the Poverty of Student Life: A Consideration of Its Economic, Political, Sexual, Psychological and Notably Intellectual Aspects and of a Few Ways to Cure It* (Detroit: Black & Red, 2000).

Jackson, Julian, Anna-Louise Milne, and James S. Williams, eds. *May 68: Rethinking France's Last Revolution* (Basingstoke: Palgrave Macmillan, 2011).

Jappe, Anselm. *Guy Debord* (Oakland: PM, 2018).

Jarausch, Konrad H. *Dictatorship as Experience: Towards a Socio-Cultural History of the GDR* (New York: Berghahn, 1999).

Jian, Chen, Martin Klimke, Masha Kirasirova, Mary Nolan, Marilyn Young, and Joanna Waley-Cohen, eds. *The Routledge Handbook of the Global Sixties: Between Protest and Nation-Building* (London: Routledge, 2018).

Jobs, Richard Ivan. *Backpack Ambassadors: How Youth Travel Integrated Europe* (Chicago: Chicago University Press, 2017).

Jobs, Richard Ivan. *Riding the New Wave: Youth and Rejuvenation of France after the Second World War* (Stanford: Stanford University Press, 2007).

Johnston, Hank, ed. *Culture, Social Movements, and Protest* (London: Routledge, 2009).

Johnstone, Chris, ed. *BIC: Behind the Iron Curtain: Review of the Institute for the Study of Totalitarian Regimes* (Czech Republic: Institute for the Study of Totalitarian Regimes, 2012).

Judt, Tony. *Postwar: A History of Europe since 1945* (New York: Penguin, 2005).

Junes, Tom. *Student Politics in Communist Poland: Generations of Consent and Dissent* (Lanham: Lexington, 2015).

Kaiser, Rolf Ulrich. *Protokolle einer Kommune und 23 Trips* (Düsseldorf: Droste, 1970).

Kalter, Christoph. *The Discovery of the Third World: Decolonization and the Rise of the New Left in France, c. 1950–1976.* Translated by Thomas Dunlap (Cambridge: Cambridge University Press, 2016).

Karcher, Katharina. *"Sisters in Arms"? Militant Feminisms in the Federal Republic of Germany since 1968* (New York: Berghahn, 2017).

Katsiaficas, George. *The Global Imagination of 1968: Revolution and Counterrevolution* (Oakland: PM, 2018).

Katsiaficas, George. *The Imagination of the New Left: A Global Analysis of 1968* (Boston, MA: South End, 1987).

Kätzel, Ute, ed. *Die 68erinnen: Porträt einer rebellischen Frauengeneration* (Berlin: Rohwolt, 2002).

Kellner, Douglas. *Herbert Marcuse and the Crisis of Marxism* (Berkeley: University of California Press, 1984).

Kempton, Richard. *Provo: Amsterdam's Anarchist Revolt* (Southport: New Autonomy, 2007).

Kenny, Michael. *The First New Left: British Intellectuals after Stalin* (London: Lawrence and Wishart, 1995).

Killingsworth, Matt. *Civil Society in Communist Eastern Europe: Opposition and Dissent in Totalitarian Regimes* (Wivenhoe Park: ECPR, 2012).

Klimke, Martin. *The Other Alliance: Student Protest in West Germany and the United States in the Global Sixties* (Princeton: Princeton University Press, 2010).

Klimke, Martin, and Joachim Scharloth, eds. *1968: Handbuch zur Kultur- und Mediengeschichte der Studentenbewegung* (Stuttgart: J. B. Metzler, 2007).

Klimke, Martin, and Joachim Scharloth, eds. *1968 in Europe: A Handbook on National Perspectives and Transnational Dimensions of 1960/70s European Protest Movements.* Transnational History Series (London: Palgrave Macmillan, 2008).

Klimke, Martin, and Joachim Scharloth, eds. *1968 in Europe: A History of Protest and Activism, 1956–1977* (London: Palgrave Macmillan, 2008).

Klimke, Martin, Jacco Pekelder, and Joachim Scharloth, eds. *Between Prague Spring and French May: Opposition and Revolt in Europe, 1960–1980* (New York: Berghahn, 2011).

Knabb, Ken. *The Situationist International Anthology* (Oakland: AK, 2006, revised and expanded edition).Leszek. *Toward a Marxist Humanism: Essays on the Left Today* (New York: Grove, 1968).

Kornetis, Kostis. *Children of the Dictatorship: Student Resistance, Cultural Politics, and the "Long 1960s" in Greece* (New York: Berghahn, 2013).

Kramer, Bernd, ed. *Gefundene Fragmente, 1967–1980* (Berlin: Karin Kramer, 2004).

Kraushaar, Wolfgang. *1968 als Mythos, Chiffre und Zäsur* (Hamburg: Hamburg Edition, 2000).

Kraushaar, Wolfgang. *1968: Das Jahr das alles verändert hat* (Munich: Piper, 1998).

Kraushaar, Wolfgang. *Frankfurter Schule und Studentenbewegung: Von der Flaschenpost zum Molotowcoctail, 1945–1995* (Frankfurt: Hamburger Edition, HIS, 1998).

Krebs, Mario. *Ulrike Meinhof: Ein Leben im Widerspruch* (Reinbek: Rowohlt, 1988).

Kugelberg, Johan, and Philippe Vermès, eds. *Beauty Is in the Street: A Visual Record of the May '68 Paris Uprising* (London: Four Corners, 2011).

Kundnani, Hans. *Utopia or Auschwitz: Germany's 1968 Generation and the Holocaust* (London: Hurst, 2010).

Kusin, Vladimir V., ed. *The Czechoslovak Reform Movement, 1968* (London: International Research Documents, 1973).

Kusin, Vladimir V. *Political Grouping in the Czechoslovak Reform Movement* (New York: Columbia University Press, 1972).

Kutschke, Beate, and Barley Norton, eds. *Music and Protest in 1968* (Cambridge: Cambridge University Press, 2013).

Labedz, Leopold. *The Use and Abuse of Sovietology* (Livingston: Transaction, 1988).

Lacoss, Don. *Surrealism in '68: Paris, Prague, Chicago* (Chicago: Black Swan, 2008).

Leech, Kenneth. *Youthquake: Spirituality and the Growth of a Counter-Culture* (London: Abacus, 1976).

Lewis, Helena. *The Politics of Surrealism* (St. Paul: Paragon House, 1988).

Lobl, Eugen, and Leopold Grunwald. *Die Intellektuelle Revolution: Hintergrunde und Auswirkungen des "Prager Fruhlings"* (Dusseldorf: Econ, 1969).

Lomax, Bill. *Hungary 1956* (London: Allison & Busby, 1976).

Lönnendonker, Siegward, Bernd Rabehl, and Jochen Staadt. *Die antiautoritäre Revolte: Der Sozialistische Deutsche Studentenbund nach der Trennung von der SPD, vol. I: 1960–1967* (Opladen: Westdeutscher, 2002).

Lotringer, Sylvere, and Christian Marazzi, eds. *Autonomia: Post-Political Politics* (Los Angeles: Semiotext(e), 2007).

Lövy, Michael. *Morning Star: Surrealism, Marxism, Situationism, Utopia* (Austin: University of Texas Press, 2009).

Lüdtke, Alf, and Peter Becker, eds. *Akten, Eingaben, Schaufenster: Die DDR und ihre Texte. Erkundungen zu Herrschaft und Alltag* (Berlin: De Gruyter, 1997).

Lumley, Robert. *States of Emergency: Cultures of Revolt in Italy from 1968 to 1978* (London: Verso, 1990).

Magri, Lucio. *The Tailor of Ulm: Communism in the Twentieth Century.* Translated by Patrick Camiller (London: Verso, 2011).

Major, Patrick. *The Death of the KPD: Communism and Anti-Communism in West Germany, 1945–1956* (New York: Clarendon, 1997).

Maravall, José. *Dictatorship and Political Dissent. Workers and Students in Franco's Spain* (Cambridge: Cambridge University Press, 1978).

Marcus, Greil. *Lipstick Traces: A Secret History of the Twentieth Century* (Cambridge, MA: Harvard University Press, 2003).

Marcuse, Herbert. *One-Dimensional Man: Studies in the Ideology of Advanced Industrial Society* (Boston, MA: Beacon, 1964).

Markovits, Andrej S., and Philip S. Gorski. *The German Left: Red, Green, and Beyond* (Cambridge: Polity Press, 1993).

Martel, Frédéric. *The Pink and the Black: Homosexuals in France since 1968* (Palo Alto: Stanford University Press, 2000).

Marwick, Arthur. *The Sixties: Cultural Revolution in Britain, France, Italy, and the United States, c.1958–c.1974* (Oxford: Oxford University Press, 1990).

Maximov, Grigori. *The Guillotine at Work in Russia* (Chicago: Berkman Fund, 1940).

Mazierska, Ewa, ed. *Popular Music in Eastern Europe: Breaking the Cold War Paradigm* (New York: Palgrave MacMillan, 2016).

McDermott, Kevin, and Matthew Stibbe, eds. *Eastern Europe in 1968: Responses to the Prague Spring and Warsaw Pact Invasion* (Basingstoke: Palgrave Macmillan, 2018).

McDermott, Kevin, and Matthew Stibbe, eds. *Revolution and Resistance in Eastern Europe: Challenges to Communist Rule* (Oxford: Berg, 2006).

McKay, George. *Senseless Acts of Beauty Cultures of Resistance since the Sixties* (London: Verso, 1996).

Melzer, Patricia. *Death in the Shape of a Young Girl: Women's Political Violence in the Red Army Faction* (New York: New York University Press, 2015).

Mett, Ida. *The Kronstadt Uprising* (London: Solidarity, 1967).

Michnik, Adam. *Letters from Freedom: Post–Cold War Realities and Perspectives* (Berkeley: University of California Press, 1998).

Michnik, Adam. *The Trouble with History: Morality, Revolution, and Counterrevolution* (New Haven: Yale University Press, 2014).

Milder, Stephen. *Greening Democracy: The Anti-Nuclear Movement and Political Environmentalism in West Germany and Beyond, 1968–1983* (Cambridge: Cambridge University Press, 2017).

Miles, Barry. *In the Seventies: Adventures in the Counterculture* (London: Serpent's Tail, 2011).

Mitchell, Juliet. *Women's Estate* (London: Penguin, 1971).

Mohandesi, Salar, Bjarke Skærlund Risager, and Laurence Cox, eds. *Voices of 1968: Documents from the Global North* (London: Pluto, 2018).

Morgan, Bill. *The Beats Abroad: A Global Guide to the Beat Generation* (San Francisco: City Lights, 2015).

Naples, Nancy, Renee C. Hoogland, Maithree Wickramasinghe, and Angela Wong, eds. *The Wiley-Blackwell Encyclopedia of Gender and Sexuality Studies* (Chichester: Wiley-Blackwell, 2016).

Navrátil, Jaromir, ed. *The Prague Spring 1968: A National Security Archive Documents Reader* (New York: Central European University Press, 1998).

Nehring, Holger. *Politics of Security: British and West German Protest Movements and the Early Cold War, 1945–1970* (Oxford: Oxford University Press, 2013).

Nicholls, Julia. *Revolutionary Thought after the Paris Commune, 1871–1885* (Cambridge: Cambridge University Press, 2019).

Nuttall, Jeff. *Bomb Culture* (London: Strange Attractor, 2018), fiftieth anniversary edition.

Oglesby, Carl, ed. *The New Left Reader* (New York: Grove, 1969).

Ohse, Marc-Dietrich. *Jugend nach dem Mauerbau: Anpassung, Protest und Eigensinn (DDR 1961–1974)* (Berlin: Christoph Links, 2003)

Orwell, George. *Homage to Catalonia* (New York: Harcourt, 1969).

Oved, Yaacov. *Globalization of Communes: 1950–2010* (London: Routledge, 2013).

Oxley, A., A. Pravda, and A. Ritchie, eds. *Czechoslovakia: The Party and the People* (London: Penguin, 1973).

Papadogiannis, Nikolaos. *Militant around the Clock? Youth Politics, Leisure and Sexuality in Post-dictatorship Greece, 1974–1981* (New York: Berghahn, 2015).

Passerini, Luisa. *Autobiography of a Generation: Italy 1968* (Middletown: Wesleyan University Press, 1996).

Perlman, Fredy. *Birth of a Revolutionary Movement in Yugoslavia* (Kalamazoo: Black & Red, 1969).

Pervan, Ralph. *Tito and the Students: The University and the University Student in Self-Managing Yugoslavia* (Nedlands: University of Western Australia Press, 1978).

Piketty, Thomas. *Capital in the Twenty-First Century* (Cambridge, MA: Harvard University Press, 2014).

Plogstedt, Sibylle. *Im Netz der Gedichte: Gefangen in Prag nach 1968* (Berlin: Christoph Links, 2001).

Poiger, Uta. *Jazz, Rock, and Rebels: Cold War Politics and American Culture in a Divided Germany* (Berkeley: University of California Press, 2000).

Pollmann, Bernhard, ed. *Lesebuch zur deutschen Geschichte*, vol. 3, *Vom deutschen Reich bis zur Gegenwart* (Dortmund: Chronik, 1984).

Quattrocchi, Angelo, and Tom Nairn. *The Beginning of the End: France, May 1968* (London: Verso, 1998).

Ramet, Sabrina Petra, ed. *Rocking the State: Rock Music and Politics in Eastern Europe and Russia* (Boulder: Westview, 1994).

Rauhut, Michael. *Rock in der DDR, 1964–1989* (Bonn: Bundeszentrale für politische Bildung, 2002).

Rauhut, Michael, and Thomas Kochan, eds. *Bye, Bye Lueben City: Bluesfreaks, Tramps and Hippies in der DDR* (Berlin: Schwarzkopf & Schwarzkopf, 2004).

Reichardt, Sven, and Detlef Siegfried, eds. *Das Alternative Milieu: Antibürgerliche Lebensstil und linke Politik in der Bundesrepublik Deutschland und Europa, 1968–1983* (Göttingen: Wallstein, 2010).

Reid, Donald. *Opening the Gates: The Lip Affair, 1968–1981* (London: Verso, 2018).

Reinders, Ralf, and Ronald Fritsch. *Die Bewegung 2 Juni: Gespräche über Haschrebellen, Lorenzentführung, Knast* (Berlin: Edition ID-Archiv, 1995).

Remington, Robin Alison, ed. *Winter in Prague: Documents on Czechoslovak Communism in Crisis* (Cambridge, MA: Massachusetts Institute of Technology Press, 1969).

Renton, David. *Never Again: Rock against Racism and the Anti-Nazi League, 1976–1982* (London: Routledge, 2018).

Reynolds, Chris. *Memories of May '68: France's Convenient Consensus* (Cardiff: University of Wales Press, 2011).

Reynolds, Chris. *Sous les Pavés, the Troubles: Northern Ireland, France and the European Collective Memory of 1968* (Bern: Peter Lang, 2014).

Robinson, Lucy. *Gay Men and the Left in Postwar Britain: How the Personal Got Political* (Manchester: Manchester University Press, 2011).

Rosemont, Penelope. *Dreams and Everyday Life: André Breton, Surrealism, Rebel Worker, SDS and the Seven Cities of Cibola* (Chicago: Charles H. Kerr, 2008).

Rosemont, Franklin, and Charles Radcliffe, eds. *Dancin' in the Streets! Anarchists, IWWs, Surrealists, Situationists and Provos in the 1960s – As Recorded in the Pages of the Rebel Worker and Heatwave* (Chicago: Charles H. Kerr, 2004).

Ross, Kristin. *May '68 and Its Afterlives* (Chicago: University of Chicago Press, 2002).

Rotaprint 25, ed. *Agit 883: Bewegung Revolte Underground in Westberlin 1969–1972* (Berlin: Assoziation A, 2006).

Rowbotham, Sheila. *Promise of a Dream: Remembering the Sixties* (London: Penguin, 2001).

Rusinow, Dennison I. *The Yugoslav Experiment 1948–1974* (Berkeley: University of California Press, 1977).

Russell, Bertrand. *Theory and Practice of Bolshevism* (London: George Allen & Unwin, 1920).

Ryback, Timothy. *Rock around the Bloc: A History of Rock Music in Eastern Europe and the Soviet Union* (Oxford: Oxford University Press, 1990).

Sander, Hartmut, and Ulrich Christians, eds. *Subkultur Berlin: Selbstdarstellung, Text-, Ton-Bilddokumente, Esoterik der Kommunen, Rocker, subversiven Gruppen* (Darmstadt: März, 1969).

Savage, Jon. *Teenage: The Creation of Youth Culture* (New York: Viking, 2007).

Schildt, Axel, and Detlef Siegfried, eds. *Between Marx and Coca-Cola: Youth Cultures in Changing European Societies, 1960–1980* (New York: Berghahn, 2006).

Schildt, Axel, Detlef Siegfried, and Karl Christian Lammers, eds. *Dynamische Zeiten: Die 60er Jahre in den beiden deutschen Gesellschaften* (Hamburg: Wallstein, 2000).

Schulenburg, Lutz, ed. *Das Leben äNewndern, die Welt veräNewndern! 1968 – Dokumente und Berichte* (Hamburg: Edition Nautilus, 1998).

Schulz, Kristina, ed. *The Women's Liberation Movement: Impacts and Outcomes* (New York: Berghahn, 2017).

Schwartz, Harry. *Prague's 200 Days: The Struggle for Democracy in Czechoslovakia* (New York, Frederick A. Praeger, 1969).

Scott, Andrew Murray, ed. *Invisible Insurrection of a Million Minds: A Trocchi Reader* (Edinburgh: Polygon, 1991).

Sedlmaier, Alexander. *Consumption and Violence: Radical Protest in Cold-War West Germany* (Ann Arbor: University of Michigan Press, 2014).

Serge, Victor. *Memoirs of a Revolutionary, 1901–41* (Oxford: Oxford University Press, 1963).

Sher, Gerson. *Praxis: Marxist Criticism and Dissent in Socialist Yugoslavia* (Bloomington: Indiana University Press, 1977).

Siegelbaum, Lewis H., ed. *Borders of Socialism: Private Spheres of Soviet Russia* (New York: Palgrave Macmillan, 2006).

Siegfried, Detlef. *Time Is on My Side: Konsum und Politik in der Westdeutschen Jugendkultur der 60er Jahre* (Göttingen: Wallstein, 2006).

Siegler, Heinrich. *Die Ereignisse in Polen und Ungarn: Eine Chronik des Geschehens von der Revolte in Posen bis zur militärischen Niederschlagung des Aufstandes in Ungarn* (Bonn: Siegler, 1957).

Skilling, H. Gordon. *Czechoslovakia's Interrupted Revolution* (Princeton: Princeton University Press, 1976).

Slobodian, Quinn. *Comrades of Color: East Germany in the Cold War World* (New York: Berghahn, 2015/2017).

Slobodian, Quinn. *Foreign Front: Third World Politics in Sixties West Germany* (Durham, NC: Duke University Press, 2012).

Smith, Evan, and Matthew Worley, eds. *Against the Grain: The British Far Left from 1956* (Manchester: Manchester University Press, 2014).

Stansill, Peter, and David Zane Mairowitz, eds. *BAMN (By Any Means Necessary): Outlaw Manifestos and Ephemera, 1965–1970* (New York: Autonomedia, 1999).

Statera, Gianni. *Death of a Utopia: The Development and Decline of Student Movements in Europe* (New York: Oxford University Press, 1975).

Steele, Jonathan, ed. *Eastern Europe Since Stalin* (New York: Crane, Russak, and Company, 1974).

Stegmann, Petra, Jennifer Burkart, and Akademie der Künste, eds. *"The Lunatics Are on the Loose . . ." European Fluxus Festivals 1962–1977* (Down with Art!, 2012).

Suri, Jeremi, ed. *The Global Revolutions of 1968: A Norton Casebook in History* (New York: Norton, 2007).

Suri, Jeremi. *Power and Protest: Global Revolution and the Rise of Détente* (Cambridge, MA: Harvard University Press, 2003).

Sviták, Ivan. *The Czechoslovak Experiment: 1968–1969* (New York: Columbia University Press, 1971).

Tarrow, Sidney. *Democracy and Disorder: Protest and Politics in Italy, 1965–1975* (Oxford: Oxford University Press, 1989).

Thomas, Nick. *Protest Movements in 1960s West Germany: A Social History of Dissent and Democracy* (Oxford: Berg, 2003).

Thomlinson, Natalie. *Race, Ethnicity and the Women's Movement in England, 1968–1993* (Basingstoke: Palgrave Macmillan, 2016).

Tismaneanu, Vladimir, ed. *Promises of 1968: Crisis, Illusion and Utopia* (New York: Central European University Press, 2011).

Tokes, Rudolph L., ed. *Opposition in Eastern Europe* (London: Palgrave Macmillan, 1979).

Varela, Raquel. *A People's History of the Portuguese Revolution* (London: Pluto, 2018).

Varon, Jeremy. *Bringing the War Home: The Weather Underground, the Red Army Faction, and Revolutionary Violence in the Sixties and Seventies* (Berkeley: University of California Press, 2004).

Viénet, René. *Enragés et situationnistes dans le mouvement des occupations* (Paris: Gallimard, 1968).

Vostell, Wolf, and Jürgen Becker. *Happenings: Fluxus, Pop Art, Nouveau réalisme* (Hamburg: Rowohlt, 1965).

Wark, McKenzie. *The Beach beneath the Street: The Everyday Life and Glorious Times of the Situationist International* (London: Verso, 2015).

Warner, Michael. *Publics and Counterpublics* (Brooklyn: Zone, 2005).

Wessel, Martin Schulkze. *Der Prager Frühling: Aufbruch in eine neue Welt* (Ditzingen: Reclam, 2018).

Whiteley, Sheila, and Jedediah Sklower, eds. *Countercultures and Popular Music* (Abingdon: Taylor and Francis, 2014).

Williams, Kieran. *The Prague Spring and its Aftermath: Czechoslovak Politics, 1968–1970* (Cambridge: Cambridge University Press, 1997).

Windsor, P., and A. Roberts. *Czechoslovakia 1968: Reform, Repression and Resistance* (London: Chatto and Windus for The Institute for Strategic Studies, 1969).

Wolin, Richard. *The Wind from the East: French Intellectuals, the Cultural Revolution and the Legacy of the 1960s* (Princeton: Princeton University Press, 2010).

Wu, Judy Tzu-Chun. *Radicals on the Road: Internationalism, Orientalism, and Feminism during the Vietnam War Era* (Ithaca: Cornell University Press, 2013).

Index